Praise and Blame in Greek Tragedy

Also available from Bloomsbury

Ancient Greece and Rome in Videogames: Representation, Play, Transmedia by Ross Clare

Classical Antiquity in Heavy Metal Music edited by K. F. B. Fletcher and Osman Umurhan

Classical Antiquity in Video Games: Playing with the Ancient World edited by Christian Rollinger

Representations of Classical Greece in Theme Parks by Filippo Carlà-Uhink

Praise and Blame in Greek Tragedy

Kate Cook

BLOOMSBURY ACADEMIC
LONDON • NEW YORK • OXFORD • NEW DELHI • SYDNEY

BLOOMSBURY ACADEMIC
Bloomsbury Publishing Plc, 50 Bedford Square, London, WC1B 3DP, UK
Bloomsbury Publishing Inc, 1385 Broadway, New York, NY 10018, USA
Bloomsbury Publishing Ireland, 29 Earlsfort Terrace, Dublin 2, D02 AY28, Ireland

BLOOMSBURY, BLOOMSBURY ACADEMIC and the Diana logo
are trademarks of Bloomsbury Publishing Plc

First published in Great Britain 2024
This paperback edition published 2025

Cover image: *Ulysses and Neoptolemus Taking Hercules' Arrows from Philoctetes*,
1800, by François-Xavier Fabre

A catalogue record for this book is available from the British Library.

A catalog record for this book is available from the Library of Congress.

ISBN: HB: 978-1-3504-1049-7
PB: 978-1-3504-1053-4
ePDF: 978-1-3504-1050-3
eBook: 978-1-3504-1051-0

Typeset by RefineCatch Ltd, Bungay, Suffolk

Contents

Acknowledgements

This book began as a PhD thesis at the University of Reading, and so I begin my thanks with recording my gratitude to the Department of Classics there and all the staff who provided guidance and support, most especially David Carter and Barbara Goff for supervising that thesis. Since then I have been fortunate in support from colleagues in multiple departments, and am especially grateful to those who have read and provided comments and criticisms on many parts of this work, including Malcolm Heath, Emma Cole, Kat Molesworth and Jon Hesk. I also thank Greg Nagy and the anonymous reader of the press for their many valuable suggestions for improvement. I am grateful to the team at Bloomsbury, especially Zoë Osman and Lily Mac Mahon, for their help in making this book an actuality.

I also count myself lucky in my friends and support groups who have provided advice and encouragement throughout the writing, including during the weirdness that was writing during a pandemic: thank you to Juli, Jenny, Toby, Ellie, Emma, Kat, Elena, Owen, Zara, Tom, Lucy, Sarah, Jane, Josh, Christine, Andy and Clare. I am particularly grateful to Stuart, who has cheered on this book through every hour of its progress, and been the best friend it or I could ask for. Finally I would like to thank my parents, who are deserving of the highest praises for all their support, and without whom this book would not have been possible.

Introduction

σὺ δ' αἰνεῖν εἴτε με ψέγειν θέλεις, ὅμοιον·

Aesch. *Ag.* 1403–4

'Praise or blame me as you like, it's all the same.' Thus Clytemnestra after the murder of her husband, in Aeschylus' *Agamemnon.*[1] But only a few lines later she will complain about the chorus doing precisely that when they criticize her (1412–15), demonstrating the insincerity of her rhetorical claim to value praise or blame so little. Furthermore, Clytemnestra frames her comment in terms of an opposition between concepts that were decidedly *not* 'all the same' to the Greeks of her external audience, let alone her internal audience, the chorus themselves, who have already demonstrated in the *Agamemnon* a keen awareness of the importance of praising to the correct extent (782–6). In doing so, they drew on one of the genres of Greek poetry established for the express purpose of distributing praise speech: epinician.[2] The chorus' awareness, as much as Clytemnestra's declared rejection of the same process, both engage with a matter of central importance to understanding Greek poetry: its function in the public distribution of praise and blame.

As this book will demonstrate, the *Agamemnon* is far from the only tragedy in which we find this kind of engagement. Throughout Greek tragedy we find characters and choruses engaged in the process of generating praise and blame discourses, often drawing on older poetic genres and expressions to do so, just as Clytemnestra and the chorus do in the *Agamemnon*. Many tragic characters and choruses demonstrate a persistent, critical engagement with these processes of praising and blaming, and the earning of both types of discourse, across the genre. As a result, tragedy demonstrates itself to be a genre that both develops and problematizes one of the key elements of Greek poetry.

Greek poetry in the archaic and classical periods has as one of its central functions the distribution of praise and blame. Aristotle describes praise and blame as intrinsic to poetry, giving two central traditions of poetry, one centred around each function, putting epic and tragedy in the category of praise, and iambic and comedy in the category of blame (*Poetics* 1448b 25). Genres such as the epinician, praise songs for athletic victors, feature singers explicitly acknowledging their poetry as designed for establishing praise in opposition to the poetry of other singers, which they associate with blame, as in the comment from Pindar in *Pythian* 2.52–6, where he opposes his own praise poetry to the iambic (blame-focused) poetry of Archilochus.[3] As Detienne's study *Les Maîtres de vérité dans la Grèce archaïque* (1969) demonstrated, however, this poetic function of praising and blaming extends far beyond specific genres, given the central role of poets as 'truth-speakers' in distributing praise and blame, which was essential for establishing the 'memory' of a warrior which would confirm his worth within his society.[4] Building on Detienne's work, Nagy has demonstrated the centrality of this as a poetic function in epic, as well as in the work of Pindar.[5] The memory of an individual established through this poetic technique becomes their *kleos*, their reputation or literally what is heard about them, itself a central poetic issue from Homer onwards.[6] Conversely, those who are not sung about, along with those who are blamed, are forgotten; without *kleos*, and without poetic praise, their fate is oblivion.[7] Much of Greek poetry concerns itself with the production of these discourses of praise and blame, establishing or denying *kleos*.

This poetic background is essential for understanding Greek tragedy. Aristotle's typology includes drama within the poetic genres, rather than separating out comedy and tragedy into a distinct category. Work on tragedy has highlighted the genre's development from older genres of poetry, so that tragedy should be seen as a continuation of the poetic tradition. Herington's 1985 work, *Poetry into Drama*, argued that tragedy is another form in the Greek poetic tradition stretching from Homer down to the fifth century BCE and beyond, and is specifically connected with earlier poetic genres.[8] More recently, there has been an increasing body of work which explores how tragedy draws on features from genres of archaic and classical poetry, such as Swift's *The Hidden Chorus*, which provides one of the most wide-ranging and thorough examples of this approach.[9]

However, this is not to say that tragedy is simply a Greek poetic genre like any other. Unlike many genres of archaic poetry – including epic, epinician or iambic – tragedy features no authoritative narratorial voice. The introduction of additional actors into tragedy, as the genre developed, makes it an essentially dialogic genre and opens up an increased possibility for competing discourses to be raised, beyond even the multivocal potential of a chorus and separate singer.[10] Aristophanes' joke that Euripides had made tragedy more 'democratic' by introducing additional speakers of varying status and identity to the plays (*Frogs* 947–51), while an exaggeration for humorous effect, does to some extent represent a genuine reflection on the multivocal nature of tragedy by Euripides' time. As Segal has discussed, this lack of a narratorial or authorial voice sets tragedy apart from other poetic genres.[11] Similarly, tragedy's production at the time of an increasingly literary culture has also been seen by Segal as allowing for a wider range of viewpoints and a less 'one-sided' presentation of a hero than choral lyric.[12] The chorus of tragedy can be seen as less representative of the community or 'civic voice' than the choral performances of lyric.[13] At the same time, according to Calame, the use of the mask, costume and ritual gestures in the performance of tragedy contribute to a 'complex polyphony' of the 'instance of enunciation', increasing the dialogic aspects of that enunciation while reducing the direct access to an 'authorial' enunciation.[14]

The potential for competing discourses of praise and blame arising from the involvement of multiple voices in its generation is already apparent in epic, in the laments of Hector's relatives at the end of the *Iliad*.[15] These allow for varying perspectives on Hector's life and achievements, and even open the possibility of voicing criticisms both of Hector and of the wider heroic system of *kleos* to be voiced.[16] However, these voices within an epic are always subordinate to the voice of the narrator,[17] and the narrator's voice in the *Iliad* has the final word on Hector's *kleos*, in the last line of the poem where he is referred to by his epic epithet: Ὣς οἵ γ' ἀμφίεπον τάφον Ἕκτορος ἱπποδάμοιο ('Thus they buried horse-taming Hector' *Il.* 24.804).

In contrast, the competing discourses of praise and blame issued in tragedy by characters and choruses are met with no such over-arching authoritative voice. As this book will show, these competing discourses therefore often lead in tragedy to damaging or destructive ends, particularly when multiple speakers are set against one another within the same tragedies. The multivocality of tragedy includes a particular element which enhances this destructive element in the production of praise and blame discourses: women's speech. In tragedy, as the Aristophanic joke indicates, the voices of women take on an additional prominence.[18] Although the voices of women which were heard in tragedy may or may not be read as representing the voices of historical women, tragedy's plurality of voices nonetheless provides additional space for the representation of a gendered discourse, which, as we shall see, is then implicated in the conflicts between praise or blame discourses which are staged in tragedy.[19]

The presence of the alternative voices in the production of epic *kleos* is also gendered: the female characters who sing the laments allow for an alternative, critical discourse in contrast to the discourse of heroic *kleos* in Homeric epic. However, there are clear signs of the right of women's voices to participate in this sphere being contested in fifth-century Athens. There is an explicit argument made in the same Athenian democratic context within which tragedy was produced, that not only should women be uninvolved in the awarding of praise and blame, but that they should be sufficiently distant from this context even to avoid receiving it. This comment appears in Pericles' much-discussed address to the Athenian war-widows:

> μεγάλη ἡ δόξα καὶ ἧς ἂν ἐπ' ἐλάχιστον ἀρετῆς πέρι ἢ ψόγου ἐν τοῖς ἄρσεσι κλέος ᾖ.
>
> Her reputation will be great, who is least spoken about among men either in praise or blame.
>
> Thuc. 2.45.2[20]

Pericles' comment draws on all of the key elements of this traditional discourse; he makes explicit reference to the potential *kleos* of women, and phrases the potential for gaining *kleos* in terms of being denied rather than awarded praise and blame.

It is important not to overestimate the significance of this comment from Pericles' idealising speech when considering wider attitudes to women's participation in praise and blame discourses. Although the extant poets most associated with praise and blame poetry are often male (such as Pindar or Archilochus), there are also potential examples of female poets composing in these spheres, particularly if Corinna was a rival poet to Pindar, and thus may have been working in some of the same or similar genres.[21] Sappho too seems to have produced poetry noted for being critical of some Andromeda (fr. 57 L–P), apparently in terms commonly used to describe iambic poetry.[22] *Partheneia*, sung (if not always produced) by women, gave choruses of women an opportunity to perform praise for female beauty.[23] In the *Iliad*, alongside the female participation in the laments of Book 24, women's association with public blame is held up as a spur to heroic behaviour for Hector, when he remarks:

> αἰδέομαι Τρῶας καὶ **Τρῳάδας ἑλκεσιπέπλους,**
> μή ποτέ τις εἴπῃσι κακώτερος ἄλλος ἐμεῖο·
> Ἕκτωρ ἧφι βίηφι πιθήσας ὤλεσε λαόν.
>
> I am ashamed before the Trojans and the Trojan wives with trailing robes, lest some other worse man than me will say: Hector, trusting in his own might, ruined his people!
>
> *Il.* 22.105–7

Helen fears blame from the Trojan women as a collective (Τρῳαὶ. . . μωμήσονται), if she joins Paris in bed after his duel with Menelaus (*Il.* 3.410–12).[24] Festivals including the Thesmophoria, festivals at Sparta, the Hybristika at Argos, and those celebrating Apollo at Anaphe and Demeter at Pellene, suggest a wider Greek context in which choruses of women could participate in mocking and criticising both men and women.[25] There is also a specifically Athenian example provided in the *Against Neaira*, when the speaker argues that the jury will face condemnation from the women in their homes, if they do not judge Neaira to be guilty (Dem. 59.110–11). Even beyond the formal genres of poetry in which poets generate this discourse, the potential for female blame of the male figures in Greek society is clear.[26]

As the second half of this book explores, however, tragedy's female speakers make full use of this potential and turn it to dangerous effect against the heroic figures of the poetic tradition, when they become participants in the generation of praise and blame discourses. In this regard, tragedy reflects a similar concern to that expressed in Pericles' speech: neither work claims against the evidence of their social and poetic contexts that women do not participate in praise and blame discourse production, but both argue that they *should* not. This exploration of the intersection of gender and praise and blame discourses is one of the most unusual facets of tragedy's interaction with these discourses, and results from its 'democratic' multivocality, and its capacity to draw on a wide range of such discourses in its absorption of other poetic genres, both those performed by male and by female poets.

The treatment of praise and blame discourses and their production in tragedy shares an additional important feature with Pericles' funeral speech: its social and historical context. Tragedy was being produced at a time when questions about the appropriate voices for praise and blame in the democratic society were being explored. As Goldhill has discussed, by the time in which Pindar was composing his praise songs for athletic victors, the increasing influence of the *polis* meant that the poet's role in establishing *kleos* through praise needed to be negotiated in new ways in comparison to the picture of the poet's role in generating *kleos* given by epic.[27] Simonides' fr. 531 *PMG* demonstrates the poet's argument for the value of poetry in commemorating and praising those who had died for their country, engaging with funerary epitaphs to prioritize poetry as the optimum source of this praise.[28] It is striking that the context in which this fragment is found, Diodorus' Siculus' *World History*, notes that both Simonides and the historians celebrated the men of Thermopylae, indicating that new genres such as prose historiography were also entering into this space of generating praise and blame.[29]

In the democratic Athens in which tragedy was produced, these questions are even more clearly implicated in the invention of the new, state-sponsored genre of praise prose: the *epitaphios*. In her 1981 study *L'invention d'Athènes*, Loraux pointed to the importance of rise of the *epitaphios*, the prose funeral speech of praise for a community of dead, as a key element in studying Athenian ideology. This specifically Athenian form of praise speech demonstrates an ongoing social concern with how individuals should be praised, especially given its potential interaction with the poetic context. Fr. 531 *PMG* of Simonides' praise elegy for the dead at Thermopylae seems to have anticipated some of the questions arising in this genre about how to praise the Athenian dead in a democracy, demonstrating their ongoing significance.[30] Loraux considers the 'official orator' as analogous to the poets who 'possess the *ainos*', the same authoritative poets identified by Detienne and Nagy as those distributing praise and blame.[31] The *epitaphios* therefore forms part of an evolving tradition of praise or blame speech, which was moving between poetic and prose forms in the classical Athenian period.[32] Yet the need to adopt such a form at all, and the noticeably more communal approach of the *epitaphios* in comparison with the traditionally individually focused genres of praise and blame poetry, demonstrates, according to Loraux, that: 'The city, then, has come between the glory of the aristocrats and that of the citizen-soldiers, and it is the city that, calling upon the orator to speak, separates him irremediably from the poet.'[33] This increased prominence of the *polis* is a characteristic shared with tragedy, whose choruses, often representing a wider citizenry, and concerns with the 'political' in its broadest sense made it a poetic genre into which the city, as in the *epitaphios*, had significantly interposed itself.[34]

As a mark of how prominent this concern with praise and blame was beyond the *epitaphios* in fifth-century Athens, we could also consider contemporary prose authors, since many of these also engaged with the question of how to manage discourses of praise and blame in the democratic *polis*, and continued to do so from the fifth into the fourth centuries. The philosophers were implicated in this discussion early on, with Protagoras apparently criticised for teaching his students to praise and blame the same person, thus impairing the value of the process.[35] Gorgias was apparently credited with following the example of Protagoras in this regard.[36] His *Encomium of Helen* also shows Gorgias in the process of engaging with a traditional, poetic discourse of blame for a mythological figure, Helen, and inverting it with his own discourse of praise.[37] He engages explicitly with the question of what should and should not be praised:

> ἄνδρα δὲ καὶ γυναῖκα καὶ λόγον καὶ ἔργον καὶ πόλιν καὶ πρᾶγμα χρὴ τὸ μὲν ἄξιον ἐπαίνου ἐπαίνῳ τιμᾶν, τῷ δὲ ἀναξίῳ μῶμον ἐπιτιθέναι· ἴση γὰρ ἁμαρτία καὶ ἀμαθία μέμφεσθαί τε τὰ ἐπαινετὰ καὶ ἐπαινεῖν τὰ μωμητά.
>
> Man and woman and word and deed and city and act should be honoured with praise if worthy of praise, and attacked with blame if unworthy: for it is the same error and mistake to blame what is to be praised, and praise what is to be blamed.
>
> Gorgias *Encomium* 1

Gorgias' own *epitaphios* shows his direct engagement with this live issue of how to praise and blame in democratic Athens, through his contribution to this developing genre.[38] Isocrates argued for the central place of praise and blame in all kinds of oratory, not solely the *epitaphios*.[39] Plato too discusses how his proposed city in the *Laws* will draw on poetic traditions of praise and blame as part of education, with the lawgiver explicitly required to ψέγειν τε ὀρθῶς καὶ ἐπαινεῖν δι' αὐτῶν τῶν νόμων: 'blame and praise correctly, by means of the laws themselves.'[40] The historians can also be seen engaging especially with epinician and its role in distributing praise, as they developed their own prose genre.[41]

Maslov has recently argued that one of the key aspects necessary for a work's participation in and establishment of a new genre is the 'redeployment of forms from prexisting genres', which were for the audience 'endowed with the meaning and social potency they had in their original context.'[42] The social potency of praise and blame discourses, particularly those established through poetry, was clear to the fifth-century Athenians, and it is therefore not surprising that with the development of genres such as the *epitaphios* or prose philosophical works, along with the ongoing developments of lyric genres, we see a repeated return to this socially-potent element.[43] As this work demonstrates, tragedy too identifies itself through redeployment of this key element, in interaction with both the lyric and epic traditions, to establish a new – often more complex – approach to these discourses suitable for the tragic Athenian stage. In some ways, tragedy's nature as a 'super genre', as Weiss has described it, capable of absorbing multiple lyric genres, makes it particularly suited to this kind of redeployment, especially of the poetic elements which orators or historians sought to replace: tragedy, with its sung passages and choral performance, could integrate these elements through generic interaction.[44] At the same time, tragedy's staging of the mythical heroes of epic and (some forms of) lyric provide the ideal format for the raising of issues related to these key discourses, without losing touch with its poetic rootedness. As with other aspects of the tradition, however, this book demonstrates that in taking on this poetic tradition, tragedy makes use of its multivocal nature to problematize aspects of praise and blame, putting them in the hands of dangerous users, or making dangerous heroes' own attempts to seek *kleos* of the 'wrong' kinds.

Fifth-century Athenian tragedy's social and historical context means it was being produced at a time when the central poetic function of establishing discourses of praise and blame was being interrogated and renegotiated: moved into new, sometimes state-controlled genres, and requiring new balances between poet and *polis*. In this multivocal genre of poetry, the production of those discourses as a process in which individuals are engaged becomes open to challenge and distortion, especially given the prominent voices of women within the genre. As a result, tragedy's interrogation of the production of discourses of praise and blame repays study. This study enables us to understand both a significant aspect of tragedy's interaction with the existing poetic tradition, and its engagement with its wider social and historical context in terms of the ongoing adaptation of the production of praise and blame. It sheds new light on the depiction of women and women's speech in tragedy, and some of its most dangerous aspects.

Identifying praise and blame

Given the range of extant tragedies available to us, this book does not aim at being a comprehensive study. Issues of praise and blame are more prominent in some tragedies than in others, and so these examples form the central case studies of this work. Examples of this prominence often feature direct engagement with alternative genres suitable for establishing discourses of praise and blame. In some plays, we see engagement with the *epitaphios* as a new genre, and with its production of praise discourses, particularly in Euripidean tragedy. I have argued elsewhere that Euripides' *Heraclidae* demonstrates explicit interaction with the *epitaphios*, proposing tragedy as its competition for the genre with a role in commemorating the myths of the city,[45] and Loraux and Foley have shown how Euripides' *Suppliant Women* also undertakes sustained engagement with the *epitaphios*. Tragedies which develop and engage with the mythological tradition of heroic figures, including those from the epic tradition, such as Philoctetes and Neoptolemus, or with major *polis*-related traditions such as Theseus or Heracles, often engage explicitly with the poetic traditions of praise which celebrate them, such as epic or epinician. This feature of tragedy – that it reuses mythical characters rather than the original characters found (predominantly) in extant comedy – marks it out as developing relationships with the poetic traditions of those figures.[46] The question of male warriors' (or 'heroes") transition from epic or other archaic genres on to the tragic stage has been much discussed,[47] with particular reference to what epic ideas about heroic qualities or values continue to be represented in tragedy.[48] However, the ways in which this tragic depiction simultaneously engages with the production of poetic praise and blame discourses which are so crucial to heroic *kleos* has not previously been considered.

Given this interaction with earlier poetic traditions, it is possible to identify and discuss praise or blame speech in tragedy, especially praise, by use of specific generic features which draw on the traditions of poetry discussed above.[49] Often, characters and choruses redeploy language and discourses from epic in their production of praise discourses, particularly in relation to epic heroes. Poetic interaction is also found especially in choral passages, where it is frequently signalled by features found in the genres of epinician and paean.[50] Triumphs may be described as athletic victories and praised in songs which draw on the epinician, such as the chorus' praise for Orestes' murder of Aegisthus (Eur. *El.* 860–5), which Electra also takes up in her celebration (866–79). Elsewhere, as in Euripides' *Heracles*, particular tropes of epinician praise – such as a focus on youth or vigour (Eur. *HF* 637–700), or a celebration which ties the 'victor' to his local community (792–7) – may evoke the genre even without the more obvious allusion set up by reference to athletic victory. Tragic use of vocabulary common in Pindar, such as the term *kallinikos* (καλλίνικος, glorious in victory), can highlight an interaction with epinician. Similarly, the paean in which Ion praises Apollo (Eur. *Ion* 113–83) is marked by a specific paeanic refrain (125–7, repeated at 141–3), as well as by references to sacred labour (esp. 134).[51] The use of these poetic features has the effect of drawing attention to the production of praise discourses.

It is not possible to identify generic interaction marking blame speech in tragedy in the same way. The genre most usually considered to be 'poetry of blame', in direct contrast with praise poetry, is iambos: Pindar claimed that Archilochus' iambic poetry should be considered as effectively opposite to his, as that poet distributed ψόγος (blame) where Pindar gave ἔπαινος (*Pyth.* 2.55).[52] Aristotle makes similar associations between blame and iambic poetry (*Pol.* 1448b). While there is undoubtedly an increased frequency of invective or mockery as a central feature of iambos,[53] other features too have been identified as key to the genre, such as a pronounced narrative element,[54] or vulgarity in treatment of sex, which is a less common element in other genres.[55] Furthermore, as with many genres of archaic Greek poetry, there is a distinct flexibility when it comes to identifying iambos: certainly it is not clear that there was any early, formal categorization of the genre.[56] Additionally, many of these generic features do not lend themselves well to tragedy itself. Explicit sexuality, for example, or the vulgar language found in Hipponax's iambic poetry, are features which, while popular in Greek comedy, will not be found in tragedy.[57] Moreover, while it is possible to identify references to epinician, for example, in the tragedians' use of the dactylo-epitrite metre, the iambic trimeter used by Archilochus and Semonides in their iambic works is the usual metre of dramatic dialogue, so that references to the earlier iambic tradition cannot obviously be distinguished by metre.[58]

However, while generic features of existing poetic genres may make instances of praise and blame more marked in Greek tragedy, these are not the only instances where this significant poetic tradition is developed in tragedy. In the examples quoted at the start of this introduction from the *Agamemnon*, while the chorus do make use of an image from epinician, Clytemnestra's framing extends beyond this kind of immediate poetic interaction to the wider context of thought about praise and blame and its poetically established opposition. The importance of the praise/blame opposition for generating *kleos* and memory in Greek thought extends throughout its literary and performance-based culture, and is not limited to particular genres of lyric or epic poetry.[59] As with Clytemnestra's example, much of the presentation of praise and blame discourses in tragedy draws on significant vocabulary even where it does not make these generic connections. Instances where speech is explicitly designated as praise or blame are particularly important, as this invites the audience to contemplate the discourse as it plays out before them.

In the same way, discourses and actions that are marked within a tragedy as contributing to an individual's *kleos* or making them εὐκλεής ('glorious' or 'of good repute') often appear in combination with features of other poetic genres. Even where they do not, the use of either the term *kleos* itself or words from the same root often invokes this significant feature of the function of poetry. As noted above, and as Detienne and Nagy emphasize, this *kleos* is intrinsically connected to poetry's production of praise and blame discourses. All bar three instances of *kleos* in extant Euripides appear in plays related to the Trojan War,[60] thus in plays with a looming Homeric context, with one further instance appearing in the *Phoenissae*, which has connections to Thebes' own epic tradition.[61] Only two appearances of the term therefore appear outside of these epic contexts.[62] Five out of six extant uses in Sophocles are in Trojan War plays,[63] and all three uses of it in extant Aeschylean tragedy are in the *Agamemnon* (487, 1098, 1356).[64]

Similarly, references to characters being *kleinos* (κλεινός – famous or renowned) in tragedy often draw on the traditional concepts of *kleos* (which sits at the root of the word *kleinos*) and invoke this poetic tradition of praise and blame. Descriptions of tragic characters or locations in tragedy as *kleinos* regularly appear in contexts which point to the epic tradition. Winnington Ingram suggested that *kleinos*, particularly in the later plays of Euripides, indicated 'belonging to the epic' and marked direct (often satirical, in his view) interaction between the tragedies and the epic tradition.[65] In response, Lee noted that by far the largest group of uses of the word *kleinos* in Euripides (more than twenty out of seventy-four uses) appears in connection to the Trojan War, and where the word appears in other contexts it is commonly associated with the storied, heroic past, especially of Athens or the heroes of Thebes, also a city and individuals with a strong epic tradition.[66] In Sophocles, just over half of all uses appear in plays connected to the Trojan War,[67] although it is not possible to see any pattern in Aeschylus, where the term appears only once in a securely Aeschylean tragedy.[68] This usage may also be reflected in the lyric context: Stesichorus' use of the term for Troy in relation to the Achaean sacking of it demonstrates a similar connection with epic (fr. 117.6–7 Finglass), and its use in Pindar is also intimately connected to the generation of *kleos*.[69]

This study therefore considers case studies where terms such as *kleos* or other poetically informed vocabulary are prominent, as these draw attention to tragedy's interaction with that poetic context. Beyond this poetically focused vocabulary, it is valuable to consider the terms used of praise and blame discourses in tragedy, where these discourses are explicitly identified as such. The verb most used for praise, αἰνέω and its compounds (particularly ἐπαινέω), appear in a wide range of contexts in tragedy, with meanings which include but extend beyond formal contexts of praise.[70] Occasionally in tragedy this vocabulary does introduce the kind of formalized, often choral, praise ode that may also be accompanied by features common to the genres of epinician or paean. In the *Oedipus Coloneus*, for example, the chorus introduces their praise ode for Colonus specifically as such:

> ἄλλον δ᾽ **αἶνον** ἔχω ματροπόλει τᾷδε
>
> And I have another word of praise for this my native city.
>
> 707

Similarly, the chorus of Aeschylus' *Suppliant Women*, in the first few lines of their departing song of praise for Athens, sing:

αἶνος δὲ πόλιν τάνδε Πελασγῶν
ἐχέτω,

And let this city of the Pelasgians have praise.

Aesch. *Supp.* 1023–4

This type of explicitly labelled praise can also be addressed by a chorus to an individual, without the same formalized sung context, as when the chorus of the *Hippolytus* directly tell Phaedra αἰνῶ δὲ σέ (Eur. *Hipp.* 483–4), for her decision to die rather than submit to her passion for Hippolytus.

It is also common in Greek to express a more general positive judgement by describing a choice or decision as one to be praised, without the same kind of indication that a formal poetic praise context is also being invoked. The use of Greek praise words for these judgements is often translated into English as 'approve' or 'agree', which demonstrates the limited scope of the English word 'praise' in comparison to the Greek, and has the result of rather subduing the weight of the statements. A clear example is the statement made by the chorus of the *Choephori,* where there is no indication that the chorus intends to begin any formal praise of Clytemnestra or Aegisthus of the kind that is introduced in the examples above:

ἀρχὰς πρέπον
βίᾳ φρενῶν αἰνέσαι,

It is proper to praise my rulers in spite of my thoughts.

Aesch. *Cho.* 78–9

Instead, the scope of what may be described as 'praise' appears to cover a far more general positive judgement or attitude. Similarly, the chorus of *Philoctetes* complain to the warrior that:

εὖτέ γε παρὸν φρονῆσαι
λωίονος δαίμονος εἷλου τὸ κάκιον αἰνεῖν.

When it was possible to think sensibly, you chose to praise the worst fate instead of the more desirable.

Soph. *Phil.* 1099–1100

Again, here, Philoctetes has not been involved in any formal praise; rather, the chorus means that he has made a positive judgement of what they consider the 'worse' fate. There are similar examples at Eur. *Alc.* 1093, *Hipp.* 483, *IT* 1023, *HF* 275.

The use of the concept of αἶνος to convey a general positive judgement is also shown in several cases where individuals express an explicit refusal to praise as a way of conferring negative judgement. In discussing the situation between Andromache and Hermione, for example, the chorus of Euripides' *Andromache* declare:

οὐδέποτε δίδυμα λέκτρ' ἐπαινέσω βροτῶν

I will never praise a double marriage-bed among mortals.

Eur. *Andr.* 465

Similarly the chorus of the *Eumenides* include among a long section of generalized advice on social morals (490–565):

μήτ' ἄναρκτον βίον
μήτε δεσποτούμενον
αἰνέσῃς·

Do not praise a life of anarchy, nor one lived under despotism.

Aesch. *Eum.* 526–8

Phaedra's Nurse taps into a common fifth-century sentiment in the expression:

οὕτω τὸ λίαν ἧσσον ἐπαινῶ
τοῦ μηδὲν ἄγαν·

And so I praise excess less than acting moderately.

Eur. *Hipp.* 264–5[71]

Phrasing negative judgements by claiming that something is found unworthy of being awarded praise is not limited to generalizations, as it can also be found in specific circumstances or applied to individuals. Tyndareus complains to Menelaus,

ἐγὼ δὲ μισῶ μὲν γυναῖκας ἀνοσίους,
...
Ἑλένην τε, τὴν σὴν ἄλοχον, οὔποτ' αἰνέσω

I hate wicked women... and Helen, your wife, I will never praise

Eur. *Or.* 518 and 520

and in the same way, Amphitryon passes a negative judgement on all of Greece for their lack of help for his son:

οὐδ' Ἑλλάδ' ᾔνεσ' (οὐδ' ἀνέξομαί ποτε

σιγῶν) κακίστην λαμβάνων ἐς παῖδ᾽ ἐμόν,

I will not praise Hellas (nor will I ever keep silent), on finding her to be most wicked towards my son.

Eur. *HF* 222–3

This formulation has its own epic roots; Penelope's suitors rather startlingly suggest that if their plot to murder Telemachus was discovered by the people as a whole:

οἱ δ᾽ οὐκ αἰνήσουσιν ἀκούοντες κακὰ ἔργα·

They will not praise us on hearing of the evil deeds.

Od. 16.380

In this epic instance, and in some of the examples shown above, the phrase might seem rather an understatement; presumably the people of Ithaca would speak against or criticize the attempt to kill Telemachus, rather than simply decline to praise it, and Tyndareus' words against Helen and Clytemnestra, when coupled with his statement of express hatred, are condemnation, rather than merely a lack of praise. Nonetheless, it is clear in the repetition of the same formula that discussing a person or a deed in terms of the praise they may or may not win was a well-established way to discuss positive or negative judgements. The ongoing centrality of this concept of being awarded praise and blame discourses in the expression of judgements thus appears throughout tragedy, beyond the cases where tragedy engages explicitly with the poetic tradition of establishing such discourses.

It is similarly possible to discuss tragic use of the typical Greek vocabulary for blame. The words associated in the poetic tradition with blame are identified by Nagy as ψόγος, μῶμος and ὄνειδος; and both ψόγος and ὄνειδος feature frequently in tragedy, especially in statements pronouncing judgement on what is seen to pass on stage.[72] As with the use of terms stemming from αἰνέω discussed above, this vocabulary for blame seems to invoke a wide range of types of negative speech. This can include comments or specific criticism directed against an individual, as when Creon characterizes Haemon's criticisms of his decisions about Antigone as ψόγοισι (Soph. *Ant.* 759), or accusations, as when Athena asks Orestes to defend himself against the Furies' ψόγον (Aesch. *Eum.* 436). Often it is equally appropriate to render the terms ψόγος and ὄνειδος as 'reproach' or 'criticism'.[73] In Euripides' *Ion*, for example, when Ion comments:

ἵν᾽ ἐσπεσοῦμαι δύο νόσω κεκτημένος,
πατρός τ᾽ ἐπακτοῦ καὐτὸς ὢν νοθαγενής.

καὶ τοῦτ᾽ ἔχων **τοὔνειδος**, ἀσθενὴς μένων
<αὐτὸς τὸ> μηδὲν κοὐδένων κεκλήσομαι.

So I shall burst in on them with two illnesses, that my father is an alien, and I am a bastard. And while dealing with this criticism, I am weak, and I shall be called nothing and son of no-ones.

Eur. *Ion* 591–4

Ion's complaint is not that he fears being blamed in the English sense of the word, implying some fault on his part, but that he fears the bad things that the citizens of Athens will say about him (he goes on to elaborate this point fully, 594–606). More explicitly, Menelaus in Euripides' *Andromache* complains of Peleus' long list of insults (590–641):

αἰσχρὰ μὲν σαυτῷ λέγεις
ἡμῖν δ᾽ **ὀνείδη** διὰ γυναῖκα βάρβαρον,

You speak words that are shameful to yourself, and criticism against me on account of a barbarian woman.

Eur. *Andr.* 648–9

In this instance, the word encompasses a wide range of accusations and abuse from Peleus. The 'blame' Ion fears is only imagined, whereas the audience experiences the criticisms of Menelaus from Peleus. Nonetheless, both examples demonstrate that a wide range of negative speech contexts can be covered by the term ὄνειδος.

There are also instances where more widespread discourses of blame are described with the use of ψόγος, particularly in connection with female characters, who complain about the 'blame' women receive from others more generally.[74] In doing so, they engage directly with the tradition of generalised blame discourses found in Greek poetry such as Semonides 7 or Hesiod's *Theogony* (592–609). Clytemnestra complains in Euripides' *Electra* that when women cheat in response to the adultery of their husbands:

κἄπειτ᾽ ἐν ἡμῖν ὁ ψόγος λαμπρύνεται,
οἱ δ᾽ αἴτιοι τῶνδ᾽ οὐ κλύουσ᾽ ἄνδρες κακῶς.

Then against us the blame shines clearly, but the men who are responsible, are not spoken of badly.

Eur. *El.* 1039–40

Similarly, Andromache complains in the *Trojan Women* that:

πρῶτον μέν, ἔνθα (κἂν προσῇ κἂν μὴ προσῇ
ψόγος γυναιξίν) αὐτὸ τοῦτ' ἐφέλκεται
κακῶς ἀκούειν, ἥτις οὐκ ἔνδον μένει,

First (whether a there is a specific accusation that exists against a woman or not) whenever she doesn't remain inside, this attracts speaking badly about her.

Eur. *Tro.* 647–9

The chorus of the *Suppliant Women* apply a similar remark to the fate of foreigners:

πᾶς τις ἐπειπεῖν
ψόγον ἀλλοθρόοις
εὔτυκος.

Everyone is ready to cast blame on those who speak another language.

Aesch. *Supp.* 972–4

In extending to generalization, these comments again demonstrate an ongoing tragic awareness of a context in which discourses of praise and blame can be widespread in society. They also accentuate the importance of praise and blame speech in the reification of social judgements.

Thus, discourses of praise and blame remain central to Greek tragedy just as they were central to other Greek poetic genres. In certain contexts, particularly those which are themselves associated with existing poetic traditions, such as those tragedies which focus on the Trojan War or Theban epic cycle, we see a particular reflection on these in terms which echo the *kleos*-focused language of earlier poetry. Elsewhere, the broader uses of terms for praise and blame come into focus, and characters and choruses identify a wider range of expressed positive or negative judgements in terms of this opposition.

This study focuses on those examples where the development and contestation of praise and blame discourses is especially marked, especially where the interaction with previous poetic traditions is especially significant. Chapters 1 and 2 explore the tragic situations of two heroes appearing in plays contextualized by the Homeric epic tradition: Sophocles' *Philoctetes* and *Ajax*. Chapter 3 moves away from the epic context to consider a hero with a prominent role in other poetic praise genres: Euripides' Heracles, whose crisis in the *Heracles* features a manipulation of praise discourses which draw heavily on the epinician and paeanic traditions. All three of these case studies demonstrate how tragedy's multivocal nature problematizes the awarding of praise discourses for these poetically situated heroes, in contrast to their traditional contexts. In the

Philoctetes, Philoctetes' successful, skilled manipulation of praise and blame discourses, and the resulting promises of *kleos* which he can offer Neoptolemus as a result, is key to persuading Neoptolemus to help him, so that Sophocles' play demonstrates even in this new genre the influence of such discourses. In both the *Ajax* and the *Heracles,* the problems of multivocality in handling discourses of praise and blame become central. For Ajax, a desire to move beyond the praise discourses of the *Iliad* to establish himself as 'best of the Achaeans', contrary to the discourses produced by those around him, leads to his self-destruction. Heracles in Euripides' *Heracles* seeks to elevate his acts of fatherhood to being praiseworthy and worthy of *kleos*, but is contradicted by those around him, particularly Amphitryon and the chorus, who draw on the epinician and paeanic traditions to insist that Heracles' heroic acts are the only aspects of his identity which should be celebrated with poetic praise. As in the case of Ajax, the conflict which results is enormously destructive: in this situation, to Heracles' identity as father, rather than his entire identity.

In the second half of this book, I consider examples where this complex, destructive multivocality becomes problematic in relation to the key aspect of tragedy raised above: gender. Chapter 4 considers first the example of the Athenian hero, Theseus, in Euripides' *Suppliant Women*. As I demonstrate, the presence of the female chorus in Euripides' *Suppliant Women* has a significant effect on praise discourses around Theseus, since they persist in manipulating these to provide a counter-discourse against his attempts to establish a tragic *epitaphios*, and prevent his own preferences for praise speech from being carried out. Their manipulation of praise leaves Theseus in the unusually negative situation of facing a distinct lack of praise discourses in comparison with other heroic figures in tragedy. Chapters 5 and 6 consider two examples of individual female characters who demonstrate a similarly damaging involvement in the production of praise and blame discourse: Deianira in Sophocles' *Trachiniae*, and Medea in Euripides' *Medea*. In both of these cases, the conflict in discourses takes different forms. In the *Trachiniae*, Deianira's resistance to and refusal to accept praise discourses around her husband, Heracles, sets up the environment which leaves him vulnerable to becoming an unpraiseworthy figure by the end of the play. Medea, as in many ways, proves a much more aggressive figure, since she actively manipulates traditional speech of blame, particularly generalized discourses of blame against women, as part of her destruction of Jason.

In all of these examples, better attention to praise and blame discourses and their production generates new readings of the individual tragedies considered. As such, this work demonstrates that appreciating this essential element of the poetic context improves our understanding of specific tragedies, especially given that this context would have been intimately familiar to the original Athenian audience. This insight brings us closer to the kinds of readings they may themselves have developed. Studying this key element of heroic identity also enables us to develop a new understanding of tragedy's handling of heroic figures from the existing poetic tragedy. While work on women's speech on tragedy has flourished recently,[75] this study is the first to integrate such work into the wider poetic context and show how women's new prominence in tragic speech develops and interacts with that context to demonstrate a further problematic aspect to the roles of women and their freedom of speech portrayed in tragedy. Across the selection of plays considered, one key pattern emerges in this multivocal genre: that the contestation of and failure to control praise and blame discourses, whether in relation to those seeking or those speaking them, is dangerous. As this work shows, praise and blame remain central issues throughout tragedy, just as they were in wider Athenian society and in both traditional and contemporary poetic production.

1

Praise and the Construction of a Hero: Neoptolemus in the *Philoctetes*

In Sophocles' *Philoctetes*, the configuration of heroic identity through generation of praise and blame poetry is a key issue. The play's setting in the Trojan War, and characters such as Odysseus, Neoptolemus and Philoctetes, place it within the realm of epic poetry, and thus connect this play with heroic poetry and with the epic concerns of reputation and *kleos*.[1] Sophocles' *Philoctetes* seems to have been the first version of the fetching of Philoctetes to introduce Neoptolemus; earlier versions of the story had either Odysseus alone, or Diomedes accompanying him.[2] The introduction of Neoptolemus into this scenario puts Neoptolemus in an unusual position and makes prominent the question of heroic identity. The *Philoctetes* represents the earliest extant moment in Neoptolemus' 'heroic career'. His actions at Troy were already well known and represented in the poetic tradition.[3] There are also at least two versions extant of his death in Pindar.[4] Neoptolemus' later career at Troy and death were also featured in Greek tragedy,[5] with his death appearing in the extant plays in Euripides' *Andromache* (1085–1165).[6] However, the *Philoctetes* seems to represent the beginning of Neoptolemus' career, since it takes place either before his arrival at Troy, or at least before the sack of the city.[7] Neoptolemus' arrival at Troy may have also been part of the poetic tradition, as his fetching from Skyros seems to have been a part of the epic cycle, but this is likely to have been narrated as a quest for Odysseus and either Diomedes or Phoenix, rather than with Neoptolemus as its focus.[8] Sophocles' *Skyrioi* may also have featured this story. If so, this would suggest that Sophocles returned twice to stage the opening events of Neoptolemus' career, demonstrating a particular interest in the beginning of an individual's 'heroic' identity. However, since the play is not extant and its plot is doubtful, it is difficult to make much of this material.[9]

Sophocles' *Philoctetes* is the earliest and fullest extant representation of Neoptolemus at the start of his heroic career. Neoptolemus' position as 'pre-heroic' is marked in the text through the emphasis on his youth and inexperience, especially as he is often addressed by other characters as 'child' or 'my son', παῖ or τέκνον.[10] As a result, the *Philoctetes* has often been interpreted in terms of the 'growing up' of Neoptolemus,[11] or his 'education' by Odysseus and Philoctetes.[12] Scholars have also noted that this education of a younger man by an older maps on to a substitute parental relationship in the *Philoctetes*, given the physical absence of Neoptolemus' dead father Achilles, yet constant references to his assumed influence on Neoptolemus' choices.[13] The choice between 'father figures' or routes through education can be seen in terms of what *type* of hero Neoptolemus will grow up to be.[14] This presentation of 'types' of heroism is often framed as being a choice between heroic models, one which prioritizes force, and the other which makes use of intelligence, deception and persuasion to achieve its aims. Achilles and Odysseus are held up as the two exemplars of these heroic 'types',[15] just as in another of Sophocles' Homeric plays, the *Ajax*, a similar distinction is made between Ajax and Odysseus.[16] The presence of Odysseus in the *Philoctetes*, as well as the prominence of Achilles as an 'alternative' model for Neoptolemus to imitate, lends itself well to the presentation of Neoptolemus' choice in this play as being one between heroic types.[17]

There is an additional aspect of heroic identity that is represented in the *Philoctetes*: the central role of praise and blame poetry. In the *Philoctetes*, we see Neoptolemus not just as a young man on the way to becoming an adult, but also as a young man on his way to becoming a *hero*.[18] In the context of Greek poetry from epic onwards, the idea of *kleos*, of gaining 'glory' or a positive reputation that is conveyed, reinforced and then remembered via poetry, is central to the concept of 'heroism': it is not possible to be a 'Greek hero' and be unmentioned by poetry.[19] The question of how a hero is to be praised or blamed by the poetic tradition is not only central to our understanding of these figures, but is represented as a concern for them as characters within their own 'heroic' worlds, too. The *Philoctetes* shows Neoptolemus on the point of recognising the importance of this tradition, and the significance of developing his own poetic reputation. As such, his behaviour is guided as much by what will be considered praiseworthy by those around him as by any judgement according to internal 'Achillean' principles.[20] In making the choices that will start him on his heroic career, Neoptolemus is choosing not simply to be a particular type of person, but also to take the type of path that will make him memorable and, most importantly, celebrated, in the poetic world he inhabits. His heroic identity is in the *Philoctetes* demonstrably under construction, and is being formed through his desire to control what is said about him in the form of poetic praise and blame.[21] As such, the *Philoctetes* forms the first example of a tragedy considered in this study that interacts explicitly with this existing poetic tradition in its handling both of the importance of praise and blame, and in the genre's demonstration of the potential for contestation of such discourses.

Promises of praise

Neoptolemus' interest in seeking praise and aiming for praiseworthy behaviour is a facet of his character from the start of the play, revealed in his responses to Odysseus' and Philoctetes' promises. Both Odysseus and Philoctetes promise that Neoptolemus can be 'praised' or achieve 'glory' for following their respective propositions, and both threaten him with the opposite when Neoptolemus seems likely to disobey. Neoptolemus expresses concern for his reputation or being blamed in his conversations with both and chooses the course that will help him avoid blame and gain praise. For Philoctetes in particular, these choices are also often framed in terms of Neoptolemus becoming the 'type of person' who is praiseworthy, so that Philoctetes explicitly shapes some of his discussion with Neoptolemus in terms of Neoptolemus' identity, and his options for constructing it through his behaviour.

The praise that Odysseus offers Neoptolemus is focused not just on Neoptolemus himself, but also on Neoptolemus' father, Achilles. Odysseus first addresses Neoptolemus not by name, but by the strength of his father, with name following:

> ὦ κρατίστου πατρὸς Ἑλλήνων τραφεὶς
> Ἀχιλλέως παῖ Νεοπτόλεμε
>
> You who were raised as the child of the mightiest of Greeks, Achilles – Neoptolemus.
>
> 3–4

The use of the superlative κρατίστου is reminiscent of the epic praise terms commonly associated with Achilles, 'best of the Achaeans', and the use of it in an address to Neoptolemus implies that the younger man might be associated with such terms.[22] Similarly, when Odysseus begins to give instructions to Neoptolemus about their task, deceiving Philoctetes, he addresses him again as 'son of Achilles' (50), and repeats the description when telling Neoptolemus that he should introduce himself to Philoctetes as the 'son of Achilles' (56–7). Along with the early superlative, the patronymic address itself has the flavour of praise poetry; both epic and epinician make much of the connection between father and son as enabling excellence.[23]

After laying out his scheme that Neoptolemus should pretend to have left the Greeks due to hatred of Odysseus and the Atreids, Odysseus acknowledges that Neoptolemus is not likely to be keen on the deceit, but concludes his speech with two possible rewards:

ἀλλ᾽ ἡδὺ γάρ τι κτῆμα τῆς νίκης λαβεῖν,
τόλμα· δίκαιοι δ᾽ αὖθις **ἐκφανούμεθα**.
νῦν δ᾽ εἰς ἀναιδὲς ἡμέρας μέρος βραχὺ
δός μοι σεαυτόν, κᾆτα τὸν λοιπὸν χρόνον
κέκλησο πάντων εὐσεβέστατος βροτῶν.

But, as it is a pleasure to take a possession through a victory, dare it, and hereafter we will be **shown to be** righteous. Give yourself to me for a few shameless hours now, and later for all time **be called** the most pious of mortals.

82–5

Odysseus' promise is based upon the positive reception of their deed, rather than the deed itself. He does not say that they will be acting righteously, rather that they will be revealed as righteous, implying an external audience who will be able to see and appreciate this appearance.[24] Similarly, the claim on which he ends his speech is one not regarding Neoptolemus' actual nature or character, but rather regards his perceived character: he will be *called* most pious.[25] As with the initial address, the superlative and partitive genitive here emphasise the exceptional, epic nature of the description that Neoptolemus will apparently receive. The parallel with Odysseus' first address to Neoptolemus also indicates that Neoptolemus can draw a comparison here between the superlatives already part of the common praise for his father, and the forthcoming praise for him.

Neoptolemus is unwilling initially to subscribe to Odysseus' plan, and one of his objections is precisely to what people will say about him; he does not wish to 'be called' a traitor:

πεμφθείς γε μέντοι σοὶ ξυνεργάτης ὀκνῶ
προδότης **καλεῖσθαι**·

I was sent as a helpmate for you, but I shrink from **being called** a traitor.

93–4

This comment is pointed given that immediately before this statement Neoptolemus has suggested assaulting Philoctetes, making the unedifying point that with only one good leg, Philoctetes will not be able to resist (91–2). He complains that trickery is not 'in his nature', and connects his own attitude explicitly with Achilles' nature, so that his heroic, epicized identity as the son of Achilles is expressed (88–9).[26] However, he combines this claim about his 'nature' with the specific concern for what kind of reputation he will attract by acting through treachery, rather than being solely concerned with his own scruples about it.[27] For Neoptolemus, therefore, his identity is bound up inextricably with the reputation he will gain, and what he will be called by others.

Odysseus launches another attempt at persuading Neoptolemus, making use of the same praise-focused tactics.[28] Once again Neoptolemus is addressed not by name, but as ἐσθλοῦ πατρὸς παῖ ('son of a **noble** father' 96), so that the praise awarded Achilles by tradition seems again to indicate the potential of Neoptolemus' own praiseworthiness.[29] Odysseus finally manages to convince Neoptolemus with the promise of two 'prizes':

O: ὡς τοῦτό γ' ἔρξας δύο φέρῃ δωρήματα.
N: ποίω; μαθὼν γὰρ οὐκ ἂν ἀρνοίμην τὸ δρᾶν.
O: σοφός τ' ἂν αὑτὸς κἀγαθὸς **κεκλῇ**' ἅμα.
N: ἴτω· ποήσω, πᾶσαν αἰσχύνην ἀφείς.

O: Yes, you would gain two gifts doing this.
N: What gifts? For if I learnt that I might not refuse to do it.
O: **You will be called** both wise and good.
N: Let it go! I will do it, throwing away all shame.

117–20

Odysseus does not say anything about Neoptolemus *being* either wise or good, simply that others will call him that.[30] While the suggestion of taking Troy (113–15), or Odysseus' excuses about tricks not being the same as lies (96–101), are not sufficient to end Neoptolemus' doubts, this final promise of two-fold praise apparently convinces him. The desire for glory at Troy is often seen as the motivating factor for this choice.[31] However, Odysseus' technique here is not to offer generalized glory from conquering Troy. Instead, the specific inclusion of the types of praise discourses that Neoptolemus will earn finally win him over.[32] Neoptolemus' concern throughout their discussion has been with how acting treacherously will earn him a reputation for being the kind of person who commits treachery. The suggestion that treacherous acts may instead earn praise and a positive reputation for wisdom and goodness is enough to overcome his earlier doubts. He also no longer attempts to try to argue for different tactics, indicating that his concern over the risk to his reputation which deception may entail, not deception itself, was the stronger influence on his responses.

Odysseus is not the only character to use promised or actual praise to persuade Neoptolemus. When Neoptolemus meets Philoctetes, Philoctetes twice uses similar tactics to persuade Neoptolemus, once attempting to convince Neoptolemus to take him home, and then when trying to reclaim his bow. Before Neoptolemus introduces himself, Philoctetes has already described both the wind that brought him to Greece and the sound of Neoptolemus' voice superlatively as φίλτατος ('most dear' 234, 237). On the discovery that Neoptolemus is Achilles' son, Philoctetes extends these superlative epithets to Achilles too, describing Neoptolemus as:

ὦ φιλτάτου παῖ πατρός, ὦ φίλης χθονός,
ὦ τοῦ γέροντος θρέμμα Λυκομήδους,

Son of the dearest father, of a dear land, nursling of aged Lycomedes.

242–3

He goes on to address Neoptolemus as 'son of Achilles' (260), using the patronymic again, along with affectionate addresses to Neoptolemus as παῖ or τέκνον (260, 268, 276). When Neoptolemus gives him the news of Achilles' death, Philoctetes celebrates Achilles as εὐγενὴς ('noble' 336).

As he switches to persuasion, Philoctetes, like Odysseus, promises substantial amounts of praise and a positive reputation if Neoptolemus will do as he is asked. This pledge comes early:

τοῖσι γενναίοισί τοι
τό τ' αἰσχρὸν ἐχθρὸν καὶ τὸ χρηστὸν **εὐκλεές**.
σοὶ δ', ἐκλιπόντι τοῦτ', **ὄνειδος** οὐ καλόν,
δράσαντι δ', ὦ παῖ, πλεῖστον **εὐκλείας γέρας**,
ἐὰν μόλω 'γὼ ζῶν πρὸς Οἰταίαν χθόνα.

For noble men, what is shameful is hateful, and being useful brings **fame.** And you will have, if you neglect this, blame, not fine at all, but if you do it, my child, a great prize in glory, if only I reach the land of Oeta alive.

475–9

Philoctetes' language here is filled with epic and poetic praise and blame terms, and significantly stronger than Odysseus' claims. The use of γενναῖος recalls his earlier praise of Achilles as εὐγενὴς. As with Odysseus' elision of descriptions of Achilles and Neoptolemus, Philoctetes' suggestion here that Neoptolemus should act according to what is valued by those 'noble men' implies that by acting as he suggests, Neoptolemus can earn a similar judgement to that given to his father. In addition, Philoctetes' promises of fame and glory make use of terms derived specifically from *kleos,* making them valuable through their association with poetic praise. The prize which Philoctetes offers, a 'εὐκλείας γέρας', draws on a term, *geras,* which is itself a central feature of epic glory, and forms the compensation for heroic death alongside *kleos.*[33]

Philoctetes explicitly juxtaposes this assurance of epicized glory with the threat of blame, ὄνειδος, if Neoptolemus will not help. This contrast between praise, leading to *kleos,* and blame, is one established as the two possible alternatives for a poetic tradition, particularly in Pindar's presentations of poetry as a memorialising force, adding significant weight to Philoctetes' threat.[34] His comments are so strong here that the chorus, in supporting and responding to his plea, invoke similar terms and claim that Neoptolemus will not be able to 'blame' them for complaining later about Philoctetes' sickness:

> ἥκιστα· τοῦτ᾽ οὐκ ἔσθ᾽ ὅπως ποτ᾽ εἰς ἐμὲ
> τοὔνειδος ἕξεις ἐνδίκως ὀνειδίσαι.
>
> Not at all: You will never be able to blame this type of blame against me fairly.
>
> 522–3

The close repetition of ὄνειδος and its cognate verb in the Greek is especially noticeable given its proximity to Philoctetes' comment, and significance as a term. The chorus are, presumably, deceiving Philoctetes here, but their close echoing of his language nonetheless shows its impact.[35] This immediate echo also has the effect of keeping Philoctetes' threat alive, and in the minds of both Neoptolemus and the audience.

Philoctetes continues to swear that Neoptolemus will receive praise through association and friendship with him. Later, once Neoptolemus has apparently agreed to take Philoctetes home, he offers Neoptolemus the chance not only to hold the bow of Heracles, but also to boast of doing so:

> θάρσει, παρέσται ταῦτά σοι καὶ θιγγάνειν
> καὶ δόντι δοῦναι κἀξεπεύξασθαι βροτῶν
> ἀρετῆς ἕκατι τῶνδ᾽ ἐπιψαῦσαι μόνῳ·
>
> Be assured, it will be allowed for you to hold it and give it back to the one giving it, and **to boast loudly** that you alone among mortals, on account of your excellence, have handled it.
>
> 667–9

Here Philoctetes invites Neoptolemus to engage in a kind of self-praise, as, according to Philoctetes' formulation of the situation, Neoptolemus will be able to celebrate his own nobility among others by boasting of it. The claim that it is an act on account of ἀρετῆς that Neoptolemus can boast of connects Philoctetes' comments to the kind of heroic excellence celebrated in poetry,[36] and to the promises of heroic excellence given by Heracles at the end of the play (1420, 1425). After the brief intermission that his pain causes, Philoctetes again describes Neoptolemus as 'noble', εὐγενής, and as sprung from similarly noble ancestors (874). Philoctetes therefore connects Neoptolemus firmly to the discourse of praise with which he had earlier celebrated Achilles, and demonstrates the proof of his earlier suggestion that Neoptolemus could earn such praise by acting as Philoctetes wished. Moreover, where Odysseus only offered such praise in the future, Philoctetes begins to enact it on behalf of Neoptolemus there and then, through his immediate praising speech. This effective move from promising praise into actually praising Neoptolemus will, as we shall see, be mirrored in the other significant aspect of Philoctetes' effective use of language, when he turns to blaming Neoptolemus in the later parts of the play.

Just as he did in conversation with Odysseus, Neoptolemus reveals his willingness to be persuaded by considerations of praise and blame in his responses to Philoctetes, and thus the impact such considerations will have on his choices. When he introduces the false tale of Odysseus depriving him of his arms, he expresses an outward-looking concern for his reputation, claiming that he wishes to take violence upon the Greek commanders:

ἵν' αἱ Μυκῆναι γνοῖεν ἡ Σπάρτη θ' ὅτι
χἠ Σκῦρος ἀνδρῶν ἀλκίμων μήτηρ ἔφυ.

So that Mycenae and Sparta **may know** that Skyros also is a mother of valiant men.

325–6

Similarly, when the chorus urges him to leave without Philoctetes, Neoptolemus almost recapitulates the promise Philoctetes made him, that he could soon 'boast' of handling the bow, but reworks it to reflect his own concerns. Now, he says, it would be a problem to be 'boasting' of his deeds while they are incomplete, and when such boasts would involve lies:

κομπεῖν δ' ἔργ' ἀτελῆ σὺν ψεύδεσιν αἰσχρὸν
ὄνειδος.

To boast of incomplete actions with lies is a shameful reproach!

842

Neoptolemus apparently fears being blamed for substituting 'false' boasts for the 'true' boasts Philoctetes had promised. Once again Neoptolemus frames this as fear that he will attract blame, ὄνειδος, such that this term continues to cluster in the speech of characters and chorus immediately after Philoctetes' threat. Similarly, the discussion of justifiable boasting refers to an idea originally raised by Philoctetes, who claimed that Neoptolemus would be able to truthfully boast of having held Heracles' bow. Neoptolemus, therefore, demonstrates a continuing awareness of the importance of maintaining the right kind of reputation in his discussion with Philoctetes. However, Neoptolemus' language around this concern is influenced by Philoctetes' terms and phrasing. Philoctetes' promises and threats appear to be directly affecting Neoptolemus' choices.

Both Odysseus and Philoctetes attempt, with varying degrees of success, to persuade Neoptolemus to take their different paths by promising praise and *kleos*. Neoptolemus proves amenable to such persuasion, although initially he is more successfully persuaded by Odysseus' promises than Philoctetes'. It is reasonable to suggest that Philoctetes' promises of praise might be judged by Neoptolemus as being of less value than those of Odysseus. Odysseus can undertake that Neoptolemus' good reputation will be widely celebrated among the Achaean army, whereas Philoctetes may pledge to celebrate Neoptolemus' good reputation, but intends to do so from the obscurity of his homeland (478–9). The glory obtained from the taking of Troy will also not be available to Neoptolemus if returns Philoctetes home, and so, overall, his chances of a lasting praise-centred tradition seem higher if he follows Odysseus' instructions.[37] However, as the play progresses, Philoctetes will reveal himself a master of the poetic alternative to praise speech, which combines with his promises of praise to prove ultimately successful.

Philoctetes: master of blame

It is the actual blame that Philoctetes delivers in response to Neoptolemus' betrayal which successfully overcomes Odysseus' influence over Neoptolemus, rather than assurances of potential future praise.[38] While forgetfulness is one alternative to being praised and having one's *kleos* remembered, the Pindaric corpus in particular makes it clear that the other poetic alternative is ὄνειδος.[39] As Detienne demonstrates, blame is in much archaic and classical poetry thought to be less memorable than praise, so that extensive blame can lead to oblivion; only praise keeps one's memory truly 'alive'.[40] As discussed above, Philoctetes introduces the possibility of blame speech into his interactions with Neoptolemus, by suggesting that he could attract it by ignoring Philoctetes' needs. This dart has clearly struck home for Neoptolemus, as both he and the chorus pick up the discussion of potential blame and reproduce it – Neoptolemus, notably, at the start of his crisis, when he reveals that he pities Philoctetes and is beginning to doubt his own decision (842).

After Neoptolemus has already indicated his susceptibility to influence by blame, he reveals his betrayal of Philoctetes, and Philoctetes gives a speech which is a tour de force of blame:

> ὦ πῦρ σὺ καὶ πᾶν δεῖμα καὶ πανουργίας
> δεινῆς τέχνημ' ἔχθιστον, οἷά μ' εἰργάσω,
> οἷ' ἠπάτηκας· οὐδ' ἐπαισχύνῃ μ' ὁρῶν
> τὸν προστρόπαιον, τὸν ἱκέτην, ὦ **σχέτλιε**;
> . . .
> . . . ὦ λιμένες, ὦ προβλῆτες, ὦ ξυνουσίαι
> θηρῶν ὀρείων, ὦ καταρρῶγες πέτραι,
> ὑμῖν τάδ', οὐ γὰρ ἄλλον οἶδ' ὅτῳ λέγω,
> ἀνακλαίομαι παροῦσι τοῖς εἰωθόσιν,
> οἷ' ἔργ' ὁ παῖς μ' ἔδρασεν οὑξ Ἀχιλλέως·
> ὀμόσας ἀπάξειν οἴκαδ', ἐς Τροίαν μ' ἄγει·
> προσθείς τε χεῖρα δεξιάν, τὰ τόξα μου
> ἱερὰ λαβὼν τοῦ Ζηνὸς Ἡρακλέους ἔχει,

> You fire, you absolute horror, and hateful masterwork of terrifying villainy, what you have done to me, how you have deceived me! Are you not ashamed, looking at me, the one who turned to you, your suppliant, o cruel one? . . .O harbours, o promontories, o community of mountain beasts, o jagged rocks, to you, for I know no-one else to speak to, to my usual companions I address this lament at the things the son of Achilles has done to me! He swore to take me home, but is taking me to Troy! He gave his right hand as a pledge and took my bow, the sacred bow of the son of Zeus, Heracles, and is holding on to it . . .
>
> 927–43

Philoctetes' language is exceptionally strong,[41] and redolent with epic and other poetic language.[42] His speech conforms with the generic markers of 'flyting', the abusive or challenging speeches levied by one Homeric hero against another often as a prelude to combat, itself a form of blame poetry.[43] The monologic style, early use of the rhetorical question,[44] identification of Neoptolemus by his patronymic,[45] and reference to past significant speech events, in this case the 'oaths' of Neoptolemus, are all typical of Homeric flyting.[46] The pattern of his initial lines – address to Neoptolemus (927–30), problem in Neoptolemus' behaviour and broader perspective for its ramifications (931) and directive proposed as a solution (932) – map on to the typical structures of Homeric rebuke delineated by Minchin.[47] Philoctetes' vocabulary too is often epic in style, and of the kind which features in Homeric invective specifically. Rehm has identified in Philoctetes' initial address to Neoptolemus, ὦ πῦρ, a web of resonances across the poetic, primarily epic, tradition, both to Neoptolemus' future fate at Troy and to alternative traditions connected to his naming.[48] The use of the term σχέτλιε to address Neoptolemus is also significant. This term has a Homeric background, yet is a description never used by the narrator of the *Iliad*, found only in speech from one character to another, as the strength of its judgement makes it unsuitable for the 'unobtrusive' Homeric narrator.[49] Philoctetes here draws on the language of Homeric invective deployed by one hero against another. Flyting is itself often associated not simply with a challenge to a Homeric hero, but also with evaluation of the hero, often in terms which find him wanting, as Parks has identified.[50] Thus Philoctetes draws expertly on an epic genre of speech ideally suited to advancing a new assessment of Neoptolemus' character and to finding it blameworthy, simultaneously enacting that blame through his invective.

Philoctetes also makes use of terms of lament in his speech, describing his language as 'ἀνακλαίομαι'. His reference to lament echoes the chorus' first description of him, when they claimed that as he arrived on stage διάσημα θρηνεῖ ('he laments clearly' 209), and in their pitiful description of his situation that he was lamenting alone with no hearer (691–5). Neoptolemus described Philoctetes in their initial conversation as having plenty of his own griefs to lament, στένειν (339–40), when Philoctetes offered to lament Neoptolemus' sorrows (338). The association between Philoctetes and lament is therefore well established in his characterization before he turns to deploying lament along with his blame for Neoptolemus here. These associations with lament are significant, given the suitability of lament for the introduction of blame speech, as seen in both epic poetry and other tragedies such as Sophocles' *Electra,* Euripides' *Trojan Women* or the *Medea*.[51] His blame for Neoptolemus successfully makes use both of language with epic connotations, and of traditional features of lament, indicating his mastery of the genre of blame.[52]

Philoctetes includes within this speech of blame an appeal to Neoptolemus to return the bow, which is, for the moment, ignored. When Neoptolemus refuses to answer him, Philoctetes again refers to Neoptolemus as 'son of Achilles'.

Earlier, that address had been combined in Odysseus' and Philoctetes' language with praise, but here Philoctetes combines this marker of identity with his majestic speech of blame, tainting its earlier positive connotations. Initially, this blame may only be spread to the landscape around Philoctetes, so is not likely to reach a wide audience.[53] Given Philoctetes' extended isolation, Neoptolemus might also have been able to rely on Philoctetes' blame being limited in its reach. However, after his brief interchange with the wavering Neoptolemus, it is possible to see Philoctetes' expressed blame successfully reaching a human target. Neoptolemus continues to indicate his doubts (965–6, 969–70), and Philoctetes continues to emphasize that Neoptolemus may receive blame, specifically, for his deception (967–8: μὴ παρῇς / σαυτὸν βροτοῖς **ὄνειδος**). Finally, Philoctetes assures him:

> οὐκ εἶ **κακὸς** σύ· πρὸς **κακῶν** δ᾽ ἀνδρῶν μαθὼν
> ἔοικας ἥκειν αἰσχρά.
>
> You are not wicked, but you seem to have come here after learning shameful things from wicked men.[54]
>
> 971–2

Immediately, however, Odysseus appears on the scene, and addresses the doubting Neoptolemus directly: ὦ **κάκιστ᾽** ἀνδρῶν, τί δρᾷς; ('Most wicked of men, what are you doing?' 974). He therefore repeats the terms implied in Philoctetes' blame for Neoptolemus. Philoctetes has just threatened Neoptolemus with similar terms of blame; in claiming that Neoptolemus is *not* quite κακὸς, yet associating the description with Neoptolemus' actions, he makes it clear that unless Neoptolemus returns the bow, this is the blame he will deserve. Yet on his appearance, Odysseus shows that the charge of κακὸς threatened by Philoctetes may already be attaching itself to Neoptolemus. Neoptolemus, apparently cowed by this rebuke, does not speak again for some time – instead, Philoctetes and Odysseus engage in an argument, before Philoctetes launches another speech of blame against Odysseus, and laments for his own fate (984–5, 1004–44). Neoptolemus remains silent until Philoctetes again calls him by his patronymic, this time 'seed of Achilles' (1066), at which point Neoptolemus instructs the chorus to stay with Philoctetes (1074–80) only due to his growing pity for the man.[55]

The next we hear from Neoptolemus, he has resolved to give back the bow. He describes his previous behaviour, both tricking Philoctetes and obtaining the bow, as acting αἰσχρῶς (shamefully), repeating the term three times in his conversation with Odysseus (1228, 1234, 1249). As has been well established, the idea of 'shame' as a motivating factor in its representations in archaic and classical Greek poetry is often connected to the judgement of others in the community,[56] so that Neoptolemus can be seen again responding to a fear of potential external judgements in his decisions. Odysseus repeats the address 'son of Achilles' in this conversation (1237) but introduces no new promises of praise or threats of blame in response to Neoptolemus' change of behaviour. Instead, he threatens Neoptolemus with violence, both individually and then via the force of the Greek army (1239, 1243, 1250, 1253, 1255). Neoptolemus resists both (1242, 1244, 1251, 1253). Despite Neoptolemus' earlier faith in violence to persuade or compel action, the tactic proves entirely useless for Odysseus.

Philoctetes is unwelcoming upon Neoptolemus' return with the bow, and persists with his blame discourse. He again combines his earlier patronymic address to Neoptolemus with blame, cursing him, and calling him:

> ἀρίστου πατρὸς ἔχθιστος γεγώς.
>
> Most hateful son of the best father.
>
> 1284

The superlative ἄριστος attached to Neoptolemus' father again draws on the epic discourse describing Achilles as 'best', and attaches it to a superlative of blame for Neoptolemus himself, ἔχθιστος. The praise that Neoptolemus could have earned previously as son of his father is contrasted with the blame that Philoctetes now awards instead. The combination of epithets seems to have its desired effect in sealing Neoptolemus' decision, as he immediately instructs Philoctetes to stop talking, and to take his bow (1286–7). The reconciliation between Neoptolemus and Philoctetes that follows is almost immediate, but features a curious exchange which demonstrates how important the issue of Philoctetes' blame has been for Neoptolemus:

> εἶέν. τὰ μὲν δὴ τόξ' ἔχεις, κοὐκ ἔσθ' ὅτου
> ὀργὴν ἔχοις ἂν οὐδὲ **μέμψιν** εἰς ἐμέ.
> Φ: ξύμφημι. τὴν φύσιν δ' ἔδειξας, ὦ τέκνον,
> ἐξ ἧς ἔβλαστες, οὐχὶ Σισύφου πατρός,
> ἀλλ' ἐξ Ἀχιλλέως, ὃς μετὰ ζώντων ὅτ' ἦν
> ἤκου' ἄριστα, νῦν δὲ τῶν τεθνηκότων.
> N: ἥσθην πατέρα τὸν ἀμὸν εὐλογοῦντά σε
> αὐτόν τ' ἔμ'·
>
> N: Well, so you have your bow, and you have no reason to be angry with me **nor to blame me**.

> Ph: I agree! You have revealed your nature, child, and the stock you came from, not from Sisyphus for a father, but from Achilles, who while he was among the living was spoken of in the best terms, but he is now among the dead.
> N: I am pleased to hear you speaking well of my father and of me.
>
> 1307–15

Along with the somewhat immature fear of Philoctetes' anger, Neoptolemus checks specifically whether Philoctetes still wishes to 'blame' him. He is reassured only when Philoctetes reasserts the now-familiar praise, tinged with epic overtones, that Neoptolemus is now certainly the son of Achilles, and that Achilles is 'by reputation' the best.[57] Neoptolemus again reveals his sensitivity to such speech in his response, when he expresses enjoyment both in hearing Philoctetes 'speak well of' himself, but also in hearing the praise attached to his father's reputation.

Therefore, where promises of praise and glory were sufficient to begin the process of persuading Neoptolemus, once combined with the effective blame speech of Philoctetes they become wholly successful. In growing up to be a 'hero', rather than simply a young man, the weight of praise and blame speech lies heavy on Neoptolemus. In the *Philoctetes*, where this process of growing up is explored, Neoptolemus' decisions around what kind of identity he wishes to establish for himself are crucially influenced by what kind of praise or blame speech he will attract through his actions. Even once the central question of the bow has been resolved, there is evidence that Neoptolemus' process of 'growing up' encompasses his increasing understanding of the importance of praise, in his attempts to convince Philoctetes to join him at Troy. Philoctetes is essential to Neoptolemus' own fame at Troy.[58] Without him, the city cannot be sacked, as Neoptolemus knows.[59] However, Neoptolemus does not attempt to use this fact to convince Philoctetes. Instead, he turns Philoctetes' own tactics partially against him, and tries to persuade him that he should come to Troy because:

> καλὴ γὰρ ἡ 'πίκτησις, Ἑλλήνων ἕνα
> κριθέντ' **ἄριστον**, τοῦτο μὲν παιωνίας
> ἐς χεῖρας ἐλθεῖν, εἶτα τὴν πολύστονον
> Τροίαν ἑλόντα **κλέος** ὑπέρτατον λαβεῖν.
>
> It is a fine addition to be counted the best of the Greeks, and first to come to healing hands, then to take mournful Troy, and obtain the highest fame!
>
> 1344–7

Neoptolemus draws here on the same praise terms that were convincing for him: he includes the offer of winning *kleos*, and the suggestion that Philoctetes might also be counted 'best' of the Greeks, judged (κριθέντ') by an implied external audience. Philoctetes, however, objects (1380), describing Neoptolemus' speech as entirely unsuitable. Faced with Philoctetes' rebuke, while Neoptolemus does attempt for a few more lines to convince Philoctetes (1381–96),[60] he does not attempt any further discussion of *kleos*, or any praise speech.[61] Similarly, Neoptolemus continues to demonstrate his own concern with how he will be spoken of, commenting that he fears αἰτίαν from the Achaeans after helping Philoctetes (1404). Yet Philoctetes' assurance that Neoptolemus should not think of it (1404) is enough to assuage this concern, as he promptly moves on to worrying about the risk of physical repercussions instead (1405). By the end of the play, Neoptolemus is willing to take Philoctetes' advice on both his own attempts to praise and his fear of blame, apparently recognising the superior influence of his older comrade in this area.

Philoctetes' strength in this arena, however, lies not only in his use of the effective specific blame discourses that I have outlined so far, nor in his being older and more experienced than Neoptolemus. Rather, Philoctetes' explicit awareness of the importance of praise speech and *kleos*, and Sophocles' portrayal of him as intimately connected to a wider network of praise-centred poetry, make him successful in deploying this kind of speech, and a valuable example for Neoptolemus.

Sophocles' Philoctetes and the praise poetry tradition

As scholars have shown, Sophocles' Philoctetes is himself an epic figure, since the play makes repeated connections between Philoctetes and epic poetry.[62] His island is described in terms that recall Odyssean islands, including Polyphemus' home and Ithaca,[63] and he is himself drawn into extensive parallels with Odysseus and Achilles.[64] However, Philoctetes' relationship with poetry is not simply that he is presented as very similar to the subjects of epic poetry; he is also presented as a character who is especially and unusually familiar with the nature and importance of praise and blame speech and its poetic background.

It is clear on his initial meeting with Neoptolemus that Philoctetes is sensitive to the value of reputation and *kleos*. He is openly dismayed that Neoptolemus has not heard already who he is, or his story, and expresses this in an exclamation of how unfortunate he must be to be unheard of:

οὐδ' ὄνομ' <ἄρ'> οὐδὲ τῶν ἐμῶν κακῶν **κλέος**
ᾔσθου ποτ' οὐδέν, οἷς ἐγὼ διωλλύμην;
...
ὦ πόλλ' ἐγὼ μοχθηρός ὦ πικρὸς θεοῖς,
οὗ μηδὲ **κληδὼν** ὧδ' ἔχοντος οἴκαδε
μηδ' Ἑλλάδος γῆς μηδαμοῦ διῆλθέ που.

Do you not understand anything of my name or the ***kleos*** of my troubles, by which I was perishing?
...
Oh most wretched me, and hateful to the gods, since no **repute** of my plight has made its way home, nor to any part of Greece.

251–2, 254–6

Philoctetes describes this story of his suffering as his own *kleos*, the reputation he should be having preserved in poetry.[65] The word he uses to describe the fate he has suffered from his troubles, διωλλύμην, is also used elsewhere in Sophocles to mean 'forgotten' or 'blotted out'.[66] The opposite of *kleos* is, in the Greek formulation of the concepts, being forgotten and consigned to oblivion. This is the fate that awaits both an individual blamed, or simply unspoken of.[67] Philoctetes recognizes that his *kleos* is lacking if his name is not being talked about among the Greeks, and expresses the result in terms of a risk of the oblivion of forgetfulness.[68] After Philoctetes has addressed this gap in Neoptolemus' knowledge by telling his own story, Neoptolemus immediately shows the effectiveness of the correction by describing Philoctetes to the merchant as the κλεινός Philoctetes (575), another word that derives from the same root as *kleos*. It would be possible to see this simply as Neoptolemus' flattery,[69] but given their earlier conversation, and the importance Philoctetes placed on correcting his lack of *kleos*, Neoptolemus' description here also suggests an immediate successful promotion of the *kleos* of Philoctetes, which is now spreading through the words of men as it should.[70]

Philoctetes' facility with song, as well as his awareness of its importance, is another persistent aspect of his characterization. As noted above, Philoctetes' first entry on to the stage is described in terms of the sounds he makes.[71] His arrival is depicted not solely in terms of sound, but in connection with *poetic* sound. The chorus say διάσημα θρηνεῖ ('he laments clearly' 209),[72] and they go on to specify:

οὐ μολπὰν σύριγγος ἔχων,
ὡς ποιμὴν ἀγροβάτας,

Not holding the note of a shepherd's pipe, like the herdsman in the countryside.

213–14

Philoctetes' shouting (βοᾷ, 216) is therefore to be contrasted with the sound of a pastoral singer, and the chorus frame the sounds he is making specifically through comparison to song rather than other types of utterance.[73] His final lines on stage, his farewell to Lemnos (1452–68), also have a poetic tinge, noticed by Vidal-Naquet, in the pastoral frame in which they cast the Lemnian landscape.[74] Given their closural function for the play, and the use of invocation in this speech, Nooter has identified these lines with a hymnal closure.[75] From start to finish, therefore, Philoctetes' speech is marked by the use, often self-consciously, of a wide range of poetic genres, including lament, hymn, epic, and allusions to pastoral. This poetic quality gives his speech significant impact and has particular effect when combined with the poetically significant genres of praise and blame. Philoctetes' facility with efficacious poetry, both in his associations with *kleos*-granting epic and through his connections to other genres thus helps to explain the persuasiveness of Philoctetes' use of both praise and blame to persuade Neoptolemus.

The relationship between Philoctetes and Neoptolemus is also framed in poetic terms. Philoctetes is clearly to be associated in the *Philoctetes* with the future praise tradition of Neoptolemus, beyond his essential presence at the sacking of Troy. Even before the reconciliation of Neoptolemus and Philoctetes, Neoptolemus acknowledges the centrality of Philoctetes to this tradition, when he claims regarding the sack of Troy:

τοῦδε γὰρ ὁ **στέφανος**, τοῦτον θεὸς εἶπε κομίζειν.

For it is he who wins the garland, he whom the god told us to bring.

841

Neoptolemus' description of the sack as a στέφανος associates Philoctetes' future victory with athletic victories, but also associates it with praise poetry. The description of the songs of Pindar as 'garlands' using the term στέφανος, is commonplace, and is found in tragedy too.[76] Neoptolemus' claim thus elides the sacking of Troy with the poetic celebrations which it will receive, making Philoctetes essential for the poetic praise as much as the deed itself.

Philoctetes' connection with Heracles and his bow makes his relationship with *kleos* especially marked. The bow is itself a significant object, and is described repeatedly in terms related to poetry.[77] When Neoptolemus first mentions the bow, he calls it κλεινά (654), invoking the fame engendered from poetry. The bow is also described by terms which are epic in their connotations by both Philoctetes and Odysseus. After the deprivation of the bow, Philoctetes twice claims that Neoptolemus is taking his 'life', βίος (930–3), drawing on a contemporary wordplay with the epic word for bow, βιός.[78] Upon his arrival on the scene, Odysseus describes the bow as a γέρας (1061), which, as noted above, has been identified by Loraux as a key epic term. In his claim that Philoctetes' γέρας may be assigned now to Odysseus as a τιμή (1062), Odysseus evokes two specific epic scenarios: the apparent deprivation of τιμή from Achilles after the reassignment of his prize, his γέρας, in the *Iliad*, and the awarding of Achilles' arms after his death, already mentioned in this play.[79] The bow is associated through its fame with celebration in poetry, and is spoken about by multiple characters in terms which evoke both the epic genre in general and the specific awarding of prizes and arms in epic poetry. Obtaining it enables Neoptolemus not only to gain his own glory via the capture of Troy, but also to become connected to this epic weaponry and the bow's own fame.

The bow also forms part of the connection between Heracles, Philoctetes, and Neoptolemus created at the end of the play.[80] This wider association with Heracles, particularly when it leads to his appearance on stage, further ties Philoctetes into a nexus of concepts associated with praise poetry. In that appearance, Heracles himself guarantees to Philoctetes that he will achieve substantial glory, prizes, and fame:

καὶ πρῶτα μέν σοι τὰς ἐμὰς λέξω τύχας,
ὅσους **πονήσας** καὶ διεξελθὼν **πόνους**
ἀθάνατον ἀρετὴν ἔσχον, ὡς πάρεσθ' ὁρᾶν.
καὶ σοί, σάφ' ἴσθι, τοῦτ' ὀφείλεται παθεῖν,
ἐκ τῶν **πόνων** τῶνδ' **εὐκλεᾶ** θέσθαι βίον.
. . .
ἀρετῇ τε πρῶτος ἐκκριθεὶς στρατεύματος,
Πάριν μέν, ὃς τῶνδ' αἴτιος κακῶν ἔφυ,
τόξοισι τοῖς ἐμοῖσι νοσφιεῖς βίου,
πέρσεις τε Τροίαν, σκῦλά τ' ἐς μέλαθρα σὰ
πέμψεις, **ἀριστεῖ'** ἐκλαβὼν στρατεύματος,
Ποίαντι πατρὶ πρὸς πάτρας Οἴτης πλάκα.

And first I will tell you about my fortunes, how many labours I endured to pass through and win eternal glory, as you can see here. And for you too, know it for sure, destiny is the same: from these labours to make your life glorious. . . You will be judged first in valour among the army, and Paris, who was the cause of these evils, you will deprive of life with my bow, taking Troy, and bringing the spoils to your home, after receiving the best prize from the army, for your father Poias to the top plain of Oeta your homeland.

1418–30

Heracles' association between his labours and his glory, and the subsequent description of Philoctetes' own sufferings also as labours, πόνων, connects the 'glory' Heracles has achieved with a promise of the same glory for Philoctetes. He goes further, assuring Philoctetes of the 'best' prizes in the war, and even that he will be judged to be the first among the Greeks while there, again associating Philoctetes with the same judgement of excellence from an external audience promised him by Neoptolemus earlier (1345). As a result, Philoctetes is also associated with the 'Best of the Achaeans' praise discourse which is a key part of the Iliadic tradition. Heracles' speech, like many of the similar guarantees made in this play, is filled with terms connected to *kleos* and epic praise.[81] It is not surprising that similar promises to those made by Neoptolemus about Philoctetes' glory at Troy are here successful, when spoken by a god.[82] The association Heracles makes between himself and Philoctetes here also has the effect of drawing a further connection between Philoctetes and praise poetry. Heracles, rather more than Philoctetes, is the frequent subject of poetic praise such as in epinician or hymns, which often celebrate the triumph over his 'labours' to reach glory.[83] In applying the same description to Philoctetes, Heracles implicates him in a similar level of celebration, given his promises of *kleos*.[84] Similarly, the prophecy Heracles makes to Neoptolemus along with Philoctetes is redolent with the language of epic, when he claims that:

οὔτε γὰρ σὺ τοῦδ᾽ ἄτερ σθένεις
ἑλεῖν τὸ Τροίας πεδίον οὔθ᾽ οὗτος σέθεν·
ἀλλ᾽ ὡς λέοντε συννόμω φυλάσσετον
οὗτος σὲ καὶ σὺ τόνδ᾽.

For neither will you have the strength to take the Trojan plain without him, nor he without you. But like kindred lions you two keep watch – him over you, and you over him.

1434–6

The description of Philoctetes and Neoptolemus as 'twin lions' ties both characters into an epic simile, as has frequently been noted.[85] Heracles' assurances therefore have a double poetic impact. To Philoctetes, he promises the praise poetry tradition which has been Heracles' own, by virtue of his sufferings.

However, by association with Philoctetes, Neoptolemus too can take up his place in the poetic tradition, in praise of his exploits at Troy.[86]

By contrast, Odysseus is remarkably distanced from his own poetic tradition or its celebration. While there are substantial parallels between the *Odyssey* and the *Philoctetes*, these parallels tend to draw connections between the Homeric Odysseus and Philoctetes, and Neoptolemus and Telemachus.[87] The Sophoclean Odysseus is often left out of this web of allusions. The only moment of his 'heroic' past which is discussed in the play is the (ostensibly false) tale of his claiming of Achilles' arms. In the *Philoctetes*, this tale is told by Neoptolemus to justify his claims to hate Odysseus and the Atreids (329–90). The recalling of this story here is likely to remind at least some of the audience of its inclusion in another Neoptoleman context, Pindar's *Nemean* 7, where the story of Neoptolemus' death is preceded with Pindar's claim that Homeric tradition has positively distorted both Odysseus' fame and, specifically, the story of the arms of Achilles:

> . . . ἐγὼ δὲ πλέον' ἔλπομαι
> λόγον Ὀδυσσέος ἢ πάθαν
> διὰ τὸν ἁδυεπῆ γενέσθ' Ὅμηρον·
> ἐπεὶ ψεύδεσί οἱ ποτανᾷ <τε> μαχανᾷ
> σεμνὸν ἔπεστί τι· σοφία
> δὲ κλέπτει παράγοισα μύθοις. τυφλὸν δ' ἔχει
> ἦτορ ὅμιλος ἀνδρῶν ὁ πλεῖστος. εἰ γὰρ ἦν
> ἓν τὰν ἀλάθειαν ἰδέμεν, οὔ κεν ὅπλων χολωθείς
> ὁ καρτερὸς Αἴας ἔπαξε διὰ φρενῶν
> λευρὸν ξίφος· ὃν κράτιστον Ἀχιλέος ἄτερ μάχᾳ
> ξανθῷ Μενέλᾳ δάμαρτα κομίσαι θοαῖς
> ἂν ναυσὶ πόρευσαν εὐθυ-
> πνόου Ζεφύροιο πομπαί
> πρὸς Ἴλου πόλιν. ἀλλὰ κοινὸν γὰρ ἔρχεται
> κῦμ' Ἀίδα, πέσε δ' ἀδόκη-
> τον ἐν καὶ δοκέοντα· τιμὰ δὲ γίνεται
> ὧν θεὸς ἁβρὸν αὔξει λόγον τεθνακότων.

I believe that Odysseus' story has become more than his actual suffering because of Homer's sweet singing, for on his lies and winged crafts rests great reverence, and his skill deceives with misleading tales. The great majority of men has a blind heart. For if they could have seen the truth, mighty Ajax would not have been angered over the arms and stuck the smooth sword through his chest. Except for Achilles he was the mightiest in battle, of those whom the friendly breezes of the straight-blowing Zephyr brought to the city of Troy in swift ships, to carry off his wife to fair-haired Menelaus. But the waves of Hades hold all in common, and fall on the unknown and the famous; yet honour belongs to those whose fair tale a god exalts once they have died.

Nem. 7. 20–32

This passage of *Nemean* 7, which argues for the importance of poetic praise in confirming reputation, also recalls the awarding of the arms of Achilles, but claims that these should have been given to Ajax as the 'best' in battle, and that Odysseus' reputation has been made unduly great by the poetic tradition, especially Homer.[88] The connection between the arms of Achilles and Neoptolemus is somewhat tenuous; however, the poem demonstrates a connection between the awarding of the arms and the value of praise poetry in establishing a reputation.[89] It connects this issue with the reputation of Neoptolemus, and presents a distinctly unflattering portrayal of Odysseus. Simultaneously, Odysseus' exclusion from the epic allusions in the play prevents the allusion to an alternative poetic tradition more flattering to Odysseus. The allusion to the Pindaric association between Neoptolemus and an unfair awarding of the arms invites the audience to see here an Odysseus who has an undeserved poetic praise tradition, and one who does not demonstrate the same effective connections with praise poetry as those maintained by Philoctetes in the play.[90]

There are also potentially allusive connections made between Philoctetes' facility for blame speech and the wider poetic tradition. When Philoctetes asks Neoptolemus about the Greek heroes, he mentions Odysseus and Diomedes (416–18), and Ajax in connection to the arms of Achilles (403–11), thus again casting a potential shadow on the reputation of Odysseus. However, he also asks about two further Greeks: Nestor and Thersites, and speaks of Thersites in negative terms:

Φ: οὐ τοῦτον εἶπον, ἀλλὰ Θερσίτης τις ἦν,
ὃς οὐκ ἂν εἵλετ' εἰσάπαξ εἰπεῖν, ὅπου
μηδεὶς ἐῴη· τοῦτον οἶσθ' εἰ ζῶν κυρεῖ;
N: οὐκ εἶδον αὐτός, ᾐσθόμην δ' ἔτ' ὄντα νιν.

Ph: I did not speak of him, but there was this person Thersites, who never chose to speak once and for all, even when no one wished him to talk: do you know if he is still alive?
N: I did not see him, but I believe that he is.

442–5

The inclusion of Thersites among Philoctetes' inquiries is interesting, especially as there is no indication in the earlier tradition that they had any relationship at all.[91] Neoptolemus' claim that he believes Thersites to still be alive is an additional problem; the audience should likely be aware that, more usually, Thersites is killed by Achilles, so he should be dead by the time of the *Philoctetes*.[92] However, the mention of Thersites introduces two significant Iliadic aspects into the discussion. Firstly, he is presented in the *Iliad* as an antagonist of Achilles, Agamemnon and Odysseus, such that some have seen Philoctetes' dislike of him here as drawing the connections between Philoctetes and the Iliadic Greek leaders more fully.[93] More importantly for Philoctetes' strength in poetic praise and blame speech, Thersites is in the *Iliad* associated explicitly with blame speech against the Greek heroes. His speech to Agamemnon in Book 2, along with his general pattern of comments about the Greek leaders, are described by the narrator as νεῖκος ('blame' 2.221, 224, 243), and Odysseus complains about the same thing while beating him:[94]

> Θερσῖτ' ἀκριτόμυθε, λιγύς περ ἐὼν ἀγορητής,
> ἴσχεο, μηδ' ἔθελ' οἶος ἐριζέμεναι βασιλεῦσιν.
> οὐ γὰρ ἐγὼ σέο φημὶ χερειότερον βροτὸν ἄλλον
> ἔμμεναι, ὅσσοι ἅμ' Ἀτρεΐδης ὑπὸ Ἴλιον ἦλθον.
> τῶ οὐκ ἂν βασιλῆας ἀνὰ στόμ' ἔχων ἀγορεύοις,
> καί σφιν **ὀνείδεά** τε προφέροις, νόστον τε φυλάσσοις.

> Thersites of babbling speech, although you are a clear speaker, restrain yourself, and do not wish to quarrel alone with kings. For I say that there is no more inferior mortal than you among all those who with the sons of Atreus came beneath Troy. So you should not hold the name of kings in your mouth as you harangue in the assembly, and cast forth **blame** for them, and watch out for a return.
>
> *Il.* 2.246-51

Nagy has connected the figure of Thersites here with the *Margites*, an alternative blame and laughter-centred tradition which rejects the values of praise poetry.[95] Even if Thersites' limited appearance in the *Iliad* is not enough to point to a separate poetic tradition, it is striking that it is a figure singled out for his tendency to blame the Greek leaders that makes his appearance here. It is also Philoctetes who remembers him and complains of his speech, and thus shows awareness of this alternative, blame-centred type of speech.

In this unexpected inclusion of Thersites in his remembrances, Philoctetes therefore introduces a further poetic allusion, which ties him into a tradition of blame, lending additional weight to his own success and fluency with blame speech. The inclusion of Nestor as the other figure remembered by Philoctetes further strengthens this aspect, since Nestor has a unique function within the *Iliad* in preserving the memories of heroes of a previous generation, and connections with poetic speech which are reflected in his epithet ἡδυεπής. Martin has discussed him as someone who both promises and bestows *kleos* with this memorializing function.[96] The combination of references to these two opposing epic speakers, therefore, demonstrates Philoctetes' ongoing, almost metapoetic, awareness of the capacity for poetry to confirm such discourses as someone's *kleos*, again demonstrating a significant factor behind his success with persuasion of Neoptolemus, who values such discourses so highly.

Therefore, in the *Philoctetes* Philoctetes is connected to a greater web of possible poetic allusions than Odysseus. Odysseus is often considered by scholars in terms of his connections with contemporary sophists – but these are not poets or generally connected to poetic content in contemporary thought.[97] As a result, the type of speech which each older man offers Neoptolemus is distinct, with Philoctetes the only one able to make use of a long tradition of poetic praise and blame. In the contest of praise and blame which both characters advance as methods of persuading Neoptolemus, therefore, it is not surprising that Philoctetes is the more successful speaker.

Conclusion

The *Philoctetes* demonstrates a persistent interest in how both spoken and sung poetic praise and blame contribute to heroic identity. The introduction of Neoptolemus into the myth allows Sophocles to present a figure whose heroic identity is as yet undeveloped, and whose reputation or *kleos* becomes a key concern to him. Faced with a choice between the ability to gain poetic praise from a poetic, influential speaker, or the sophistic *seeming* good offered by Odysseus, Neoptolemus chooses poetic praise and *kleos*, taking the first steps towards a fully heroic identity. However, by choosing to pursue the actions which will lead to a heroic praise-poetry tradition, he has signed up to its most negative aspects in relation to his *own* poetic tradition, as Heracles' final warning makes clear.

Attention to the development of poetic praise and blame speech in the *Philoctetes* has ramifications for the figure of Philoctetes, as well as illuminating Neoptolemus' choices. The web of poetic connections surrounding Philoctetes, both epic and epinician, and his facility in making use of language from lament to epic, make him an influential speaker of both praise and blame speech. This influence enables him to persuade Neoptolemus, and will eventually lead to his own poetic rehabilitation, from a man with apparently no *kleos*, to one promised celebrations as extensive as those praising Heracles himself.

2

The Best of the Rest: Ajax Thwarted

Sophocles' *Ajax* shares the epic context of the *Philoctetes*, and, like that play, makes the role of praise and blame in establishing a heroic identity a central issue. In contrast to the *Philoctetes*, however, the focus of the *Ajax* is on an already established heroic character, whose concerns with *kleos* and praise discourses centre on that which should already have been won, rather than that yet to be achieved. In the *Ajax* the contestation of these discourses has destructive, damaging effects far beyond those seen in the *Philoctetes*, demonstrating the problems with the uncontrolled, multivocal aspects of praise and blame as it appears in Greek tragedy.

Issues around *kleos* are central to the *Iliad*, especially as the praise or blame allotted heroes through epic poetry itself establishes *kleos*.[1] In the *Iliad*, the most celebrated warrior and target for this praise is Achilles, whose wrath opens the action, and whose status and glory is central even when he is physically removed from the action, partly due to his own claim that his wrath stems from Agamemnon's failure to treat him as 'Best of the Achaeans' (1.410–12).[2] Ajax, son of Telamon, who leads the fighting when Achilles is absent, and is named 'Best of the Achaeans – after Achilles' (2.768) stands in second place to Achilles. In the following lyric tradition, Ajax maintains a similar status; in Alcaeus (fr. 387 *PLF*) he is described as τὸν ἄριστον πεδ' Ἀχίλλεα, and an Athenian drinking song similarly calls him:

> ἐς Τροΐαν ἄριστον ἐλθεῖν Δαναῶν μετ' Ἀχιλλέα
>
> The best of the Greeks who came to Troy, after Achilles.
>
> 898.2 *PMG*

In the *Ajax*, however, Ajax's place and reputation have become contested; the play takes place after Achilles is dead, yet in the contest for his arms and his legacy Ajax, second to him in the *Iliad*, is not the winner. Instead Odysseus has been awarded Achilles' arms, which are marked as a prize for the Greek who is the 'best in prowess', ἀριστόχειρ (935). In the *Ajax*, Ajax's failure is represented not simply as a failure to win Achilles' arms, but rather a failure to appropriate the whole discourse of praise which positions and identifies him as the 'Best of the Achaeans'. Ajax claims a right to the praise Achilles received, to be himself praised as the 'best'. Yet those around him demonstrate that this claim is inappropriate, and so he fails. Instead, Ajax continues to receive praise couched in the same terms as that he is given in the *Iliad*. He is described as strong, and great, but he remains second best, and cannot inherit the language used to describe Achilles, even when he is rehabilitated at the end of the play.

The destructive violence that breaks out as a result of Ajax's failure to maintain his identity within this particular discourse of praise corresponds to the situation which Moore has described as 'thwarting':

> Thwarting can be understood as the inability to sustain or properly take up a gendered subject position, resulting in a crisis, real or imagined, of self-representation and/or social evaluation.[3]

Moore notes that the process of thwarting regularly involves violence as a response to this failure to sustain a particular subject position.[4] Moore's analysis recognizes that such a crisis can be connected to a challenge to identity which results in the loss of assets, such as Achilles' arms. Ajax's failure to secure these thus confronts him with his simultaneous failure to position himself as 'Best of the Achaeans' within the poetic praise discourse that establishes this identity, and he experiences thwarting. As a result, he turns first to attempted external violence against the Atreids, and then finally to suicide. Therefore, scholars who argue that Ajax is rehabilitated after his death, as a result of Odysseus' willingness to praise him,[5] have not fully acknowledged that this praise is not the *kind* of praise language which Ajax has sought. Instead, Odysseus continues only to position him within the same discourse of praise as is found describing Ajax in both the *Iliad* and Sophocles' *Ajax*. Ajax is described as best only after Achilles, so that Ajax's attempt to position himself as now best outright remains unsuccessful. The failure of the people around Ajax, including the chorus, to reproduce his claim in their own praise, or to consistently produce any praise assimilating him to Achilles, makes his claim impossible. As a result, the *Ajax* demonstrates acutely how the dialogic, multivocal nature of tragedy can create conflict in the generation of and desire for praise language within the genre.

Ajax: Best of the Achaeans?

A key part of praise of Greek heroes as it is presented in the *Iliad* is the ranking of heroes against one another in allotting praise.[6] This ranking language in the

Iliad contributes to a judgement of which hero is to be labelled the 'Best of the Achaeans'.[7] The contest for the arms of Achilles brings this Iliadic context directly to the foreground of the *Ajax*; Achilles is proclaimed by the *Iliad* to be the best of the Achaeans, and so a contest among the heroes after his death to judge the most worthy to receive his weapons also raises the idea of judging which hero is most worthy to stand as his successor in that role. Both Ajax (443) and the chorus (935) specifically connect the prize of the arms with the idea of who is ἄριστος, best, so that the weapons become connected to the position and title Achilles has held, as best of the Achaeans, a title confirmed through poetic praise.[8] At the start of the *Ajax*, therefore, this Iliadic title of 'best' seems to be at issue, and it is this title, established through poetic praise, which Ajax has failed to have confirmed through a successful transferral of Achilles' arms to his possession.

Ajax himself makes an explicit claim to this highest title available in epic praise poetry, when he claims:

οὐκέτ' ἄνδρα μή
τόνδ' ἴδητ' – ἔπος
ἐξερῶ μέγα –
οἷον οὔτινα
Τρωία στρατοῦ
δέρχθη χθονὸς μολόντ' ἀπὸ
Ἑλλανίδος·

No longer shall you look upon a man – I will speak a great word – such as no other of the army that Troy saw come from the land of Hellas!

421–6

By claiming to be a Greek such as no other, Ajax's 'great word' recalls the typical Iliadic framework that judges the 'best' hero among the Greeks, and which places Ajax as mightiest after Achilles.[9] It is not immediately framed in extreme terms; Ajax does not state whether his remark refers to his status as exceptional only now that Achilles is dead, nor does he draw a comparison directly between them. However, in his next speech, Ajax does invoke Achilles deliberately and sets up a comparison between the two of them by introducing him as a judge for the award of his arms:

εἰ ζῶν Ἀχιλλεὺς τῶν ὅπλων τῶν ὧν πέρι
κρίνειν ἔμελλε κράτος **ἀριστείας** τινί,
οὐκ ἄν τις αὔτ' ἔμαρψεν ἄλλος ἀντ' ἐμοῦ.

> If Achilles were still alive and intended to judge the prize in excellence for someone in a contest for his own arms, no other would take that prize instead of me.
>
> 442–4

The claim is rather awkward, as presumably if Achilles were still alive, he would not be giving his arms away at all. However, through the naming of Achilles in this context, Ajax reminds his hearers of his claim, which he tried to assert twenty lines earlier, not only to the arms belonging to Achilles, but also his epithet, and identity, as best of the Achaeans. The use of ἀριστείας, closely related to the praise term ἄριστος, indicates the praise he seeks, and is evocative of the close connection with Achilles demonstrated in Ajax's language. By conjuring up the awkward image of Achilles awarding his own arms to Ajax, Ajax almost creates a slippage between their two identities; Achilles cannot possibly award the arms to Ajax yet carry them himself, unless they are to be identified as the same person.[10] In his language around his claim to the arms of Achilles, Ajax therefore attempts to establish a simultaneous claim to Achilles' typical praise discourses, specifically, to the identification as 'Best of the Achaeans' which had described Achilles while he was alive.

Ajax does not only assert his own right to this type of praise, but also emphasizes his father's ability to claim such a title. The vocabulary he uses makes it even clearer that he seeks Achilles' praise and title, rather than solely the physical prize of Achilles' weapons. His father's success in becoming 'the best' among an Achaean army particularly seems to chafe for Ajax. He says,

> ὅτου πατὴρ μὲν τῆσδ' ἀπ' Ἰδαίας χθονὸς
> τὰ πρῶτα καλλιστεῖ' **ἀριστεύσας** στρατοῦ
> πρὸς οἶκον ἦλθε πᾶσαν **εὔκλειαν** φέρων·
> ἐγὼ δ' ὁ κείνου παῖς, τὸν αὐτὸν ἐς τόπον
> Τροίας ἐπελθὼν οὐκ ἐλάσσονι σθένει,
> οὐδ' ἔργα μείω χειρὸς ἀρκέσας ἐμῆς,
> ἄτιμος Ἀργείοισιν ὧδ' ἀπόλλυμαι.

> . . . I, whose father came home from this land of Ida after winning the army's finest prize for **excellence**, and bringing every kind of **glory**. But I, his son, came to the same place, Troy, with no less strength, and having performed with my own hand no less great deeds, I am destroyed, dishonoured by the Argives.
>
> 434–9

The formulation of the remark about his father's prize once again recalls the epic praise which Ajax seeks, with its use of the word ἀριστεύσας. This statement is tied directly into the praise Ajax's father received for his exploits, by use of the word εὔκλειαν and the fame which Telamon's excellence has gained him.[11] Ajax claims a right to the praise his father received for what he sees as deeds of equal greatness, in terms which also strongly echo the kind of praise which Achilles deservedly claimed in the *Iliad*.[12] Similarly, when Ajax attempts to decide what he can possibly do after the slaughter of the flocks, he asks,

> καὶ ποῖον ὄμμα πατρὶ δηλώσω φανεὶς
> Τελαμῶνι; πῶς με τλήσεταί ποτ' εἰσιδεῖν
> γυμνὸν φανέντα τῶν **ἀριστείων** ἄτερ,
> ὧν αὐτὸς ἔσχε στέφανον **εὐκλείας** μέγαν;

> And what kind of expression shall I show to my father, Telamon, when I appear? How will he ever bear looking at me when I appear naked, without the prize for **being the best**, when he himself got a great crown of **glory**?
>
> 462–5

Ajax again demonstrates his preoccupation with the same ideas, even repeating the same phrases in his use of ἀριστείων and εὐκλείας. Ajax's concern is not simply that his father had won renown or prizes which he himself did not; it is the *type* of prize which his father had been able to claim which upsets him. His father had won a prize for the ἄριστος Greek, one which comes with a στέφανον εὐκλείας, a phrase particularly evocative of praise poetry.[13] Telamon, therefore, had successfully won the same prizes and been honoured in the same way as Achilles, while Ajax in seeking that prize has been entirely unsuccessful. Ajax is not the only one to suggest the parallels between Achilles and the kinds of prize which Telamon had won, and which Ajax has failed to gain. In a description of his parentage, Teucer claims:

> ὃς ἐκ πατρὸς μέν εἰμι Τελαμῶνος γεγώς,
> ὅστις στρατοῦ τὰ πρῶτ' **ἀριστεύσας** ἐμὴν
> ἴσχει ξύνευνον μητέρ', . . .

> I am born from my father Telamon, who as the army's best prize for excellence won my mother for a bedfellow.
>
> 1299–1301

The nature of the prize described here – that is, that it was Hesione – acts as a further reminder of Achilles, who also had a woman as a 'prize', Briseis, the loss of whom sparked the central conflict between him and Agamemnon in the *Iliad*, and which Achilles himself connects explicitly to Agamemnon's failure to honour ὅ τ' ἄριστον Ἀχαιῶν (*Il.* 1.410–12). Teucer's description strengthens the links between Telamon and Achilles, emphasizing that living up to his father's praiseworthy status means Ajax claiming the same kinds of praise and honour as Achilles.

Ajax's view of the position 'best of the Achaeans' therefore seems to suggest that it is one which is desired partly to meet the expectations of excellence passed on from father to son. His father had successfully maintained this position, established through a praise discourse surrounding his exploits in war and confirmed by the gifting of a prize, and Ajax demonstrates a keen awareness of his comparative failure to do the same.[14] Early on in the play, the chorus do suggest that Ajax might claim to have lived up to his father's identity of 'best', when they describe him as:

> ὅς εἷς πατρῴας ἥκων γενεᾶς ἄρι-
> στα πολυπόνων Ἀχαιῶν,
>
> He who is the best of the much-suffering Achaeans, in relation to his lineage.
>
> 636–7

However, the chorus' speech expressly goes on to state that whatever good situation Ajax might previously have been in, it no longer applies (639–40). In comparison, when Teucer talks of his own heritage, he identifies himself to Agamemnon:

> . . . ὧδ' ἄριστος ἐξ ἀριστέοιν δυοῖν
> βλαστὼν
>
> I, the best son from two of the best people.
>
> 1304–5

As with Ajax's claims about their father, Teucer creates the impression that his quality as ἄριστος, in which he is entirely secure despite Agamemnon's insults, is closely related to his father's own success at being ἄριστος. However, unlike Teucer, Ajax has apparently failed to live up to the expectations inherited from his father, that Ajax should match Telamon's identity of 'best'.

Not only has Ajax's failure to maintain this identity interrupted this succession of expectations, however, it is also possible to see a similarly interrupted succession in his failure to secure the arms of Achilles themselves. In her persuasive analysis, Goff has shown that the apparent failure in the transmission of the arms of Achilles, combined with Ajax's later concern for the disposition of his own arms, raises significant questions about Ajax's identities as son and father, both of which are disrupted through the failed transmission of the arms.[15]

Ajax's Iliadic identity as 'best . . . after Achilles' almost positions him as Achilles' successor, and his attitude in the *Ajax* to the disrupted passage of the arms from Achilles to Ajax presents this passage as a rightful inheritance.[16] His inability to properly 'inherit' his arms therefore also disrupts this aspect of his identity, compounding his inability to live up to his father's identity of 'best', established through praise.[17] Ajax proves to be unable to live up to the position expected of him as a result of his paternal inheritance, as he fails to inherit the physical symbols of that identity from a substitute paternal figure, Achilles.

The weight of the poetic tradition also lurks behind both Ajax's desire to live up to Telamon's example as a praiseworthy figure, and the connection developed between Telamon and Achilles as Ajax's paternal exemplars in the *Ajax*, adding additional pressure to the situation. Fathers play a significant role throughout the *Iliad* in the construction of heroic identity; several times characters represent themselves as acting in particular ways to live up to their fathers' standards, either at their instruction, or when compared to them by others.[18] Sophocles' representation of Ajax's concern with establishing his identity as 'best of the Achaeans', established within a discourse of praise poetry as Telamon's was, draws heavily on this tradition, so that Ajax's failure to establish his identity of 'best of the Achaeans' is one which is framed by the Iliadic context as much as the tragic. There are additional examples indicating the strength of the tradition behind this comparison between Ajax, Achilles and Telamon in the lyric tradition, in the Athenian drinking song noted earlier and its pair, which explicitly include Telamon as part of the formulation that places Ajax second to Achilles, and contrast Telamon's status and Ajax's:

> παῖ Τελαμῶνος Αἶαν αἰχμητά, λέγουσί σε
> ἐς Τροΐαν ἄριστον ἐλθεῖν Δαναῶν μετ' Ἀχιλλέα.
>
> They say that you, Ajax son of Telamon, were the best of the Greeks to come to Troy, after Achilles.
>
> *PMG* 898

> τὸν Τελαμῶνα πρῶτον, Αἴαντα δὲ δεύτερον
> ἐς Τροΐαν λέγουσιν ἐλθεῖν Δαναῶν μετ' Ἀχιλλέα.
>
> They say that Telamon was the first, and Ajax the second, after Achilles, of the Greeks to come to Troy.
>
> *PMG* 899[19]

In Sophocles' *Ajax*, therefore, Ajax carries with him a weight of pressure from both epic and lyric traditions of praise which insist that he must attempt to live up to Telamon's example and become 'best', like Achilles. These traditions indicate the impossibility of such an endeavour for Ajax, who is always framed as second best, in a way which, as we shall see, endures in the *Ajax* itself.

The poetic identity 'best' should, in Ajax's eyes, have been one which is expected of him because of his inheritance, from his father, and should have been confirmed through the award of Achilles' arms, yet Ajax's crisis and experience of thwarting comes because neither method has been successful. Ajax is unable to live up to his father's much-praised identity, and simultaneously unable to properly secure the inheritance and transmission of Achilles' arms, which further undermines his attempts at establishing this identity. The poetic tradition, while indicating the connections between these figures in Ajax's tradition, nonetheless also argues for the difficulty of such an attempt for Ajax. However, in Sophocles' *Ajax* itself it proves to be primarily in the praise and blame of those around him that Ajax's failure to sustain his attempted subject position is realized. Even characters friendly to Ajax refuse to position him within the necessary praise discourse to establish the identity of 'best'. Instead, they only reproduce Iliadic discourses of praise, repeatedly positioning him as second best. The types of praise given Ajax in the *Ajax* demonstrate repeatedly how even his most celebrated qualities are not sufficient to make him the next Achilles.

Praising Ajax and Achilles

There are clear similarities in the types of praise Ajax and Achilles are given in the *Iliad* and the wider tradition. Both are praised for their physical strength and prowess, in contrast with heroes like Odysseus who receive a wider range of praise.[20] However, although both heroes fall into a specific 'type' of praise discourse, there are significant differences in the way each is described in the *Iliad*, with these differences recurring and becoming more problematic for Ajax's claim in the *Ajax*. The differences between Ajax and Odysseus mean that Sophocles' *Ajax* has often been discussed in terms of 'types' or 'styles' of heroism, with many scholars seeing the distinction between Ajax and Odysseus as one between an archaic, strength-based, individualistic heroism and a classical, democratic heroism which relies on rhetoric and persuasion.[21] However, there is also a series of differences in the praise discourses within which Ajax and Achilles are positioned in the *Ajax*, so that even if they fall into the same 'category' or 'type' of hero, the distinctions between them are persistently drawn out. As a result, Ajax's claim to their equivalence becomes problematic, especially as the play continues.

The main vocabulary used in praise of Ajax in the *Iliad* is the word μέγας – great. Often the word appears as part of a standard identification of Ajax along with the patronymic, so that it becomes part of his name, as in the form μέγας Τελαμώνιος Αἴας (e.g. *Il.* 5.610, 12.364, 13.321, 14.409, 15.471, etc.). This praise is also applied to his shield, also an important part of his heroic identification, at 11.572. It is common for Homeric epithets to denote particularly praiseworthy aspects of a warrior's identity, so that rather than being a purely neutral descriptor, they repeatedly invoke a positive context, celebrating speed, as with πόδας ὠκὺς Ἀχχιλεύς, or beauty, in λευκώλενος Ἥρη.[22] When this epithet is transmitted to tragedy, and used in descriptions of Ajax in the *Ajax,* this positive aspect of the description is intensified, since it is repeatedly found in contexts specifically related to positive, praising descriptions of Ajax.

Throughout Sophocles' play the descriptor μέγας is shown to be an integral part of Ajax's identity, and is an essential part of the praise vocabulary used by others in the play. When the chorus of sailors describe his role in relation to them, they praise his support for their efforts in their comment,

καίτοι σμικροὶ **μεγάλων** χωρὶς
σφαλερὸν πύργου ῥῦμα πέλονται·
μετὰ γὰρ **μεγάλων** βαιὸς ἄριστ᾽ ἂν
καὶ **μέγας** ὀρθοῖθ᾽ ὑπὸ μικροτέρων.

And indeed, small men who are separated from great ones become uncertain protection for a wall: for it would be best for small men to be set straight by great men, and great men by those who are smaller.

158–61

And a few lines later, follow this with,

μέγαν αἰγυπιὸν <δ᾽>, ὑποδείσαντες
τάχ᾽ ἄν, ἐξαίφνης εἰ σὺ φανείης,
σιγῇ πτήξειαν ἄφωνοι.

They would quickly shrink in fear before the great vulture, if you were to suddenly appear, and would cower voiceless, in silence.

169–71

The image of Ajax as a vulture not only has epinician connotations,[23] it also praises Ajax through representing him as more important and influential than the Atreids, described as chattering sparrows (167–8). Tecmessa uses the same word to praise Ajax, calling him μέγας at 205, and the even stronger μέγιστον ἴσχυσε στρατοῦ a few hundred lines later (502). It is perhaps understandable that Tecmessa would focus particularly on Ajax's physical strength – her presence in the camp is, after all, a direct result of his martial prowess, as she is a military captive. However, the focus on the word μέγας also particularly recalls the Iliadic context of praise for Ajax, suggesting that he is to be celebrated in the same way in the *Ajax* as he was in that epic context.

Unlike Ajax, Achilles is described only once in the *Iliad* as μέγας (21.108), and the term appears in his taunts to Lycaon before he rejects his supplication and kills him, so the comment is made in his own words, rather than his being described in these terms by the narrator or any character around him. Achilles elsewhere in the poem receives an elevated level of praise, being described by such terms as δῖος or διίφιλος. As the epic goes on to the later books, he is praised in terms beyond those deserved by a more 'normal' hero.[24] In comparison, Ajax's key word, μέγας, seems limited, drawing a distinction between the two heroes simply through the vocabulary deemed suitable for praising them. The lack of the word μέγας to describe Achilles in the *Iliad* does not reflect a difference in their physical attributes; Achilles notes when his armour has been lost that only Ajax's gear might suit him as a replacement (*Il.* 18.192–3). The rejection of this term to describe Achilles, therefore, in favour of more extreme alternatives of praise, creates a clear distinction between the heroes, and develops contrasting identities for each of them, a contrast which is re-established in the *Ajax* through the maintenance of this discourse of praise for Ajax, despite Ajax's claims to deserve the same praise as Achilles instead.

As well as praise for physical attributes, both Achilles and Ajax receive acclaim in the *Iliad* which focuses on descriptions of their roles in the army, and particularly the roles they perform in relation to other soldiers. Both are described in terms of defence – they are called a shield, or bulwark, and said to stand between the Greeks (or a particular group of them) and disaster. Achilles is named by Nestor as:

> ὃς μέγα πᾶσιν
> ἕρκος Ἀχαιοῖσιν πέλεται πολέμοιο κακοῖο
>
> He who is for all of the Achaeans a great bulwark against evil war.
>
> 1.283–4

Less than a hundred lines later, Achilles himself characterizes his role as

> ἀεικέα λοιγὸν ἀμῦναι
> τοῖς ἄλλοις
>
> Warding off loathsome destruction from the others.
>
> 1.341–2

In the *Iliad,* Ajax too is marked as a defender of the army: he is named Αἴας πελώριος ἕρκος Ἀχαιῶν (3.229) by Helen, when she identifies him to Priam, and later called by the same epithets (6.5). However, in the parts of the *Iliad* where this description is combined with a more active role in the narrative, there is a significant difference. When Ajax steps forward to take part in the duel with Hector, thus in an aggressive role, he is described once more as the 'bulwark of the Achaeans' (7.211). However, when Ajax features in a *defensive* role, a description of his famous shield is included as an additional detail:

> Αἴας δ᾽ ἐγγύθεν ἦλθε φέρων σάκος ἠΰτε πύργον
> χάλκεον ἑπταβόειον, ὅ οἱ Τυχίος κάμε τεύχων
> . . .
> ὅς οἱ ἐποίησεν σάκος αἰόλον ἑπταβόειον
> ταύρων ζατρεφέων, ἐπὶ δ᾽ ὄγδοον ἤλασε χαλκόν.
>
> Ajax came from nearby, carrying his shield that was like a tower, a shield of bronze with sevenfold bull's hide, which Tychius made, working hard . . . who had made him his flashing shield of seven hides of sturdy bulls, and over it had worked an eighth, bronze layer.
>
> 7.219–23

Similarly, at 15.405ff he is instrumental in warding off the Trojans from the Achaean ships. His defence of Patroclus' corpse also includes a specific description of his shield:

> Αἴας δ᾽ἐγγύθεν ἦλθε φέρων σάκος ἠΰτε πύργον . . .
> Αἴας δ᾽ ἀμφὶ Μενοιτιάδῃ σάκος εὐρὺ καλύψας.
>
> But Ajax came up, carrying his shield that was like a tower . . . Ajax covered the son of Menoetius with his broad shield around him.
>
> 17.128, 132

What is particularly notable in this passage is the difference between how Ajax's and Achilles' respective defensive qualities are highlighted in the Greek. Achilles is *himself* a 'bulwark' or shield; Ajax acts as one, but the focus is on the physical item he carries.

In Sophocles' *Ajax,* this idea of Ajax as maintaining a defensive role is repeated, with the chorus as the first to describe Ajax as their protector or shield, when they say:

> μετὰ γὰρ μεγάλων βαιὸς ἄριστ᾽ ἂν . . .
> χἠμεῖς οὐδὲν σθένομεν πρὸς ταῦτ᾽
> ἀπαλέξασθαι σοῦ χωρίς, ἄναξ.

> Little men are best [supported by] the great . . . and we, for our part, have no strength at all to defend ourselves against them apart from you, lord.
>
> 160, 165–6

Similarly, Teucer says scathingly of Agamemnon,

> οὗ σὺ πολλάκις
> τὴν σὴν προτείνων προὔκαμες ψυχὴν δορί·
>
> You [Ajax] often defended this man, offering up your own life to the spear!
>
> 1269–70

The *Ajax's* chorus even claim rather emotively, once they fear disaster has come to him,

> καὶ πρὶν μὲν ἐννυχίου δεί-
> ματος ἦν μοι προβολὰ καὶ
> βελέων θούριος Αἴας·
>
> And before, furious Ajax was my shield against nightly fear and arrows.
>
> 1211–13

In all these examples, the chorus or Teucer represent Ajax himself as a shield, rather than focusing on the shield he carries. However, Ajax himself explicitly resurrects the difference found in the wording of the *Iliad*, even to the point of linguistic echoes, when he discusses his legacy for his son. As a result, he attempts again to reframe the types of praise language used around him by the chorus and Teucer. Ajax insists on passing his shield on to his son, even though his other weapons will be buried alongside him (575):[25]

> Εὐρύσακες, ἴσχε διὰ πολυρράφου στρέφων
> πόρπακος ἑπτάβοιον ἄρρηκτον <u>σάκος·</u>
>
> Eurysakes, carry my unbreakable shield of seven hides, turning it about by its well-sewn handle.
>
> 575–6

The word σάκος is doubly significant here: it is the same term used in the *Iliad* to describe Ajax's shield,[26] and Ajax claims that it is also this word which forms the basis for his son's name (574). It is further clear that Ajax sees this moment as an intrinsic part of passing his own heroic qualities on to his son along with the shield:

> ἀλλ' αὐτίκ' ὠμοῖς αὐτὸν ἐν νόμοις πατρὸς
> δεῖ πωλοδαμνεῖν κἀξομοιοῦσθαι φύσιν.

> ὦ παῖ, γένοιο πατρὸς εὐτυχέστερος,
> τὰ δ' ἄλλ' ὅμοιος·
>
> But immediately it is necessary to break him in accordance with the harsh laws of his father, and make his nature quite the same as mine. My child, become more fortunate than your father, but the same in all other respects!
>
> 548–51

For Ajax, therefore, his shield is an essential part of his heroic identity. Not only is it worth naming his son for, almost in the manner of a patronymic, it is a key part of the instructions to those who will raise him after Ajax's death, such that those instructions – that Eurysakes should carry Ajax's shield and be exactly alike him in nature – become closely intertwined.[27] The passing on of his shield becomes, in this way, an essential part of imparting that set of values and qualities which Ajax wishes to see inculcated in his heroic offspring. As Melissa Mueller demonstrates, in the handing on of his shield Ajax is also effectively handing on his own heroic identity and past.[28] In contrast, Achilles is given an entirely new shield during the course of the *Iliad* (18.478–608), and while this shield is extraordinary and god-made, it is not envisaged at any point as a part of Achilles' heroic identity. The loss of Achilles' original armour is more meaningful for Hector, who steals it, and will then die in it, than it is for Achilles himself.[29] Achilles is shield and defender of his people by his own nature.[30] Although Ajax claims the same role, it is his only by virtue of the enormous shield he carries, something external and alienable to him, and not as clearly part of his inherent qualities, which are in the tragedy almost displaced into the shield and his son rather than Ajax himself.[31] The ways in which Ajax is praised in Sophocles' *Ajax* reveals the persistence of praise which distinguishes between Ajax and Achilles, in this case even borne out in Ajax's own words and attitude, and which makes Ajax's earlier claims to the same praise-established title questionable.

The presentation of Ajax as shield and protector in Sophocles' *Ajax* is not uncomplicated. Unlike Teucer, who refers in the most part to Ajax's past glories, the sailors focus their praise on a role which Ajax fulfils for them in the present, at least, that is, until he is dead. Once Ajax has died, they are forced to bewail the loss of his protection; the quality their praise was focused on no longer exists, and their praise therefore must cease. Ajax's role as protector is only praiseworthy while he still lives and can fulfil it; once his protection is removed, the sailors will not be able to praise him in the same terms.[32] Their emphatic positioning of πρίν at 1211 makes it clear that their praise is very specifically directed at the past, to a situation which no longer applies. The strength of reversal is also demonstrated in Tecmessa's response to Ajax's death, when she describes a need to protect him rather than seeing him as protector:

> . . . νιν περιπτυχεῖ
> φάρει καλύψω τῷδε παμπήδην . . .
>
> I will cover him entirely with this cloak folded about him.
>
> 915–16

With his death, therefore, Ajax not only loses his heroic role of protector, but also finds his situation entirely reversed. He has gone from being able to cover Patroclus' corpse for its protection in the *Iliad*, an act described with the same term as Tecmessa uses (καλύπτω *Il.* 17.132), to needing to be covered himself in his death. However, no warrior stands over him in this moment; instead Ajax must be covered and protected by a woman's cloak, hidden away from the eyes even of his friends. In contrast, when Achilles in the *Iliad* also voluntarily withdraws his protection and shielding qualities from the Achaeans, his withdrawal results only in an increase of his honour, gifts, and an increased right to praise for his glorious deeds once he returns. Ajax's absence results in almost entirely opposite results; he must be hidden as if shameful, in the garments more usually used to hide away women from the eyes of others.[33]

The idea that Ajax's previously praiseworthy protective attribute now belongs firmly to the past is mirrored in statements made by both the chorus and Ajax in response to the dishonour he claims to have experienced from the Atreids. Both Ajax (446) and the chorus (616–20) claim that his previous deeds of excellence are themselves being erased by his present suffering. Clearly Ajax's deeds cannot literally be undone, or cease to have happened, so the process which the chorus and Ajax describe is one which must be the result of the blame that Ajax faces for his more recent deeds. O'Higgins argues that their description refers to the lack of praise that Ajax is now receiving for those deeds, since 'Deeds may not establish or re-establish *kleos*. In themselves they may have no meaning whatsoever', and must therefore be given context and meaning through speech.[34] In the *Ajax*, those around Ajax have refused to perform this function and confirmation of Ajax's deeds, in not awarding him the arms or the identity 'best of the Achaeans', which should have been confirmed through praise precisely of those deeds. Instead of having his exploits celebrated as the cause for naming him 'best', Ajax is facing blame, censure, rumour and disgrace, and any hopes he held for establishing such an identity for himself are entirely overturned, forcing him through the process of thwarting that Moore recognises in such crises of attempts to establish a particular identity.

Second best of the Achaeans

That Ajax's crisis and withdrawal from the Achaean army attracts extensive blame is the final and most significant way in which his claim to be 'best' like Achilles fails in the tragic context of Sophocles' *Ajax*. Ajax's insistence on being honoured as the 'best of the Achaeans' has precisely the opposite effect to that experienced by Achilles, who gains additional gifts and recognition from the Achaeans, particularly Agamemnon.[35] Rather than successfully claiming increased honour and establishing his identity as 'best' through the praise of those around him, Ajax instead faces blame and censure from those who remain after his death, which further destabilizes any attempt to position him as 'best', by positioning him instead in discourses of blame rather than praise.

His suicide has a further destabilizing effect on his identity. Once dead, Ajax cannot continue to take part in any discursive practices as a means of constructing an identity; he is reliant on those left alive, and cannot intervene to challenge their generation of discourses of blame in particular. It is also possible that Sophocles' *Ajax* is the first version of Ajax's madness to feature the attack on the Greek commanders.[36] If so, Ajax is at a further, metapoetic risk of damage to his reputation via poetic speech, since the tragedy itself contributes a new, negative aspect to the poetic tradition, adding further blame to his already darkened name.

Sophocles' *Ajax* is in fact not the first poetic work to indicate how significant the poetic praise and blame traditions could be for Ajax's *kleos*, since he appears in a similar position in two works of Pindar. In *Nemean* 7, Ajax's fate is associated directly with the power of poetry to ensure a positive reputation and *kleos* (11–33), and the positive reputation gained for Odysseus as a result of 'sweet-speaking Homer' and his 'misleading tales' (21, 23). Through this poetry men have been encouraged to believe wrongly about Ajax (24–5), leading to his death.[37] In *Nemean* 8, Ajax's fate is again connected with the influence which positive poetry can have to protect from oblivion (23–5) and 'deceptive tales', μύθοι, are associated with 'rotten glory', here κῦδος (33–5) and the distribution of blame, ὄνειδος (33). Ajax appears again in *Isthmian* 4 as a cautionary tale against the strength of the influence of poetry, which Pindar claims the audience will 'know' of (35), again in connection with the poetry of Homer (35–9), this time more positively described as having 'made him honoured' (37–8).[38] The example of *Isthmian* 4 is also particularly interesting, as the Ajax is described briefly either as himself blaming the Achaeans or, in a scenario which is key to Sophocles' account, as being blamed by the Achaeans (36b).[39] Bacchylides too makes Ajax a key example of the way poetry may preserve fame after death, including a celebration of the defence of the ships which is a key part of Teucer's defence of Ajax (Bacchyl. 13.100–81), which demonstrates significant engagement with Homer's account in the *Iliad*, even if Bacchylides does not engage in the same kind of direct argument with Homer as Pindar does in his presentations of Ajax.[40]

In this context, the capacity for tragic poetry to further impact Ajax's *kleos*, and the risks of blame arising through poetry, make the focus on blame in Sophocles' *Ajax* particularly potent.[41] Pindar's extensive engagement with the Homeric tradition in his Ajax poems also suggests recognition of the potential for alternative traditions formed by praising or blaming Ajax through poetry, as discussed by Nagy.[42] It also suggests that in focusing in his own tragedy on many of the same issues, particularly through Ajax's own desire to change 'his' poetic praise discourses, Sophocles was participating in an ongoing discussion between poets, and demonstrating how tragedy too could be part of the same process of establishing praise and blame traditions, adding further metapoetic weight to Ajax's struggle in the *Ajax*.[43]

Odysseus makes it clear that Ajax's shame is public, widespread, and likely to lead to reputational damage, as he says to Athena that,

> τήνδ᾽ οὖν ἐκείνῳ πᾶς τις αἰτίαν τρέπει.
>
> Everyone assigns the blame for this [the slaughter] to him.
>
> 28

Ajax is already facing widespread discussion of his guilt and associated blame, before the full situation has even been ascertained. The culture of blame which surrounds Ajax after his slaughter of the beasts is further indicated by the chorus' early talk of bad rumours (137–200), in which they repeatedly make it clear that the main risk to them and Ajax is not the deed itself, but rather the speech being used to describe the situation across the camp. Their initial explanation for their anxiety raises the spectre of when

> ζαμενὴς
> λόγος ἐκ Δαναῶν κακόθρους ἐπιβῇ
>
> A raging story arises from the evil-speaking Danaans
>
> 137–8

significantly, comparing this risk of dangerous speech even with the 'πληγὴ' of Zeus (137) and demonstrating quite literally the impact of such speech. As they continue their explanation of their emotional state, the chorus further refer to:

μεγάλοι θόρυβοι κατέχουσ' ἡμᾶς
ἐπὶ δυσκλείᾳ

Great shoutings against us which bring dishonour.

142–3

It is striking that the chorus attach these shouts specifically to *kleos* with their use of the term δύσκλεια. This term is rare in tragedy, particularly in Sophocles, where it appears only here in extant plays.[44] The chorus' language therefore develops an explicit connection between poetic praise and blame and the speech about Ajax's deeds, indicating the strength of the impact they envisage for this language, as well as its sphere of influence. The poetic context within the tragedy itself further strengthens this poetic resonance, since the δύσκλεια the chorus foresee is in fact being enacted before the audience partly through their own song. After a brief description of the slaughtering of the herds (141–7) the chorus immediately return to the theme of speech, by claiming that these are the ψιθύρους λόγους of Odysseus (148), a description which recalls Pindaric comments about the secretive nature of hostile talk (*Nem.* 4.39–41, *Pyth.* 2.74–6).[45] As Hesk has pointed out, the chorus' wider comments about the risk which negative speech can pose to small or great men further draw on the language of *Odyssey* 11, imbuing them with a Homeric flavour alongside the other poetic elements here.[46] Their claim that the Argives are chattering like birds (168) is similarly focused on the negative *speech* surrounding what has happened, and they contrast this with the wish that Ajax would appear with the result that:

σιγῇ πτήξειαν ἄφωνοι.

They would crouch in silence, voiceless.

171

Their focus is therefore on the speech of the Greeks and how it is damaging Ajax; they do not wish for the Argives to be punished beyond falling silent, nor for Ajax to commit any violence against them (presenting a rather ironic contrast with Ajax's own original intentions). Instead, their focus is on the importance of this public blame speech circulating against Ajax. Similarly they wish for Zeus and Apollo to stop the φάτιν (186) and Ajax to come out to stop the μύθους of the Atreids and Odysseus (188) so that Ajax does not maintain a κακὰν φάτιν (191), and conclude their comments with a further reference to the γλώσσαις of Ajax's enemies. From the start to the end of their first ode, therefore, the chorus' concern is repeatedly not with what Ajax has or has not done, but with *what is being said* about it – the rumour, which they describe as contributing to his poor *kleos*. The choral *parados* further has significant epinician echoes, adding a sense of poetic weight to the extent of the blame the chorus portray as having attached itself to Ajax's night-time expedition.[47]

The messenger makes it clear that the chorus are right to fear this new focus on blame for Ajax among the Greeks, once Teucer has returned to the Greek camp. He says of Teucer:

κυδάζεται τοῖς πᾶσιν Ἀργείοις ὁμοῦ.
στείχοντα γὰρ πρόσωθεν αὐτὸν ἐν κύκλῳ
μαθόντες ἀμφέστησαν, εἶτ' ὀνείδεσιν
ἤρασσον ἔνθεν κἄνθεν οὔτις ἔσθ' ὃς οὔ,
τὸν τοῦ μανέντος κἀπιβουλευτοῦ στρατῷ
ξύναιμον ἀποκαλοῦντες, ὡς τ' οὐκ ἀρκέσοι
τὸ μὴ οὐ πέτροισι πᾶς καταξανθεὶς θανεῖν.

He was reviled by all the Argives together. For they learned that he was approaching from afar and stood around him in a circle; then every single one of them assailed him with blame here and there calling him the brother of the man who, mad, had plotted against the army, and saying that they would not be content until he was dead, mangled to death with stones.

722–8

The scene is described dramatically, and the messenger's language makes it explicit that it is blame which is being directed against Ajax here (724, 725), before the violence seems likely to break out. Teucer clearly cannot have been involved in Ajax's actions, since he is described throughout the play before then as having been away, and even the Messenger's speech focuses for the first two lines (719–20) on making Teucer's previous absence and his present return extremely clear. The Argives cannot have thought that Teucer was involved in what has happened; it is clear from the description of the accusation they make (726–7) that their anger is really directed at Ajax. In this scene, therefore, Teucer as Ajax's closest relative and companion in the camp, stands in for Ajax and receives the blame that is directed at him. It is also notable that this blame is widespread, communal, and not the result of any individual enmities; Ajax and the chorus have both previously announced their expectations of taunts and blame from Odysseus, but the audience have seen precisely the opposite. The first instances of blame come from a much wider source – the Argives as a whole – and cannot be dismissed as an example of an individual's bias. The scene depicted here provides a counterweight to the united community represented by the chorus. Here, a group is similarly described as sharing in a common discourse which could contribute to Ajax's reputation and heroic identity, but this time of blame. The image of their united, communal role in distributing blame is strengthened by the representation of their standing in a circle, with Teucer isolated (723), just as when on stage individual actors may stand out against the grouped chorus. Starobinski is right therefore to point to Ajax's anger and rejection of the community as springing from the community's failure to proclaim him as the first among the Achaeans. The community of the Greek army does not simply fail to acknowledge or confirm Ajax's claim, however, they do precisely the opposite with this shared discourse of blame.[48]

At the same time as experiencing this increase in communal blame, Ajax faces a failure on the part of those speakers who might preserve his *kleos* against these attacks, or provide an alternative heroic *kleos* which would uphold his claim to be 'Best of the Achaeans'. Immediately after the crisis has taken place, Tecmessa describes the situation as 'unspeakable', simultaneously referring to Ajax's existing reputation by describing him as κλεινός (216):

πῶς δῆτα λέγω λόγον **ἄρρητον**;
θανάτῳ γὰρ ἴσον πάθος ἐκπεύσῃ.
μανίᾳ γὰρ ἁλοὺς ἡμὶν ὁ **κλεινὸς**
νύκτερος Αἴας ἀπελωβήθη.

So how shall I tell an unspeakable story? For the suffering you shall hear of is equal to death. For during the night our glorious Ajax was seized by madness and grievously injured.

214–17

The juxtaposition of Tecmessa's description of the crisis as 'unspeakable' and Ajax's previous fame brings the two elements into direct contrast; Ajax was once praised sufficiently to become κλεινός, but now, according to Tecmessa, does only what is unspeakable. This inability to speak on Ajax's behalf further presents a direct contrast with the rumours, blame and negative speech of the Achaeans, partly as it follows closely on the chorus' concern, but also as the chorus then explicitly confirm that the subject Tecmessa finds unspeakable is the subject which is so amplified by the Danaans' rumour, their μέγας μῦθος (226). Tecmessa's account is further limited by Ajax's own desire to silence her (293), which she connects with a gap in her tale to the chorus (295), so that her account is marked twice by its inability to be full or spoken clearly. When Ajax arrives on stage, the chorus reflect a similar unease with how to communicate about such things, since they first try to stop him talking entirely (μηδὲν μέγ' εἴπῃς 387), and then indicate their own uncertainty about what they can contribute since neither restraint nor sensible speech seems possible:

> οὔτοι σ' ἀπείργειν οὔθ' ὅπως ἐῶ λέγειν
> ἔχω, κακοῖς τοιοῖσδε συμπεπτωκότα.
>
> I am not able to restrain you and I do not know how to let you speak, since you have met such troubles as these.
>
> 428–9

Ajax's action seems to have not only damaged his *kleos* and caused δύσκλεια to arise from the blame the Achaeans have awarded him, but also are so terrible that they prevent his friends, both Tecmessa and the chorus, from speaking in his favour. As a result there is no possibility of an alternative strand of poetic praise being developed for him in the tragedy.[49]

Once Ajax is dead, the concern with Ajax's reputation, status and identity becomes the central focus of characters other than Ajax and the chorus. Teucer, Menelaus and Agamemnon all make long speeches in the second half of the play which attempt to position Ajax within discourses of praise or blame respectively, as a way of confirming his identity posthumously, contrary to the views of the opposing parties. Ajax is subjected to great deal of blame and personal attack, particularly from the two leaders of the army, Menelaus and Agamemnon. Menelaus calls him ἐχθίω Φρυγῶν ('More an enemy than the Phrygians' 1054), κακοῦ (1071) and claims,

> . . . πρόσθεν οὗτος ἦν
> αἴθων ὑβριστής, . . .
>
> Formerly he was heated in his insolence
>
> 1087–8

Agamemnon's arguments are more concerned with Teucer, although he also calls Ajax μηδέν (1231), and explicitly asks,

> οὐκ ἆρ' Ἀχαιοῖς ἄνδρες εἰσὶ πλὴν ὅδε;
>
> Are there not men for the Achaeans, other than him?
>
> 1238

This comment directly reflects Ajax's earlier claim, and the issue of the praise which he has grasped after, in its deliberate setting of Ajax as simply another man among the Achaeans. Far from being called the best, he is not even marked as outstanding; instead he is dismissed by Agamemnon as on a par with all the other unnamed Achaeans. Agamemnon himself also claims to be the heroic equal of Ajax (1236–7), definitively refusing to sanction Ajax's desire to be named the new best of the Achaeans.

A particular problem arises in the speeches of Teucer and the chorus after Ajax's disaster, and their lack of appropriate poetic praise. In the *Philoctetes*, it is the poetic fluency of Philoctetes himself, along with the influential μῦθος of Heracles, which enables Neoptolemus to take up his place in the epic praise tradition. Similarly, as we shall see, in other tragedies such as Euripides' *Heracles*, characters and choruses with additional poetic fluency are able to provide influential discourses of praise. Yet in the *Ajax*, as Nooter has demonstrated, the character who makes most use of poetic genres in his speech is Ajax himself, and this lyric fluency has the effect of isolating him from those around him, rather than rehabilitating or connecting him to his community.[50] Nooter argues that this isolation from his community enables his renewal of communication with the gods via hymnic and other religious poetic language. However, this isolation also has a particularly strong effect on the failure to integrate Ajax within the poetic praise discourses he seeks, despite this being Ajax's own priority. According to the messenger, Ajax expressed his confidence in grasping *kleos* without the aid of the gods (769), and yet it proves precisely his desired *kleos* which is *not* successfully transmitted through his own and his entourage's use of poetry, whereas his connection to the gods is restored.

There is in fact already some indication of the problem that Ajax will face in his own first conversation in the play, when he discusses the deeds he thinks he has achieved with Athena. In answer to Athena's question as to whether he has 'stained his sword in the blood of the Argive army', Ajax responds:

> κόμπος πάρεστι κοὐκ ἀπαρνοῦμαι τὸ μή.
>
> The boast is there, and I shall not deny it!
>
> 96

However, as the audience already knows and Ajax will soon discover, the boast is *not* there for Ajax: he has not achieved what he claims to be able to boast of, as the Argive leaders are alive (and will survive Ajax himself). Ajax's association of this 'boast' with the belief that the Argive leaders will never again dishonour him (98) and his own right to the arms (100) shows the shaky foundation of speech on which his claims will be demonstrated to rest throughout the remainder of the play.[51] While Ajax thinks he can praise himself in such a way as to prevent his future dishonour and demonstrate his claim to the arms and the epithet of 'best', in fact the opposite is true, and the chorus' and Teucer's language only continues to reinforce this impression of shakiness conveyed at the start by Ajax himself.

The chorus' inability to speak about Ajax's new situation, discussed above, is met with no answering poetic praise for his rehabilitation. Instead, the chorus' most poetic moment comes during their celebration of what they believe to be Ajax's change of heart. Following Ajax's 'Deception Speech' the chorus break into an ode with multiple poetic features. They describe themselves as 'leaping' (694) and invoke the god Pan with a ritual cry, which associates him specifically with dancing and choral activity:

> ἰὼ ἰὼ Πὰν Πάν,
> ὦ Πὰν Πὰν ἁλίπλαγκτε, Κυλ-
> λανίας χιονοκτύπου
> πετραίας ἀπὸ δειράδος φάνηθ', ὦ
> θεῶν χοροποί' ἄναξ, ὅπως μοι
> Μύσια Κνώσι' ὀρ-
> χήματ' αὐτοδαῆ ξυνὼν ἰάψῃς.
> νῦν γὰρ ἐμοὶ μέλει χορεῦσαι.
>
> Hail, hail, Pan, Pan! O Pan, Pan wandering over the sea, appear to me from the snow-beaten rocky ridge of Cyllene, oh lord and chorus-leader among the gods, so that you may begin along with me the dances, the Mysian and Cnosian steps that you taught yourself. For now I intend to dance!
>
> 694–701

The chorus here connect their celebration to dance and choral performance through their address to Pan, drawing on a poetic air for the ode.[52] They refer to their own plans to dance a chorus, adding a further explicitly choral element to the ode.[53] Yet the second part of their ode contains no attempt to celebrate Ajax himself, only celebrating his reconciliation with the gods and the Atreids, with no mention of his excellence or more general *kleos*.[54] There is a significant contrast, therefore, with the chorus' handling of celebratory odes surrounding heroes such as Heracles in Euripides' *Heracles*, or in Sophocles' *Trachiniae*.[55] The chorus' celebration is misplaced; their belief that Ajax's reconciliation with the Atreids is shortly to follow is overturned in the next scene, when the Messenger will arrive and reveal Calchas' dire prophecy (719–83).[56] The main thing to which the chorus attach any praise vocabulary in their odes is not Ajax, but Salamis, which they describe as κλεινά and περίφαντος αἰεί (596, 598). Where they do refer positively to Ajax's past deeds, his μεγίστας ἀρετᾶς, it is explicitly as things which are now being dropped or forgotten by his 'friends' in the army

(619–21). The chorus further talk negatively about πόνος, elsewhere in tragedy a central source of praise, when they connect it to the fruitless search for Ajax (866).[57]

Even the Trojan War itself, usually a source of epic poetic praise and celebration for heroes, becomes in the odes of *Ajax*'s chorus a source of blame, reproach, and misery (600–7, 1185–220).[58] In their second ode the chorus complain not only about their own experience of the war, but also explicitly describe the Trojan war as δύστανον **ὄνειδος** Ἑλλάνων, 'a wretched reproach for the Greeks' (1191). As a result they overturn its usual connection with praise for heroes to make it a source of the opposite: blame, for all of the Greeks involved. In the same song they reflect on the fact that the war has separated them from garlands (στεφάνων 1199), cups and pipes (1200–1). The chorus' comment encompasses locations of song as one of the key things from which the war has separated them, rather than war providing a source of inspiration for their songs. Their explicit complaint that it is στεφάνων from which they have been separated has an additional resonance given Ajax's earlier complaint that Telamon had received a στέφανον εὐκλείας (465). The chorus should be able to convey garlands of praise-song to their hero, Ajax,[59] yet the chorus of the *Ajax* claim that the very source of his great deeds has prevented them from doing so, and instead provided only a source of blame. Finally, the chorus' inability to connect with and fully support Ajax is clearly demonstrated by the unusual staging of his suicide, which takes place after the chorus have left the stage, with Ajax returning entirely alone.[60] As a result, while the chorus of the *Ajax* make explicit the risks to Ajax's *kleos* which results from the blame spread by the Argives, they do not, in contrast to other tragic choruses, participate in themselves rehabilitating or even establishing that *kleos* through praise celebrations of Ajax, leaving his praiseworthy status in a much more vulnerable position.

Teucer does attempt a more thorough rehabilitation of Ajax's reputation, and, significantly, draws directly on epic poetry to do so, in his discussion with Agamemnon (1273–97), when he raises both Ajax's duel with Hector and his protection of the Greek ships. Both episodes appear in the *Iliad*, although they are slightly reformulated in Teucer's account.[61] There are also significant Homeric formulations in Teucer's description of Ajax's deeds, particularly Teucer's complaint of Agamemnon's lack of remembrance (1269–70), which echoes Achilles' similar complaint in the *Iliad* (9.322).[62] There may also be a significant connection with the tragic Achilles, as Teucer's defence of Ajax's achievements is very similar to that apparently given by Achilles of his own deed in Aeschylus' *Myrmidons* (fr. 132c *TrGF*).[63] However, as noted above, Ajax's situation is rather different from Achilles'; while Achilles' withdrawal causes the Achaeans to appreciate his value, Ajax's seems to have had precisely the opposite effect. Ajax, unlike Achilles, is also dead, and must rely on Teucer to make this defence on his behalf. The connection between the two heroes therefore presents a contrast as much as an image of likeness. Teucer's speech has puzzled some interpreters by diverging from the tradition of the *Iliad* in subtle ways, primarily through the attempt to emphasize Ajax's participation in each event as part of his defence.[64] Both of Teucer's speeches to Menelaus and Agamemnon are at times rather more concerned with attacking the Atreids than celebrating Ajax (1093–1110, 1115–17, 1123, 1135, 1137, 1150–8, 1290–8).[65] Hesk has rightly associated Teucer's speech with the epic speech genre of flyting, so that it *is* part of a poetic tradition, but not a speech genre of celebration or praise.[66] It is effective for raising Teucer's status and for dismaying both Agamemnon and Menelaus, but does not contribute effectively to the praise discourses surrounding Ajax, thus representing a missed opportunity to praise the hero. Teucer's speech also proves unconvincing for its hearers and is criticized as αἰσχίστους λόγους (1320) by Agamemnon.[67] Teucer's speech, and its use of epic narratives and styles, can by drawing on the *Iliad* only rehabilitate Ajax so far as that tradition had allowed him to go: that is, Ajax may be restored to 'second best', and no further, as the final scene confirms.

In the last scene of the play, after this discourse of blame has played out fully and its results of denying Ajax the identity 'best' are felt, Odysseus makes his reappearance. As the audience have already seen in his dialogue with Athena, he is unexpectedly sympathetic to Ajax, presenting a sharp contrast with Ajax's and his supporters' previously expressed fear (148–50, 379–82, 955–60, 971) that Odysseus will mock him and damage his reputation. Instead, Odysseus denies any desire to 'dishonour' Ajax at all, and his argument as to why Ajax should be buried directly picks up on the same rhetoric of praise that Ajax laid claim to earlier:

> οὔ τἄν ἀτιμάσαιμ᾽ ἄν, ὥστε μὴ λέγειν
> ἕν᾽ ἄνδρ᾽ ἰδεῖν ἄριστον Ἀργείων, ὅσοι
> Τροίαν ἀφικόμεσθα, πλὴν Ἀχιλλέως.
>
> I would not so dishonour him as to not say or realise that he was the best man among the Argives, of those who came to Troy, except for Achilles.
>
> 1339–41

Odysseus' statement clearly mirrors the claim Ajax made to the title granted to Achilles in the *Iliad* so that to begin with, it seems as though he is ready to grant that title in its entirety to Ajax. However, once again Ajax's attempt to claim the identity 'best' is prevented, as Odysseus insists on including the traditional exception for Achilles. It is not until the very end of his statement that he makes the exception clear, so that the hope is built up by both the phrase itself and the comment that it covers all those who came to Troy that Odysseus will concede this title to the dead Ajax.[68] However, Odysseus' final note makes it clear that he had no intention of making the statement without the traditional, Iliadic exception. Ajax is the best only after Achilles, and the way in which this part of the remark falls last, makes it appear a very final judgement.[69] As the praise comes from someone who claims not to be a friend of Ajax (1336–7), it is given a greater validity in Greek eyes.[70] Odysseus comes very close to repeating this judgement in his comments to Teucer a little later, when he states that the funeral rites should be those appropriate to ἀρίστοις ἀνδράσιν (1380). The use of ἀριστοις would seem a concession to Ajax's claims, except for the fact that it appears in the plural, in a generalizing comment, so that once again Ajax becomes one of several best men, and not the sole 'best of the Achaeans'. At this stage of the play, too, no one chooses to argue this point – it becomes the final assessment of Ajax's status and the sorts of praise he can claim a right to. In fact, Teucer finally seems to confirm the appropriateness of this judgement, by naming Odysseus ἄριστ' Ὀδυσσεῦ, in his acknowledgement of Odysseus' help. While this comment does not appear with the full, traditional formulation, by naming Odysseus alone as 'best', with no qualifier or generalizing plural, Teucer fails to make any further claim to the exceptionalism of Ajax, praising Odysseus as 'best' instead of his brother. Teucer explicitly marks his comments as praise (ἐπαινέσαι 1381), formalizing this judgement. As a result, it seems clear that Ajax's attempt has failed. He is limited after his death to the same status he was granted in the *Iliad*, and in the wider poetic tradition, and has been unable to move beyond it either as a result of the death of Achilles or through his transition into the new tragic genre.

Conclusion

In Sophocles' *Ajax*, Ajax experiences the process of 'thwarting', due to his failure to establish the desired identity for himself of 'Best of the Achaeans', through a discourse of praise. Ajax argues for his right to such an identity on the basis of his father's same claim, and his own claim to be Achilles' successor, and recognizes in his failure to secure the arms of Achilles a physical symbol of his failure to secure Achilles' desirable identity. Despite Ajax's claims, the other characters and chorus in the *Ajax* repeatedly fail to position him as 'best', instead repeating the traditional praise discourse of the *Iliad* within which he is instead positioned as different from Achilles rather than equivalent to him. Any attempts to claim further praise are met with the blame of Agamemnon and Menelaus, and the only identity which is successfully rehabilitated and maintained against their competing discourse is that confirmed by Odysseus, 'best . . . after'. Ajax's violent response to this crisis in the identity he fails to secure is typical of thwarting, and rather than rehabilitating him, his suicide leaves him vulnerable to positioning by those characters who arrive on the stage after his death, and without recourse to further attempts to participate in constructing his own identity.

3

Euripides' Heracles, 'Glorious' How?

In Euripides' *Heracles*, it is possible to see a very similar process at work in the identity crisis faced by Heracles to that of Ajax.[1] Like Ajax, Heracles faces a conflict in the kind of praise which he seeks, in that he attempts to establish for himself a praiseworthy identity in terms of his fatherhood. The conflict that results causes an eruption of violence and almost leads to his suicide, as with Ajax. Yet unlike Ajax, Heracles is eventually able to accept the identity constructed for him by the praise of those around him, and thus ends the play still alive and reintegrated into a new community with his heroic identity successfully reconstructed, even if his attempt to encompass a more family-focused aspect into his praiseworthy identity ends in violence and fails.

Recognition of these two aspects to Heracles' heroic identity in Euripides' *Heracles* is not entirely new, as scholars have argued that the play stages an adjustment of Heracles' identity, from semi-divine hero of renown, to mortal, fallible and destructive father, forced to rely on friends rather than his own qualities of excellence.[2] Many aspects of the play lend themselves to a recognition of these two distinct strands of Heracles' identity, or two separate subject positions which he takes up, one as a mortal, family-focused individual, the other as the larger-than-life, glorious Heracles of the mythical labours. The split between these two distinct subject positions can be seen in the frequent discussion of the issue of dual parentage,[3] and, when the end of the tragedy is considered, in regard to the future of Heracles' ambivalent weapons, both symbols of his heroic victories and representative of the murder of his family.[4] The idea of the two identities of Heracles also reflects the complex representations of his nature in the literary tradition on which tragedy draws. In epic Heracles is a figure of contrasting values, as likely to break the bounds of hospitality and moral codes as to protect them.[5] Epinician poetry makes a significant move towards rehabilitating him, presenting him as a more humanized character, and one whose moral virtue was as supreme as his valour and physical strength.[6] Such a transition in Euripides' *Heracles* would therefore be reflecting and continuing the trend in the representations of his character found in other genres, presenting a tragic portrayal that continues and dramatizes the process of bringing Heracles back to earth as a more mortal figure rather than the destructive hero of enormous dangerous potential.[7]

However, with closer attention to the role and propagation of poetic praise in the *Heracles*, a rather different picture emerges of Heracles' developing identity over the course of the play. Heracles does attempt to prioritize his family life in the middle section of the play, but his attempt to effect any repositioning of himself as praiseworthy father and protector of his family is in the end entirely unsuccessful, as a result of the reactions of the chorus and characters around him. His actions in this section receive no praise and are undermined by blame aimed at his acts both here and elsewhere in relation to his family. His departure for Athens with Theseus comes with the promise of a status as an object of praise once more, and as a glorious hero, who leaves his uncelebrated family life behind him, precisely as he had done during his praiseworthy labours. As with the *Ajax* and the *Philoctetes*, Euripides' *Heracles* makes persistent use of existing poetic techniques to enforce the failure of this new type of discourse, particularly in the speech of the chorus, so that the 'traditional' quality of praise for Heracles, that is, celebration for his labours, is maintained against his will, just as the epic praise for Ajax was maintained. As a result, Euripides' *Heracles* provides a further example of a play in which the manipulation of existing techniques and topics of poetic praise works against a tragic hero, who cannot break free into a new discourse despite his appearance in a new genre.

Renown and identity

The importance of praise and renown to an interpretation of Euripides' *Heracles* is, as with the *Philoctetes* and the *Ajax*, made clear throughout the play by the presentation of praise by both characters and chorus. Euripides' *Heracles* demonstrates a clear preoccupation with the value of renown, and of establishing and maintaining a particular identity through discourses of praise and blame. Often at moments when the plot might invite a focus on family or domestic issues, the chorus or characters instead focus on praise of heroic deeds or comment on the reputation gained by such deeds, particularly as a way for characters to decide which actions they can pursue and how they should represent themselves. The characters of the *Heracles* explicitly make a connection between praiseworthy, heroic deeds, the reputation gained by these, and identity, by explicitly identifying themselves with reference to such deeds.

The importance of renown and reputation as a method of expressing identity is brought immediately into focus by Amphitryon's introduction at the start of the play:

> Τίς τὸν Διὸς σύλλεκτρον οὐκ οἶδεν βροτῶν,
> Ἀργεῖον Ἀμφιτρύων',
>
> Who among mortals does not know me, the man who shared his wife with Zeus,
> Argive Amphitryon?
>
> 1–2

He announces his renown among all mortals, and the deed for which he gains this renown, even before his name, and represents it as a key part of his identity. Similarly, when Megara enters, she addresses him first by recalling his celebrated deeds, rather than addressing him through recognition of their family connection:[8]

> ὦ πρέσβυ, Ταφίων ὅς ποτ' ἐξεῖλες πόλιν
> στρατηλατήσας κλεινὰ Καδμείων δορός
>
> Old sir, you who once took the city of the Taphians, famously leading the army of the Cadmeians.
>
> 60–1

Megara's address particularly emphasizes the quality of renown in association with Amphitryon's deeds, in the flattering description of his leadership as achieved κλεινά, so that even this initial address prioritizes not simply Amphitryon's actions, but the *kleos* he has won from them. In this way, she reflects Amphitryon's own concern with his fame and reputation, demonstrating a consistent approach of prioritising renown and reputation across Heracles' family members.

In several situations the value of that renown, or an individual's reputation, is given a great deal of weight in arguments or situations where characters seek to decide how to act, with Lycus as the only exception. Megara manages to convince Amphitryon to support her decision to leave the altar with an argument based on what is worthy of their renowned status. First she reflects a common heroic attitude to reputation and judgement by others, when she claims that death by fire would mean their ἐχθροῖσιν γέλων διδόντας ('giving laughter to our enemies' 285).[9]

She goes on to focus specifically on the fact that the children's deaths must not happen in such a manner as to mar Heracles' glorious reputation:

οὑμὸς δ' ἀμαρτύρητος εὐκλεὴς πόσις;
ὃς τούσδε παῖδας οὐκ ἂν ἐκσῶσαι θέλοι
δόξαν κακὴν λαβόντας· οἱ γὰρ εὐγενεῖς
κάμνουσι τοῖς αἰσχροῖσι τῶν τέκνων ὕπερ·
ἐμοί τε μίμημ' ἀνδρὸς οὐκ ἀπωστέον.

Is my glorious husband unwitnessed? He would not want to save these children if doing so brought them a bad reputation: for noble parents are distressed by the shames of their children: and I must not reject my husband's example.

290–4

Her argument here is bracketed by emphatic references to Heracles' reputation, so that the way her children must behave is clearly to be understood as being dictated by that reputation. Megara argues that Amphitryon's own reputation, independent of his son's, must also preclude such a death for him,

σὲ μὲν δόκησις ἔλαβεν εὐκλεὴς δορός,
ὥστ' οὐκ ἀνεκτὸν δειλίας θανεῖν σ' ὕπο·

You obtained a glorious reputation as a warrior, so that it is unbearable for you to die like a coward.

288–9

As with her initial address to him, Megara again refers to Amphitryon's reputation with language that is connected to *kleos*, therefore making use of the poetic background of such a reputation, in her description of it as εὐκλεὴς. Similarly, Megara's reference to her husband as motivating her behaviour described him specifically as εὐκλεὴς (290), so that she repeatedly draws on terms directly associated with poetic praise to highlight the importance of this element in guiding both her and Amphitryon's behaviour. Megara's argument is successful, and there is no suggestion within the play that it is anything other than correct or persuasive to appeal to renown and reputation in this manner.[10] Megara and Amphitryon thus not only explicitly identify individuals by their heroic exploits and reputation, but also consider these as an essential aspect in the ongoing maintenance of identity, even to the extent of considering what kind of death is suitable for an individual with their projected reputation.

The issue of reputation and renown becomes key in relation to Heracles himself in the scenes following Lycus' entrance, when Lycus makes sustained efforts to dismiss the importance of the absent Heracles' renown as part of his attack on Heracles' family. Although he does bring up the unlikelihood of Heracles' being able to rescue his family (144–6), his main argument against Amphitryon and Megara is not concerned with this question. Instead, he focuses at length on destroying the reputation Heracles has attained (in his view, unreasonably) for his renowned labours.[11] Lycus insists on stressing family ties in his initial address to Megara and Amphitryon, ignoring the praise-focused identification Megara had used, and identifying them as τὸν Ἡράκλειον πατέρα καὶ ξυνάορον ('father and wife of Heracles' 140). He then claims that Heracles' reputation is undeserved, and unworthy of attention, asking:

> τί δὴ τὸ σεμνὸν σῷ κατείργασται πόσει,
>
> What awesome thing has your husband even achieved?
>
> 151

While questioning the reputation of Heracles' deeds, Lycus identifies him solely by the family relationship of 'husband', just as he had prioritized these ties when addressing Megara and Amphitryon. He refuses to accept Heracles' reputation as a valid part of his identity at all, arguing instead that he knows the reality of what sort of person Heracles is, and it does not match his reputation:

> ὁ δ' ἔσχε **δόξαν** οὐδὲν ὢν εὐψυχίας
> θηρῶν ἐν αἰχμῇ, τἄλλα δ' οὐδὲν ἄλκιμος
>
> Heracles, despite being nothing special, has got a **reputation** for courage from spearing beasts, although in other things he is not at all brave.
>
> 157–8

Lycus does not contradict the tradition that Heracles killed the Nemean lion or ὕδραν ἕλειον ('marsh snake' 152), but he rejects the reputation Heracles has gained as a result, taking aim at Heracles' renown, not his deeds.

Given the importance of renown to Amphitryon, it is not surprising that this is the aspect of Lycus' speech against which he objects, complaining:

> ἐμοὶ μέλει
> λόγοισι τὴν τοῦδ' ἀμαθίαν ὑπὲρ σέθεν
> δεῖξαι· κακῶς γάρ σ' οὐκ ἐατέον κλύειν.
>
> It is my concern to show the ignorance in the words of this man in relation to you [Heracles]: for to hear you spoken badly of is not to be borne.
>
> 171–3

The first part of his defence does not focus only on attesting that Heracles' glorious reputation is deserved; he accentuates that reputation's widespread nature, as if its very excessiveness is self-validating. Amphitryon suggests that Lycus could hear of Heracles' renown from the gods (176 and 180), the Centaurs (181) and even Mt. Dirphys (185), indicating that even mythological races of great fame, the gods and monumental landmarks will lend their voices to praising Heracles. When he criticizes Lycus for his own lack of deeds, this too focuses on his deeds as praiseworthy or not. He notes that Lycus has done nothing glorious, going on to say that he has done nothing noteworthy even to his own people, let alone those further afield:

> οὐκ ἄν σέ γ' αἰνέσειεν· οὐ γὰρ ἔσθ' ὅπου
> ἐσθλόν τι δράσας μάρτυρ' ἂν λάβοις πάτραν.
>
> You would certainly not be praised, for you have not done anything good anywhere for which you could take your homeland as a witness!
>
> 186–7

It is not until Amphitryon has dealt sufficiently with these issues of λόγοι that he finally turns to Lycus' intended deed (205), thus making Heracles' reputation his most urgent concern. Amphitryon's focus here gives a clear indication of his priorities in how he identifies Heracles, in that his public, 'heroic' reputation is the main concern, and comes before his concern for Heracles' family, himself included.

In response, Lycus rejects not just Amphitryon's argument, but rather his entire approach, commenting:

> σὺ μὲν λέγ' ἡμᾶς οἷς πεπύργωσαι λόγοις.
> ἐγὼ δὲ δράσω σ' ἀντὶ τῶν λόγων κακῶς.
>
> You go on saying these words to me with which you have fortified yourself, but I will actually do something bad to you in return for your words.
>
> 238–9

Lycus' conclusive remark indicates his contrasting priorities. He rejects the idea that words and renown can be meaningful or valuable enough to engage with further, and instead demonstrates his view that acts, in this case violence, are more significant. His lack of concern for reputation can be seen demonstrated elsewhere in his behaviour, making this a consistent pattern of his characterization. The very act of threatening to burn suppliants around an altar suggests a disregard for the disapprobation such behaviour would earn him: the chorus' own disapproval and horror suggests what the wider public view would be of such an act (252–67). Megara even comments to Heracles, in her discussion of Lycus' conduct:

αἰδώς; ἀποικεῖ τῆσδε τῆς θεοῦ πρόσω.

Shame? Why, he lives far away from that goddess.

557

Concepts of αἰδώς can often be strongly linked with an idea of what is considered conduct likely to bring external criticism rather than honour, and so Lycus' rejection of this idea demonstrates a clear dismissal of the value of public reputation and praise, as he has no apparent fear of attracting blame instead.[12] Unlike Megara and Amphitryon, Lycus refuses to accept renown or reputation as a central aspect of identity, and does not concern himself with reputation or public opinion when presenting his own identity to others.

Yet Lycus' claim to authority is entirely undermined by the play, with the result that his attitude to reputation and public opinion is not upheld by the characters around him. The chorus complain of the inappropriateness of his current position of power (252–7) and later his *hubris* (740–1), thus undermining any authority his position might supply for his speech, and Heracles and Megara make it clear that his behaviour has been shameful (556–7). His decision to burn Megara and the children on the altar at which they are supplicating (716, 723–5) further discredits his attitude, since it demonstrates willingness to engage in behaviour a Greek audience would have considered disgraceful.[13] Moreover, the attitudes of all the other characters and the chorus to praise and reputation emphasize that Lycus' approach is wrong, even if it were not made problematic by their direct reactions to his words and deeds. These rejections have the effect of setting Lycus up to be isolated in his opinion. Unlike the community of Argives who blame Ajax in the *Ajax*,[14] or the communal choral praise offered Heracles within this play, Lycus is not shown in the *Heracles* to be supported by anyone else in his attitudes, indicating the extent of his incorrect decision-making. This also has the effect of making his blame speech seem individually motivated and less effective than the shared speech of the other characters, who all share a discourse which values praise and renown and demonstrates its significance as a motivating force for them.

The prominence and weight given to a reputation for heroism is reinforced throughout the first half of play by all the characters and the chorus, bar the exceptional and mistaken Lycus. It is treated as an important aspect of identity, and something which must be considered when it comes to making even life or death decisions. It is in this renown-focused context that Heracles' attempt to reframe his own reputation and renown takes place upon his arrival on stage. Heracles' return to his family and responsibilities is accompanied by an attempt to change what may bring poetic praise and what may be considered 'glorious' through an effort to argue that his protection of his family too may fall within this category. However, this attempt proves utterly unsuccessful and ultimately destructive to that family, due to the persistence of traditional ideas about what may bring *kleos* for him among all the surrounding characters and the chorus.

Heracles, glorious in fatherhood?

As soon as he arrives on stage, Heracles begins to counteract the effect of the chorus, Amphitryon and Megara's earlier focus on his heroic deeds to the exclusion of his role as a father, with an attempt to integrate his deeds as a father into the same scheme of praise earned for his heroic deeds and the reputation gained by them. Heracles chooses to focus his attention on the situation of his family, and connects that focus with the claim that saving his family should be considered as important as his labours. He dismisses the importance of his heroic labours to his own identity and reputation, in contrast to his wife and father, since he declares, χαιρόντων πόνοι ('farewell to my labours' 575), and goes on to argue,

> μάτην γὰρ αὐτοὺς τῶνδε μᾶλλον ἤνυσα.
>
> In vain I accomplished them rather than the tasks here.
>
> 576

Heracles attempts to argue that any reputation for his labours must be contingent on his successful completion of the defence of his family, when he claims that unless he defends his family,

> οὐκ ἄρ' Ἡρακλῆς
> ὁ καλλίνικος ὡς πάροιθε λέξομαι
>
> I shall not be called Heracles, glorious in victory, as I was before.
>
> 581–2

The word καλλίνικος is one laden with praise and carries with it the full extent of Heracles' heroic reputation.[15] In declaring that this term can now be applied only after a successful defence of his children, he attempts to transfer that quality of glory and reputation on to his domestic work, presenting this defence as itself a heroic labour worthy of receiving praise, and even suggesting that his existing *kleos*, consisting of how he is described favourably by others, cannot stand without this additional task being completed. Heracles could reasonably have celebrated his overthrow of Lycus as a socially beneficial heroic task, since he is ridding Thebes once again of wrongful treatment and domination.[16] However, this option is prevented by the hero's own presentation of the situation, which is persistently family focused. On leaving the stage, he takes hold of his children and leads them carefully into the house, focusing specifically on their welfare and remarking:

> καὶ γὰρ οὐκ ἀναίνομαι
> θεράπευμα τέκνων.
>
> I do not refuse to care for my children.
>
> 632–3

Heracles emphasizes that his children and family, not the city, are his priority here. His gnomic statement which follows, claiming that 'all mortals love their children' (634–6), attempts to make this behaviour sound as reasonable and as widely praiseworthy as his monster-slaying deeds, while making use of a technique which is itself common in praise and blame speech in archaic and classical poetry.[17] Heracles attempts to move the focus away from public heroism, even drawing in the wider audience of 'the whole race of mortals' as his support, and to subsume care for his children under the umbrella of *kleos*-gaining deeds, of the kind on which his heroic reputation for being καλλίνικος is founded.

However, despite the confidence of Heracles in this scene, it is clear from both the reactions of the other characters and the events of the play that this attitude is complicated at best. The use of gnomic statements in poetry can often be a claim to an authoritative position, backing up an argument or opinion with the strength of generally acknowledged wisdom.[18] Yet the Greek of this statement is ambiguous: πᾶν δὲ φιλότεκνον γένος (636) could indicate either that all mortals love children, or that all mortals love only their own children. Any authority given to the more general statement is undercut by Heracles' act in the next part of the play: he will kill the children he believes to be Eurystheus' offspring with relish and an excess of violence, even indicating his delight in doing so:

> ὁ δ' ἠλάλαξε κἀπεκόμπασεν τάδε·
> Εἷς μὲν νεοσσὸς ὅδε θανὼν Εὐρυσθέως
> ἔχθραν πατρῴαν ἐκτίνων πέπτωκέ μοι.
>
> He raised a warcry and boasted aloud in this way: 'This is one chick of Eurystheus' dead, he has fallen to pay me back in full for his father's hostility!'
>
> 981–3

Heracles does not act in grim silence; he shows no qualms about killing young children – indeed he is represented by the messenger as triumphing in doing so – and thus there is clear difficulty with setting this delight in child-killing alongside any statement that claims universal love between mortals and children.[19] A similar ambiguity occurs even in the statement by which he declares his intention to save his children:

> τῶν δ' ἐμῶν τέκνων
> οὐκ ἐκπονήσω θάνατον;
>
> Shall I not labour against the death of my children?
>
> 580–1

The construction's ambiguity arises from the implication of precisely its opposite; grammatically, Heracles could also be asking whether he should labour to bring about the deaths of his children.[20] Given that he will end up accomplishing precisely that, this doubled meaning is particularly significant. The combination of problems here make Heracles' attempt at gnomic wisdom uncertain at best.

Even without considering the ambiguous nature of Heracles' statements, or any acts committed under a god-sent madness, there are clear problems throughout the play with the child-and-family-focused attitude he attempts to claim as glorious and praiseworthy. Unlike the glory bestowed for heroic acts, Heracles receives only mild criticism for his decisions in relation to caring for his family. As noted above, Amphitryon's focus in his discussion with Lycus was primarily maintaining praise associated with Heracles' public heroic reputation, not Heracles' status as a member of a family under threat. Conversely, his comments about Heracles' role within his immediate family are more critical. Amphitryon remarks rather pointedly on Heracles' decision to leave his family behind to undertake his labours:

> λιπὼν δὲ Θήβας, οὗ κατῳκίσθην ἐγώ,
> Μεγάραν τε τήνδε πενθερούς
>
> Leaving Thebes, where I had settled, and leaving Megara and his in-laws.
>
> 13–14

Logically it does not need to be stated that Heracles must have left Thebes to go elsewhere and perform labours, but Amphitryon frames this point in terms that make it clear that by doing so Heracles has also abandoned both sides of his family, natal and marital. When talking about the responsibilities this has left Amphitryon himself with, he is almost scornful, calling himself a τροφὸν τέκνων ('children's nursemaid' 45), an incongruous description for a famous warrior. Amphitryon's comments suggest either that Heracles is disingenuous to claim that all men would agree that his family must come before his labours, or at the very least that Heracles' resolution is rather a case of too little too late, since up until now he has concentrated on his labours to the detriment of his family. Therefore his attempt to claim a care for family as being as glorious a pursuit as his previous labours is complicated by the blame which Amphitryon introduces for this element of his identity, which contrasts rather sharply with the play's praise for his labours. Amphitryon's persistent concern with renown and reputation makes his comments pointed; like Philoctetes in the *Philoctetes*, Amphitryon has been presented in the *Heracles* as someone who clearly appreciates the value of reputation and renown, and prioritizes it both in guiding his own behaviour and in protecting his son and preserving Heracles' reputation. His voice is therefore lent extra authority within the context of the play, so that his criticism and the disappointment he expresses in Heracles' deeds within the family sphere strengthen the contrast with the praise he was eager to maintain for the heroic deeds of Heracles.

Even in the moments meant to portray Heracles' care for and devotion to his family, there are some uncomfortable juxtapositions. Megara, immediately before her anticipated death, describes her grief for her children by talking of the happy and hopeful lives they have led. However, when she talks of Heracles playing with his children, each of them is given an inheritance won by martial deeds, and the first two are lent one of his weapons or heroic tools as a toy (462–75). Perhaps this would be less concerning in the heroic age than in the more safety-conscious modern era, were it not for the fact that the next time the children encounter these weapons, it will be in their father's murderous hands.[21] This troubled connection between Heracles' children and his heroic weapons is at the heart of the conflict embodied in this play between his heroism and his family life. Once his children are dead, he faces his weapons in full awareness of this fact, imagining that they speak to him, and remind him of how they killed his children in graphic terms:

Ἡμῖν τέκν' εἷλες καὶ δάμαρθ'· ἡμᾶς ἔχεις
παιδοκτόνους σούς

You killed your children and wife through us, and you still hold us, your child-slaying weapons.

1380–1

Simultaneously he acknowledges that to give them up means repudiating his heroics:

ἀλλὰ γυμνωθεὶς ὅπλων
ξὺν οἷς τὰ κάλλιστ᾽ ἐξέπραξ᾽ ἐν Ἑλλάδι

But shall I strip off my weapons with which I achieved my most glorious exploits in Greece?

1382–3

In attempting to unite his identity as father of children with his identity as public monster-slayer under the same umbrella of the καλλίνικος Heracles, Heracles has seen the more dangerous, heroic side of him destroy his priorities in a mortal, domestic world. This conflict of what to do with the weapons represents his recognition that the two must once more be separated. In combination with his conversations with Theseus, his decision to bear the weapons once more will mark a decision to return to the 'heroic world,' that is, to focus solely on martial, heroic *kleos*-gaining deeds for his ongoing identity and reputation. His children's early association with the weapons will spell disaster in his attempt to combine the two aspects of his identity.

Heracles attempts to establish for himself an identity as family-focused man, and further endeavours to represent this identity as one which, like his heroic identity, can be established through discourses of praise. Yet even from the earliest moments of the play, Heracles' attempted family-focused identity features in no such discourses of praise from those around him. Instead it is established as problematic, worthy only of blame, even from close supporters such as Amphitryon. It is particularly significant in this context that the labours occurring before Heracles' madness is a Euripidean innovation.[22] In other versions of the myth, Heracles does not leave his family to complete his heroic deeds, since they are already dead when these take place. As a result, this type of blame from Amphitryon, and warning signs from Megara, about the negative consequences for Heracles' family of his renowned exploits is unique to the situation Euripides has created.[23] Euripides has effectively forced a situation in which Heracles' treatment of his family, even before his madness, can be called into question or face outright blame, problematizing his desire to be praised for caring for them.

Heracles, glorious in heroism

Heracles' claims are also undermined by the fact that the chorus and other characters in the *Heracles* repeatedly insist on positioning him within discourses of praise which succeed only in constructing his identity as heroic, glorious and monster-slaying, and ignore any other aspects of his identity, such as fatherhood, entirely. As discussed above, praise and reputation are seen to be essential in establishing and maintaining identity for both Megara and Amphitryon even before Heracles' arrival. However, there are also noticeable examples of places where they are privileged expressly above family concerns, both by the chorus and by the members of Heracles' family who appear on stage. Heracles' identity as loving father is never securely established in the discourses of praise in which the chorus and characters position him, and instead his identity as glorious hero is constructed repeatedly in relation to his labours, without any apparent ability to encompass the family-focused labour of protecting them that Heracles himself proposes, and which will go so entirely wrong in the attempt.

As has already been discussed, Amphitryon is clearly concerned with his own and his son's reputations for past glories, and it is notable that on two separate occasions he turns his focus to these even when that focus becomes somewhat forced as a result. The first time this happens is in what he believes will be his final goodbye to the chorus, when he expects Lycus to return and kill them. He has already called Zeus to aid Heracles' family, and made much of his own service to them (339–47, and 497–502). But in his final moments, when he turns to say goodbye to the Theban elders who have shown themselves to be eager friends to the family (unlike Zeus, according to Amphitryon), he suddenly drops this concern with the family, instead demonstrating that in his final farewell, his reputation and previous glory are his lingering concern:

> ὁρᾶτ' ἔμ' ὅσπερ ἦ περίβλεπτος βροτοῖς
> ὀνομαστὰ πράσσων . . .
> ὁ δ' ὄλβος ὁ μέγας ἥ τε δόξ' οὐκ οἶδ' ὅτῳ
> βέβαιός ἐστι . . .
>
> Look at me, the man who was once admired from all sides by mortals, doing famous deeds . . . But great wealth and reputation – I do not know how that can ever be secure.
>
> 508–12

In his generalization, Amphitryon asks the chorus to recognise in him not a father, husband or grandfather, but rather someone who has done glorious deeds. He makes it an essential aspect of his identity, and one which is so dominant that it is almost proverbial, unlike any family-oriented aspect of his identity. Later, Amphitryon demonstrates the same focus when talking to his newly arrived son. Although he originally advises Heracles to focus on his home, greeting his household gods and protecting his family (599–605), he actually ends up significantly delaying his son in doing so by asking prolonged questions about Heracles' previous deeds in Hades, Eurystheus, and Theseus (610–20). The effect is rather wrenching – at this time of apparent crisis, despite his own advice, Amphitryon is almost lured away from his focus on Heracles' family to dwell on his son's labours, and heroic deeds, and the fellow hero he met in accomplishing them. It is Heracles himself who forces the scene back on to his domestic focus, preventing further questions from his father by addressing his children instead (622).

This focus from Amphitryon forms part of a persistent pattern across the *Heracles* which suggests that Heracles' identity should be solely heroic, and which is focused on praise which constructs solely that identity, allowing for no alternative. The other examples of this pattern come from speakers with significant authority: the chorus, and the goddess, Lyssa. The chorus' identity in the *Heracles* has the effect of giving them an almost metatheatrical role much closer to that of the non-tragic chorus, as authoritative public singers of Greek society.[24] The chorus introduce themselves as ἰηλέμων γέρων ἀοιδὸς ('an aged singer of lament' 110–11), labelling themselves immediately as singers rather than elders or counsellors.[25] They thus imbue their speeches both with the authority of a public chorus, and, given their focus on their old age, with the authority of age, even if they comment on their lack of physical vigour (e.g. 107–9, 268–9).[26]

This idea of the chorus both as authoritative speakers and as being closely associated with public choral performance is maintained throughout the play, such that it is constantly drawn to the audience's attention. In lines 673–700 they give a more formalized lyric announcement of their role as singers, which explicitly identifies them with choral performance and the performance of song. This second strophe and antistrophe pair are entirely bound up with the chorus' role as performers of song, beginning with a hymnic invocation to the Graces and the Muses.[27] The chorus describe themselves self-referentially as dancing in a chorus (685)[28] and as wreathed (677) aged singers (γέρων ἀοιδὸς 692),[29] and describe their ode specifically as in the group of hymns (695) and paeans (691). They further associate themselves with mythologically significant singers, in the form of the Delian Maidens (687–8) and the swan (692).[30] Their reference to the Delian Maidens introduces a further association with choral performance, as the maidens are described as dancing beautiful choruses (εἱλίσσουσαι καλλίχοροι 690).[31] Their song is repeatedly associated with praise, and with the reference to Mnemosyne, invokes the idea of the function of sung praise in preserving memory:

ἔτι τοι γέρων ἀοιδὸς
κελαδῶ Μναμοσύναν,

I still, even though I am an old singer, sing celebrations of Mnemosyne.

678–9

As Detienne has demonstrated, the poetic functions of praise and blame are in Pindar and other poets contrasted with aspects of memory and oblivion, with praise song having the ability to confirm memory of an individual and his deeds.[32] The choral invocation of Mnemosyne here, therefore, ties the chorus' ode immediately into this functional context of praise song. Immediately following this remark, they claim:

ἔτι τὰν Ἡρακλέους
καλλίνικον ἀείδω

I still hymn Heracles' glorious victory.

680–1

The chorus connect their position as singers with the function of praising Heracles and his 'victories', as in an epinician ode.[33] Their explicit reference to Mnemosyne preceding the promise of further sung praise for Heracles marks the significance of their role in creating and establishing his *kleos* and the memory of him that will endure. They invest that same victory ode with 'the power of right' in the claim that follows shortly (694–5), in a comment which once again makes explicit reference to their ode as τοῖς ὕμνοισιν. The chorus thus insist on emphasizing their authoritative position, and tying this explicitly to their function as singers beyond their involvement in specific 'character' roles.

Their third stasimon is similarly poetic and again explicitly involves the chorus introducing themselves as participating in choral dancing: πρὸς χοροὺς τραπώμεθα (761).[34] There are frequent references to song (ἀοιδάς 767, συναοιδοὶ 788, κελάδῳ 793) and garlands (the river Ismenus becomes στεφαναφόρει 781). Even the city and landscape itself is invited to join in the choral performance along with the chorus, particularly in the evocative start to the second strophe, where they cry χοροὶ χοροί (763).[35] The connections of the city and landscape into this proposed choral celebration particularly highlight the function of the *Heracles*' chorus as a public chorus rather than a group associated solely with Heracles' household, and thus institutionalize and make officially public their speech.[36] This public choral function is tied explicitly once again to celebration and praise for Heracles, as the chorus invite celebration again of his καλλίνικον ἀγῶνα (789), and describe his 'shining strength' (λαμπρὰν ἀλκάν 805–6). The chorus even insist on framing Heracles' defeat of Lycus in a similarly self-referential context of song, describing his cries as a μέλος (750), and claiming that their own third stasimon arises from the silence which has fallen upon the ending of this song of Lycus' death cries (761).[37] All of the choral stasima are explicitly self-referential and invoke the powers and gods of song and of the chorus in conveying their message, making their comments both more poetic and more authoritative in their choral performances than a chorus who do not make such connections.

It is not surprising that the chorus' main focus in relation to Heracles is his praiseworthy status as a hero; given their function as public singers, they have an important role in conveying mythical material and exempla to the society they serve.[38] The chorus' explicit decision to sing praise songs for Heracles means that they participate in the construction of this identity through the performance of praise songs throughout the play.[39] Their first major ode is even sung explicitly as a victory hymn for Heracles, describing his success in glorious labours (355–435). It is highly decorative, invoking Phoebus and the lyre at the start in a way which mimics epinician odes,[40] and describing many of Heracles' tasks with adjectives which recall gold, glory and similarly attractive ideas (e.g. 368, 375, 386, 396, 414, etc.). The chorus expressly describe their song as στεφάνωμα μόχθων, a particularly Pindaric way of referring to a praise-song.[41] It is entirely reasonable for Heracles' labours to be considered a suitable topic for the first choral ode, often focused on mythological background,[42] but the decorative and glorious style is significant here. The epinician context positions Heracles within a praise discourse which typically compares winning athletes to glorious, mythical heroes,[43] but here Heracles is himself the hero, so that the effect is undiluted by comparison. With this ode, the chorus draw on that generic context and identifies Heracles purely by his heroic, glorious deeds, without making any reference to family or other aspects of his identity, making his own introduction of those aspects somewhat of a surprise on his entry.

The second stasimon, in harking back to this first ode through the comment that the chorus ἔτι . . . ἀείδω for Heracles (680–1), intensifies this effect. This stasimon is replete with details which focus on the chorus as singers and the role of their song in praising Heracles. Parry has described the ode as an *encomium*, drawing on Pindaric and hymnic features to celebrate Heracles in song.[44] This stasimon celebrates Heracles' sudden return and, coming immediately after his arrival on stage and his promise to protect his wife and children, has far more reason than the first to celebrate the anticipated salvation of his family rather than his past exploits. However, the chorus instead digress into a celebration of

Heracles' glory more generally, even concluding with a specific focus on his labours,

> Διὸς ὁ παῖς· τᾶς δ' εὐγενίας
> πλέον ὑπερβάλλων <ἀρετᾷ>
> μοχθήσας τὸν ἄκυμον
> θῆκεν βίοτον βροτοῖς
> πέρσας δείματα θηρῶν.

> He is the son of Zeus: but he has fully overtaken even this good lineage in his excellence, and has laboured and made life peaceful for mortals, and slain terrible beasts.
>
> 696–700

Rather than concluding with a triumphant statement of his ability to save his family, the chorus appear to dismiss that family entirely, naming his divine parent instead of Amphitryon, and concluding with praise of his deeds overcoming 'monsters'. In their reference to Heracles' slayings of θηρῶν the chorus even pick up Lycus' earlier dismissive complaints that Heracles has earned a glorious reputation through killing beasts (157–8), and effectively refute them.[45] Given the meaning of Lycus' name (wolf), there is an implication of Heracles' forthcoming deed,[46] but rather than celebrate this as a new action associated with the rescue of his family, the chorus subsume it into their celebrations of his labours: Lycus becomes one more 'terrible beast', and Heracles' family vanish entirely from the song.

In the same way, immediately after Lycus' death, the chorus sing a brief hymn addressed to Thebes (764–96), before concluding with a description of Heracles and his triumphs. Once again, they explicitly claim to be seeing proof of divinity and super-mortal status in Heracles' acts (802–3), and almost dismiss Amphitryon and Heracles' mortal family ties entirely – although the 'double marriage' is noted, Amphitryon is not named in this passage, and Zeus is named twice as Heracles' father (800, 803). Here there does appear some socially focused praise of the dispatch of Lycus in terms of an overthrow of a usurper of Thebes (769–70), and the return of a more appropriate king (809–14). Yet the chorus frame this praise entirely in combination with their celebration of Thebes itself, including the city's 'shining' inheritance from the Sown Men (793–7). Their celebration of Heracles makes no explicit mention of the role he has simultaneously played in saving his family or rescuing his wife and children, which earlier the chorus twice claimed to be a key concern of theirs, and of Thebes (131–7, 253, 261–3). When it comes to this formal, poetic celebration of

Heracles, however, while Thebes remains, the children and their importance to Thebes has entirely vanished, giving the impression that the chorus are only willing or able to sing in praise of the public-oriented deeds which Heracles has accomplished. Similarly, there is a further association developed with Heracles' heroic labours in this song, since the chorus raise the aspect of the events which is most related to these, the fact that:

ὃς γᾶς ἐξέβας θαλάμων
Πλούτωνος δῶμα λιπὼν
νέρτερον.

You came out from the depths of the earth, leaving behind Pluto's home below.
806–8

Some scholars have argued that it is this mortality-defying deed of Heracles' in returning from the underworld which causes his destruction, and that the chorus' description here points to this reading.[47] However, in this formal celebration of Heracles' return and defeat of Lycus, the chorus remain focused on Heracles as a public, heroic figure – his service to Thebes and his labours are the only aspects of his deed celebrated here, and there is no recurrence of his family among the chorus' concerns. As a result, while we see here precisely the kind of sung praise which establishes *kleos* and confirms Heracles as καλλίνικος. Heracles' own wish that that glorious reputation could be associated with the protection of his children is left unfulfilled: that action remains unsung.

The same persistent identification of Heracles by his heroic exploits rather than family relationships is shown by the goddess Lyssa, in her argument as to why Heracles should not be attacked by Hera. It is made clear by Iris that Heracles' punishment is intended by Hera to be one that will be linked intimately with his family, when she states,

Ἥρα προσάψαι κοινὸν αἷμ᾽ αὐτῷ θέλει
παῖδας κατακτείναντι, συνθέλω δ᾽ ἐγώ

Hera wants him to be bound up with kindred blood, from killing his children, and I want that too.
831–2

However, in her argument against the punishment, Lyssa entirely ignores this aspect, choosing instead to spotlight his role as a glorious hero, and his wonderful deeds:

ἀνὴρ ὅδ᾽ οὐκ ἄσημος οὔτ᾽ ἐπὶ χθονὶ
οὔτ᾽ ἐν θεοῖσιν, οὗ σύ μ᾽ ἐσπέμπεις δόμους·

> ἄβατον δὲ χώραν καὶ θάλασσαν ἀγρίαν
> ἐξημερώσας θεῶν ἀνέστησεν μόνος
> τιμὰς . . .
>
> The man into whose house you are sending me is hardly insignificant, either on land or to the gods: for he tamed the untrodden land and savage sea, and alone restored the honour of the gods.
>
> 849–53

The reference to Heracles' being 'not insignificant on land or to the gods' recalls Amphitryon's earlier descriptions of the extent of Heracles' reputation, so that Heracles' deeds again appear in combination with his reputation. Lyssa could also have argued that slaying his own family is too harsh a punishment, or unfair on their part, but she does not mention Heracles' family at all, instead talking only of the significance of Heracles' deeds and heroism. Lyssa effectively lends divine support to the idea that Heracles should be identified primarily through the praise won for his heroic deeds.[48] It is therefore not solely the chorus who add authority to the expressions of this idea: even the only sympathetic divine figure to appear in the play also insists on reinforcing this type of identity for Heracles, above all else.

Several times in the play the characters and chorus reject opportunities to focus on or value Heracles' relations with his family, instead drawing attention repeatedly back to his heroic labours and his reputation. This attention is emphasized through the explicit formal choral celebrations of the chorus, and the divine speaker in the form of Lyssa. As a result, Heracles' attempt to reframe being καλλίνικος as including the care of his children is attempted against multiple significant voices arguing for the opposite: that Heracles is καλλίνικος purely as a result of his heroic labours and the reputation gained for it. Following the destruction of his family, this argument is reiterated and finally confirmed in the rehabilitation which Theseus affects, and through which Heracles' family identity and any attempt to celebrate it is finally abandoned to be replaced only with the heroic Heracles.

Reconstructing the heroic Heracles

In the final scenes of the play, Heracles and Theseus both make a point of rejecting the domestic ties Heracles had briefly tried to prioritize, in a movement led by Theseus from his entry to the play. Instead, they focus on his heroic identity as a way of moving forward, and in particular, as a way of becoming the celebrated Heracles once more. The violence which breaks out as a result of the identity crisis Heracles experiences has had a destabilizing effect on Heracles' identity, so much so that his friend Theseus is unable to correctly identify him on his entry to the stage.[49] Theseus reveals himself as being entirely unable to recognize who Heracles is, asking Amphitryon:

> τίς δ' ὅδ' οὑν νεκροῖς, γέρον;
>
> Old man, who is that in among the corpses?
>
> 1189

In the descriptions which follow, Theseus and Amphitryon participate in a process of reconstructing Heracles' identity which makes him recognizable once more. This process is accomplished through their positioning him within discourses of praise which celebrate his heroic identity as a monster-slayer, and leaves his identity as family-focused man aside. Theseus and Amphitryon therefore reiterate the same praise discourses through which Heracles' identity has been constructed throughout the play to perform this reconstruction. Heracles' survival enables him to participate in this reconstruction through his discussion with Theseus, and unlike Ajax he proves able to be persuaded to accept the discourse of others, finally returning to his identity as praiseworthy hero, and abandoning any attempt to establish a praiseworthy role as family protector.

Amphitryon begins this process immediately in response to Theseus' question, by identifying Heracles:

> ἐμὸς ἐμὸς ὅδε γόνος ὁ πολύπονος, ὃς ἐπὶ
> δόρυ γιγαντοφόνον ἦλθεν σὺν θεοῖ-
> σι Φλεγραῖον ἐς πεδίον ἀσπιστάς.
>
> That is my son, the man of many labours who came with the gods to the plain of Phlegra, where many giants fell, as a warrior to fight.
>
> 1190–2

Amphitryon does describe Heracles by their relationship, but immediately passes over it, referring to Heracles' labours and then progressing to a detailed description of one of Heracles' heroic exploits as a means of identifying him to Theseus. In addition, Amphitryon continues the description of Heracles by declaring,

> οὐκ ἂν εἰδείης ἕτερον
> πολυμοχθότερον πολυπλαγκτότερόν τε θνατῶν.

> You will not learn of another more-labouring or more-wandering among mortals.
>
> 1196–7

The comment explicitly evokes Heracles' heroic labours (along with his present suffering) in the term πολυμοχθότερον and establishes these as a further element of his identity by which Theseus can recognize him.[50] These comments may seem somewhat redundant: Theseus and Heracles have a previous relationship of which Amphitryon is already aware (619–20), and so Theseus should not need to hear more than Heracles' name to have his question answered. Yet in his state of absolute despair, as Theseus will later state, Heracles is 'not himself' (1414), so in taking more pains over identifying him, Amphitryon and later Theseus begin the process of revealing who that 'self' is and who he is to be in the future, after the violent crisis in identity he has experienced.[51]

Once Heracles is identified to Theseus, they begin the conversation which is often accredited with being part of Heracles' acceptance of a mortal life or lifestyle.[52] However, there are frequent hints that precisely the opposite is taking place. To begin with, Theseus describes Heracles' misery as spanning far more than just the mortal earth:

> ἅπτῃ κάτωθεν οὐρανοῦ δυσπραξίᾳ
>
> In your misery, you overtake heaven from down below.
>
> 1240

From then on, he actively rejects Heracles' repeated attempts to continue claiming an association with his family, now an association with extreme grief rather than celebration, as he reflects the destabilization of Heracles' identity as part of the violence he has experienced. Theseus has already indicated some disinclination to allow further speech about Heracles' family in attempting to prevent Amphitryon from giving an 'ill-omened' description of the events (1185), and this trend increases in his conversation with Heracles. He begins his comments by remarking dismissively of Heracles' grief:

> εἴρηκας ἐπιτυχόντος ἀνθρώπου λόγους
>
> You have spoken the words of some common person.
>
> 1248

In the face of Heracles' enduring despair, however, Theseus is forced to amend his judgement; Heracles is not simply speaking *like* some ordinary person, he has temporarily become someone other than himself. Theseus is forced to acknowledge a disjunction between the identity he expects, and the one which Heracles is displaying to him:

> ὁ πολλὰ δὴ τλὰς Ἡρακλῆς λέγει τάδε;
> . . .
> εὐεργέτης βροτοῖσι καὶ μέγας φίλος;
>
> Does the much-enduring Heracles say these things? 1250
>
> Is this the benefactor and great friend to mortals? 1252

Faced with Theseus' questions, Heracles begins to re-establish his heroic identity for himself, talking of his lineage (1258–68), and dwelling on his labours and successful monster-slayings (1269–79). However, here he is once more distracted by his desire to focus on family, and indicates that his killing of his children has undermined the identity that he had begun to re-establish, claiming that he will be unable to move in society (1281–6), and since the earth itself will reject his presence (1294–1300), he may as well be dead (1301). In his complaints about Hera, he argues that she has destroyed him (1303–10). Heracles claims that the man he once was exists no longer, that that identity has been overturned by Hera's sending of the madness, and despite his acknowledgement of its existence, it cannot be re-established. Once he has acknowledged the previous existence of this heroic identity, however, Theseus makes sure to have Heracles remember and continue to maintain it, asking:

> οὕτω πόνων σῶν οὐκέτι μνήμην ἔχεις;
>
> Do you thus no longer hold on to the memory of your labours? 1410

when he would linger, and accusing:

> ὁ κλεινὸς Ἡρακλῆς οὐκ εἶ νοσῶν.
>
> Distressed, you are not the famous Heracles. 1414

Theseus' comment explicitly acknowledges the crisis in Heracles' identity caused by the violent clash between his two potential subject positions.[53] He does not complain that Heracles is not behaving *like* a famous individual, rather that Heracles now *is* not his famous, heroic self. Yet Theseus states this not only as a reflection on the situation; his remark is intended as a reproach to Heracles, and succeeds in stinging Heracles to a response which recalls his own triumph in the underworld as opposed to Theseus' failure (1415–17), thus re-connecting Heracles with his heroic identity. It is particularly striking that Theseus' comment describing Heracles as not the κλεινὸς Heracles starts this process, along with reference to the memory (μνήμην 1410), of Heracles' deeds. As discussed above, the choral performances of celebration for Heracles' labours connect the chorus' songs to the memory established through performance of poetry, which makes individuals such as Heracles κλεινὸς. As a result, Theseus' comments here remind Heracles of these poetically celebrated labours, those confirmed in memory and established as part of his fame, rather than any actions connected with his family.

Theseus does not rely solely on Heracles' remembrance of his past heroic identity, however; he also offers a situation which will re-establish that identity for the future, and it is this which causes Heracles to give up on his planned death, and agree to Theseus' suggestions (1322–3). Theseus at no point suggests that Heracles should have any further concern for domestic or family matters. The life he maps out for Heracles in Athens includes the important assurance that,

> θυσίαισι λαΐνοισί τ' ἐξογκώμασιν
> τίμιον ἀνάξει πᾶσ' Ἀθηναίων πόλις.
> καλὸς γὰρ ἀστοῖς στέφανος Ἑλλήνων ὕπο
> ἄνδρ' ἐσθλὸν ὠφελοῦντας εὐκλείας τυχεῖν.
>
> The whole city of the Athenians will raise you up as revered with sacrifices and monuments of stone. For it is a fine crown for the citizens in the view of the Greeks to gain renown for aiding a noble man.
>
> 1332–5

It is clear that Theseus is not offering a domestic life; he talks of honours and prizes in recognition of heroism, and a life associated with that.[54] The close juxtaposition of the terms στέφανος and εὐκλείας evoke the context of praise poetry once more, so that Theseus' words here reflect the chorus' earlier epinician odes for Heracles, and tie his ongoing life in Athens into that context.[55] Similarly, one of Theseus' complaints in their shorter conversation expressly connects Heracles' current behaviour with the lack of praise which he can earn for it:

> εἴ σ' ὄψεταί τις θῆλυν ὄντ' οὐκ αἰνέσει.
>
> If someone sees you being feminine, he will not praise you.
>
> 1412

As a result, Theseus' promised gifts of celebrations in the context of praise poetry contrast sharply with the complete lack of praise which Heracles' despair over his family can earn, in Theseus' view. These gifts are offered in return for another heroic act which Heracles has committed – rescuing Theseus from the underworld (1336–7). Theseus presents an ongoing life for Heracles in which he continues to live and behave according to his heroic identity, and his identity as father is entirely left behind. This guarantee is then taken up by Heracles' agreement to leave with Theseus, so that even before they reach Athens, the path they embark upon will take them back to Heracles' heroic labours: the incomplete task of delivering Cerberus to Eurystheus (1386–8).[56] This decision is even represented in the staging of the scene. Heracles makes the rather symbolic move on stage away from his family: his father is left standing on stage alone, with the bodies of Heracles' wife and children around him, once more solely responsible for their care (in this case their burial 1358–65), and unable to follow Heracles to his return to heroic labours and a praiseworthy life.

Heracles explicitly accepts the idea of maintaining his heroic identity when he takes up his weapons to leave with Theseus. However, even before that, he shows growing concern for this aspect of his identity, and willingness to take it up in preference to his family disasters, in his responses to Theseus' final offer. When he agrees to accept Theseus' gifts, he does so partly with the reasoning,

> ἐσκεψάμην δὲ καίπερ ἐν κακοῖσιν ὤν,
> μὴ δειλίαν ὄφλω τιν' ἐκλιπὼν φάος·
>
> I realised that although I am in the midst of troubles, I have not incurred some charge of cowardice by leaving the light.
>
> 1347–8

This statement is not obviously connected to Theseus' arguments so far, but it is a symbol of his acceptance of the heroic identity which Theseus offers and promotes instead of his role within a family. He allows concern for reputation and renown to hold sway, and it is in association with this reason that he accepts Theseus' offer to go on living as a hero in Athens. Given the prominence with which reputation and renown are treated throughout the play, this comment is not meant simply as a subordinate concern. Rather Heracles' comment marks a return to those heroic values which have dominated throughout the *Heracles* for many of the characters, and which Heracles tried unsuccessfully to move beyond when he attempted to make tending to his family part of establishing and preserving such a reputation. Heracles' acknowledgement of the destruction of that family, which appears immediately before his decision to retain his weapons, explicitly recognises how Heracles' glory has proved contrary to his efforts to protect his family, despite his hopes:

> . . . οὐδ' ὤνασθε τῶν ἐμῶν καλῶν,
> ἁγὼ παρεσκεύαζον ἐκμοχθῶν βίου
> **εὔκλειαν** ὑμῖν
>
> [Children,] You did not benefit from my fine deeds, which I undertook for a **glorious** life for you from my labours.
>
> 1368–70

In this lament Heracles explicitly recognizes the failure of his labours to provide glory and glorious lives for his children, demonstrating the realization of his failure to encompass their fates within the category of what is glorious and what is praised within poetic speech. Heracles' choice to live and go with Theseus is a return to the glorious, public-facing Heracles, as Heracles grasps the impossibility of his earlier attempt to encompass his family life within the compass of what is glorious for him.

This impossibility is demonstrated starkly in the formal context of song which the chorus have demonstrated throughout. Immediately after Heracles' murder of his family, they attempt to put his deeds into an appropriate context through song. However, although they attempt to begin with two different mythological examples – the Danaids, and Procne's story – they reject both as unsuitable, and eventually appear to give up the attempt entirely, crying in perplexity,

> αἰαῖ, τίνα στεναγμὸν
> ἢ γόον ἢ φθιτῶν ᾠδάν ἢ τίν' Ἅι-
> δα χορὸν ἀχήσω;
>
> Alas, what groaning or wailing or song for the dead or chorus of Hades shall I sound?
>
> 1025–7

Heracles' acts have become effectively impossible for them to sing; they cannot relate a suitable mythological example, and they cannot even work out what type of sound they should make to best begin their song, suggesting and failing to take up in turn a groan, a wail, and even a chorus of Hades. Their confusion and inability to handle the situation is emphasized by Amphitryon's repeated attempts to silence them (1042–4, 1048–51, 1052, 1053–4, 1060). The chorus – so formal and authoritative earlier in the play – are now silenced and unable to perform their appropriate function in this new situation; the destruction of his family that has become the climax of Heracles' attempt to pursue domestic concerns, has made him an impossible target of song. Yet with his promised rehabilitation in Athens, this too will be transformed, as the rites of honour that Theseus offers are closely related to the earlier context of praise songs within which the chorus had repeatedly positioned Heracles. It is also significant in this regard that, even in his despair, it proves impossible for the chorus to identify Heracles as anything other than καλλίνικον (1046). Despite Heracles' earlier hope, they do not indicate that this quality can have any association with his family relationships, since they are unable to sing or speak of these, and by this stage in the play his children are dead, and cannot be a part of his being καλλίνικος. They do explicitly recognize the family relationships involved in Amphitryon's suffering (1039–41).

This lack of a possible poetic celebration of Heracles' identity as a family man is also borne out in the song-focused language which surrounds his family only at its crisis point. Describing Lyssa's attack, the messenger calls Heracles' children a χορὸς ... καλλίμορφος (925), but this chorus, intimately connected with Heracles' family life, are silent for the audience and destroyed shortly afterwards, so that the only choral theme which ever dominates is that spoken by the chorus of the tragedy, who celebrate the heroic aspects alone. Along similar lines, Iris describes the children of Heracles as καλλίπαιδα στέφανον ('a garland of fair children' 839), explicitly mirroring the language used in the celebration which the chorus had earlier offered of Heracles' labours, when they describe their formal song of praise as a στεφάνωμα for his labours (355). Yet this description comes as Iris describes the plan for Heracles to murder his children (838–41), so that as with the silenced chorus, it becomes clear that this type of garland will not endure for Heracles. Lyssa even describes Heracles' madness as if she were making him dance:

> τάχα σ' ἐγὼ μᾶλλον χορεύσω καὶ καταυλήσω φόβῳ.
>
> Soon I shall set you dancing even more, and charm your ears with a pipe of fear.
>
> 871

The chorus similarly describe Heracles as 'set to dance' (χορευθέντ') to the 'pipe of madness' (878–9) and talk ominously of his attack as it begins as a dance:

> κατάρχεται χορεύματ' ἄτερ τυπάνων
> Βρομίου κεχαρισμένων θύρσῳ ...
>
> The dancing starts, without the drums which add delight to the thyrsus of Dionysus...
>
> 889–90

The language of choral dancing here is part of an image of corrupted song which Foley has connected to the collapse of ritual in the play, and to a discrediting of the poetic tradition of Heracles which takes place across the *Heracles* before the establishing of a new type of Heracles who can exist in Athens.[57] The perverse context of this 'dance', however, also has the more specific effect of literalising the impossibility of song and dance becoming part of a celebration of Heracles' family efforts, as he wished. The combination of choral celebration and Heracles' family instead only occurs when madness is involved, and proves entirely destructive.

The same terms associated with the choral praise of Heracles' labours, choral dancing and garlands, are here associated with Heracles' 'labour' connected to his family, as he described it earlier (581). Yet this labour was double-edged, and while Heracles describes it as a potentially glorious labour *against* the death of his children, it could equally be read as the labour *for* the death of his children, as noted above. And in fact, it is the latter which applies, so that these choral celebrations of dance and crowns also become celebrations only of a labour which entirely eradicates Heracles' family, rendering the impossibility of his being called καλλίνικος for its preservation, despite his wishes. The only chorus associated with this labour is the chorus of his children, who do not survive the event. Only the garlands, dance and song associated with Heracles' heroic identity and public labours can persist following their death; any celebration of his family-focused efforts does not. As a result, these alternative, family-associated choruses and garlands are abortive; briefly mentioned only in the moment of their destruction, they can have no ongoing impact on Heracles' reputation or identity. Instead it is only the public praise for the glorious, heroic Heracles, established by the chorus through their formal celebrations, and promised by Theseus upon Heracles' translation to Athens, which will endure. In such a context, it is not surprising that when Theseus works with Heracles to reconstruct Heracles' identity and provide him a way of moving forward with his life, it is achieved only in relation to his publicly praised heroic actions. Despite Heracles' own wishes, no alternative is made possible by the play's extensive poetic presentation of Heracles' renown and its roots.

Conclusion

In Euripides' *Heracles*, the eponymous hero attempts to expand the definition of what is glorious and celebrated in song, by arguing that he should be καλλίνικος for labouring to preserve his family, rather than solely for his traditional heroic labours. Yet the play presents a persistently hostile context for such an argument, and the combined efforts of the strong choral voice and other characters instead demonstrate a recurring concern only with public heroism as a suitable topic for song. As a result, Heracles' efforts to promote an alternative fail, and the alternative target of such song is entirely destroyed, leaving him with a choice between only death and a return to the praiseworthy, public hero of song. As with the *Ajax* and the *Philoctetes*, poetic praise becomes a key issue of this hero-focused play, and as with Ajax, Heracles' attempt to claim a type of poetic praise which cannot stand is a key factor in the destructive events in the play. The *Heracles*, like the *Ajax*, demonstrates how the existing poetic traditions for praise in tragedy can develop destructive and dangerous effects, particularly when their subjects, in this case Heracles, attempt to step beyond the existing tradition to seek new types or topics of praise for themselves.

In all three plays considered so far – the *Philoctetes*, the *Ajax*, and the *Heracles* – tragedy demonstrates an ongoing engagement with existing traditions of praise and blame, particularly through their interaction with the poetic tradition. The multivocal genre of tragedy presents a new challenge to these traditions, in that the multiple voices involved can challenge or contest the production of discourses of praise and blame around these central figures. The involvement of individual heroes in seeking after those discourses of praise, particularly in the cases of Ajax and Heracles, but also in the case of Neoptolemus, poses particular dangers when this search runs against the discourses perpetuated by others. In the following section, an additional dangerous element will be introduced by tragedy into this seeking, and into the multivocal context created by tragedy: the speech of women, when female characters and choruses begin themselves to become participants in this contestation of praise and blame discourses.

4

Euripides' *Suppliant Women* and the Female Subversion of Praise

Thus far, an examination of the tragic development of the poetic praise and blame tradition has demonstrated how it becomes problematic for the heroic figures seeking it, particularly as a result of the involvement of other, non-narratorial, voices in this dialogic genre. The interaction between the genre of tragedy and other genres of praise and blame is especially interesting when we turn to the case of Euripides' *Suppliant Women.* Described as an 'encomium of Athens' in its hypothesis, this play has been examined for its presentation and celebration of Athens and Athens' 'ideal' king, Theseus, since antiquity.[1] However, the play's development of praise and blame language is not as straightforward as this description might imply. Direct praise for Theseus is limited in the *Suppliant Women*, and when it does appear, praise speech is primarily directed at both Theseus and Athens to flatter and persuade, as a rhetorical strategy designed at achieving the speaker's aims, rather than as an outpouring in celebration.[2] At the same time, a rather more problematic strain of poetic praise begins to develop throughout the play, celebrating the fatal 'achievements' of the Seven, the threatened violence of their sons against Thebes, and the spectacle of violence that Evadne enacts against herself.

The increasingly problematic element is also distinctly gendered: it is created by the involvement of women in the generation of praise and blame. The *Philoctetes* is notable for featuring no female characters or chorus in the play. In the *Ajax*, two female characters are present, Athena and Tecmessa, and Athena in particular contributes to the competing nature of the discourses surrounding Ajax. In the *Heracles* similarly, a female character, Megara, does appear, and as discussed in Chapter 3 contributes to the problematic praise discourse surrounding Heracles, particularly by her emphasis on the 'life or death' nature of reputation and praise speech. Like the *Ajax*, the *Heracles* also features divine figures, Lyssa and Iris, who are concerned with Heracles' reputation and praiseworthiness. In each of these plays, however, the female presence is limited by the constant presence of a male chorus. In the *Suppliant Women*, the chorus are female, and the play also features both divine and multiple mortal female figures with differing roles, in Athena, Evadne and Aethra. As a result, in almost every scene the male voice is tempered by a female voice, either in the presence of the chorus or in the female characters who appear at the beginning and end of the play, bracketing its action.[3] Some aspects of the clash between male and female in the *Suppliant Women* which result from this female presence have been fruitfully explored in scholarship.[4] In particular, discussions of the role of the female chorus in perpetuating lament, and of Aethra in providing the persuasive form of discourse which causes Theseus to help the Argives have added a great deal to readings of the play which had previously focused on its political aspects.[5]

There is a further significant factor to the speech of women in the *Suppliant Women* which demonstrates a gendered problem in the production of tragic praise discourses. As well as producing laments, a type of speech closely associated with the generation of *kleos*,[6] the female characters are the group in the *Suppliant Women* most concerned with praise speech and its effects. It is primarily the female characters who persuade Theseus, through poetic-flavoured praise, to help the Argives. As the play progresses, this subversion of praise by women generates additional violence, in the actions of Evadne, the declaration of war by the sons of the Seven and its sanction by Athena. As a result, the *Suppliant Women* demonstrates how female involvement in poetic praise speech can have problematic, dangerous consequences for male characters in tragedy, even in connection to the apparently idealized subject of the treatment of suppliants by Athens' hero-king.

Theseus unpraised

The *Suppliant Women* begins with Aethra describing the situation of the Argive mothers (8–19), who have come to ask Theseus' help to retrieve the bodies of their dead sons. Aethra expresses pity for the women (34–5), who plead for her help (42–86) before Theseus arrives (87). Before his arrival, neither Aethra nor the chorus make any effort to celebrate or praise Theseus; he is described simply as Aethra's son (3, 55, 60, 66, 68) or by name (37) with no praise attached.[7] Once Theseus arrives on stage, Adrastus and the chorus engage in applying praise vocabulary to him. Throughout their discussion, however, this language is used to express what they hope Theseus will be, and how they wish to persuade him to act, rather than reflecting a purely celebratory tone. Adrastus begins his plea to Theseus with praise in strong poetic terms:

ὦ καλλίνικε γῆς Ἀθηναίων ἄναξ,
Θησεῦ, σὸς ἱκέτης καὶ πόλεως ἥκω σέθεν.

Theseus, glorious in victory, lord of Athens, I have come as a suppliant to you and your city!

113–14

The word καλλίνικος is most used elsewhere in tragedy to describe Heracles, and evokes him here, both as a familiar comparison with Theseus,[8] and more generally as an exemplar of excellence. The adjective is frequently found in epinician poetry, where it can describe victors of all kinds, or celebrations associated with victory.[9] It therefore evokes two contexts of praise within which Theseus could be celebrated. However, Adrastus' use of this comment is intertwined with his request to Theseus. Adrastus moves immediately from praise to supplication, and Theseus clearly recognizes this context, as he responds only by asking what Adrastus wants from him. Adrastus therefore praises Theseus with the intention to persuade, partly to flatter him into agreeing to Adrastus' request, and undoubtedly partly with reference to his end goal, that Theseus will be 'victorious' in retrieving the bodies from Thebes, at which point Adrastus would be able to laud him in these terms. The lack of praise involved in earlier mentions of Theseus therefore becomes clear; before he is on stage, there is little point in attempting to flatter or persuade him by this method.

The next piece of praise for Theseus is again spoken by Adrastus, here combined with a formal supplication:

ἀλλ', ὦ καθ' Ἑλλάδ' ἀλκιμώτατον κάρα,
ἄναξ Ἀθηνῶν, ἐν μὲν αἰσχύναις ἔχω
πίτνων πρὸς γόνυ σὸν ἀμπίσχειν χερί
[πολιὸς ἀνὴρ τύραννος εὐδαίμων πάρος]·
ὅμως δ' ἀνάγκη συμφοραῖς εἴκειν ἐμαῖς.

But, most mighty man in Greece, king of Athens, although I hold it to be shameful, to be falling on the ground and grasping your knees with my hands, [an old man, who was formerly a fortunate king]: nonetheless I must give way to my disasters.

163–7

Once again, the praise is connected directly to Adrastus' appeal, in this case even accompanied by the physical act of supplication, combining the praise and the attempt to persuade. This praise also focuses on Theseus' status as king of Athens, and represents him as strong and potentially successful in battle, which foreshadows the role Theseus will have to play to fulfil Adrastus' appeal. Adrastus goes on to praise Theseus in connection with his city when he explains why he has come to ask Athens for help:

πόλις δὲ σὴ
μόνη δύναιτ' ἂν τόνδ' ὑποστῆναι πόνον·
τά τ' οἰκτρὰ γὰρ δέδορκε καὶ νεανίαν
ἔχει σὲ ποιμέν' ἐσθλόν· οὗ χρείᾳ πόλεις
πολλαὶ διώλοντ', ἐνδεεῖς στρατηλάτου.

Only your city could undertake this labour: for it sees pitiable things clearly, and it has you, a young, noble chief: in need of which many cities have been utterly destroyed, through wanting such a general.

188–92

Theseus is again described in terms which emphasize potential in battle, particularly in the reference to other cities lacking such a 'στρατηλάτης'.

In all of his early addresses to Theseus, Adrastus praises Theseus for strength or for the strength of his city, and only in connection with his attempts to persuade Theseus. It is perhaps not surprising, therefore, that when Adrastus' request is rebuffed, he gives up on praise, moving in almost the opposite direction when he complains about Theseus' response to him (253). However, the chorus take up the attempt and imitate his tactic:

πρός <σε> γενειάδος, ὦ φίλος, <ὦ φίλος>,
ὦ δοκιμώτατος Ἑλλάδι <γαίᾳ>,
ἄντομαι ἀμφιπίτνουσα τὸ σὸν γόνυ
καὶ χέρα δειλαία, . . .
. . .
μηδ' ἀτάφους, τέκνον, ἐν Κάδμου χθονὶ χάρματα θηρῶν
παῖδας ἐν ἡλικίᾳ τᾷ σᾷ κατίδῃς, ἱκετεύω.

By your beard, friend, <friend>, most excellent man in <the land of> Greece, I beg you, embracing your knees and hands, wretched me . . . do not, child, look away in your prime of life, and leave our sons unburied in the land of Cadmus, a delight to wild beasts, I beseech you.

277–83

Like Adrastus, the chorus entwine their praise with their supplication, and focus on praise which indicates what they expect of Theseus: his strength and physical vigour as qualities of his excellence.

The chorus have no more success than Adrastus did, and Aethra, Theseus' mother, is the next to try. Aethra continues the same tactic of combining praise language with persuasion, although she is more explicit about the rewards which Theseus can win by doing as Adrastus wishes.

ἐρεῖ δὲ δή τις ὡς ἀνανδρίᾳ χερῶν,
πόλει παρόν σοι στέφανον εὐκλείας λαβεῖν
δείσας ἀπέστης,

Someone will say that out of unmanliness you remained hands-off, instead of seizing a crown of glory for your city.

314–15

Aethra connects praise explicitly to Theseus' future deeds, rather than his past, and in framing her comment as what 'someone will say' is clearer about this aspect than Adrastus. This time, perhaps due in part to this more explicit approach, the technique is effective. Theseus picks up her inference immediately, commenting,

. . . πολλὰ γὰρ δράσας καλὰ
ἔθος τόδ' εἰς Ἕλληνας ἐξεδειξάμην,
ἀεὶ κολαστὴς τῶν κακῶν καθεστάναι.
οὔκουν ἀπαυδᾶν δυνατόν ἐστί μοι πόνους.
τί γάρ μ' ἐροῦσιν οἵ γε δυσμενεῖς βροτῶν,

For having done many fine deeds I have declared this kind of habit to Greece, always to appoint myself a punisher of evil deeds. Therefore it is not possible for me to refuse labours. For what will hostile mortals say about me?

339–43

Theseus frames his concern in relation to what people will say, suggesting the importance of his reputation, and echoing his mother's phrasing. While Theseus does mention his past exploits for the first time, both he and his mother indicate that any reputation which rests solely on them is insecure. His current decisions are presented as if they might erase any praise he has earned from past exploits, so that it is only his future actions which can make him praiseworthy.

Although the *Suppliant Women* seems to open with a great deal of praise for Theseus, therefore, all of it is deployed as persuasion rather than praise alone, and is concentrated on his future actions rather than his past successes. It is also relevant that when the chorus respond to Theseus' guarantee of aid, they have returned to calling him simply 'king' (ἄναξ 367), abandoning their earlier flowery phrases once the cause has been won. They also begin instead to praise the city, saying:

καλὸν δ᾽ ἄγαλμα πόλεσιν εὐ-
σεβὴς πόνος χάριν τ᾽ ἔχει
τὰν ἐς αἰεί.

A pious labour is a beautiful ornament for cities, and gains gratitude forever.
373–4

The 'labour' which Theseus had previously agreed to is transferred to the city as a source of glory. Even this comment, however, comes in the context of seeking to persuade others to help them. Theseus says that he will need to seek agreement from the city's people before he can act, and the chorus make this comment as their response. The chorus cannot directly address 'the city' while they remain in the orchestra, but nonetheless, they are here responding to the possibility of further persuasion, and offering praise as a reward for future actions, this time to Athens.

The situation for Theseus in the *Suppliant Women* is thus strikingly different to those experienced by Heracles or Ajax. Theseus is praised only in connection to persuasion, and in reference to his future actions. His past successes and 'labours' remain uncelebrated, so that he enjoys none of the kind of praise used to celebrate Heracles after his equivalent labours in the *Heracles* and *Trachiniae*. In this regard, the situation is like that of Neoptolemus in the *Philoctetes*, who also receives a great deal of praise aimed at persuading him to future actions, rather than celebrating past success. However, Neoptolemus in the *Philoctetes* is young and has not achieved any significant heroic work, whereas Theseus has already achieved at least his initial series of heroic 'labours' by the time of the *Suppliant Women*.[10] The lack of celebration for Theseus' achievements is therefore surprising, particularly given the centrality of Theseus to Athenian self-glorification. Furthermore, in the *Suppliant Women* a major, gendered, difference from these plays is established. Throughout the play, it is the female characters who demonstrate the most concern for the power of poetic praise speech, and who manipulate it most successfully. This manipulation becomes subversive: for the men involved, including Theseus, there are negative consequences to this female involvement in the poetic praise sphere.

Women and praise

As Mendelsohn has shown with relevance to space, the question of gender is key to interpreting Euripides' *Suppliant Women*.[11] The play is filled with female characters, some of whom, including Aethra and Evadne, are introduced unexpectedly, or have mythologically novel backgrounds that draw attention to their presence.[12] The contrast between the female chorus of mourning mothers and the responses of the two male leaders to the deaths of the Seven spotlights the significance of gender to an interpretation of this play. In considering poetic praise speech, gender too is significant. Throughout the play, it is the female characters who are most explicitly concerned with either themselves or other characters earning poetically marked praise. This concern leads to problematic behaviours, particularly in the case of Evadne, whose language of glory and poetic praise leads her to suicide over her husband's pyre. It also establishes a pattern of future wars and violence to be carried out by the sons of the Seven, with this future violence confirmed in the prophecies of Athena.

The phrase with which the Argive mothers introduce their persuasive praise of Theseus, 'ὦ δοκιμώτατος Ἑλλάδι' (278) is strongly outward-looking, since it celebrates Theseus as one who is approved of by others – here, all of Greece – rather than celebrating his inherent qualities. When Aethra takes up the attempt to persuade Theseus, this external focus becomes stronger, and she combines her comments about benefits to Theseus' reputation with phrasing from praise poetry. Aethra's promise of a στέφανον εὐκλείας (315) for Theseus, as well as being concerned with his reputation, is similar to the language used in Pindar to describe poetic praise, offered as a 'crown' for the victor.[13] Her comment that it will be a reward for εὐκλείας connects it to the discourse of *kleos* and poetic celebration inherent in the root of the word. Aethra further connects her persuasion to what others will say about Theseus (314), thus attaching her persuasion specifically to the kinds of voiced praise he may earn. Aethra's comments are also the first to discuss Theseus' potential action in terms of a labour, πόνος, when she claims that others will say that his fighting the boar was a trivial labour, whereas fighting a war would not be (317–19). This language of labour connected to the Athenians' task is associated with a contemporary discourse about Athens' toil in the face of others' inaction.[14] However, it also has strong connections with praise poetry, and the celebrations which a hero may obtain by completing specific tasks – most famously, Heracles.[15]

Aethra's speech is also concerned with her *own* reputation in a way which Adrastus' appeals are not, and this speech is markedly gendered, as the concern arises from whether or not it is right for her to be speaking publicly at all.[16] Aethra notes that if she kept silent, she might have cause to blame herself in the future:

οὔτοι σιωπῶσ᾽εἶτα **μέμψομαί** ποτε
τὴν νῦν σιωπὴν ὡς ἐσιγήθη κακῶς

I shall not keep silent and then later blame myself for that silence on the grounds that it was wrong to keep silent.

297–8

Aethra's persuasive praise is therefore bound up with a discourse which not only refers to promises of poetic, heroic praise for her son, but also repeatedly shows awareness of the power of what others might say, either in the form of praise or blame. It is not unheard of for mothers, particularly heroic mothers, to be concerned with their son's public status, although the more usual pattern is for fathers to be the main drive behind this motivation in tragedy.[17] However, Aethra's awareness begins to associate Theseus with the more problematic aspects of this discourse as it operates in the *Suppliant Women*, and with the dangerous ways in which women become involved in it.[18]

The next female character to appear on stage is Evadne, whose appearance is unexpected, and whose self-presentation swiftly becomes extremely problematic.[19] Unlike Aethra, Evadne has no reasonable excuse for her presence, and the audience will shortly learn that she is there partly because she has escaped the guards set over her by her father (1040–3).[20] Evadne promptly reveals her and Aethra's shared perspective, in that she is persistently concerned both with reputation, and with the language of praise poetry.[21] This concern is also peculiarly gendered, as although this perspective is not traditionally one demonstrated by female characters, in the *Suppliant Women* it is repeatedly represented as a female perspective. In the case of Evadne, this perspective is taken to such dangerous extremes that it not only leads to future violence, but to fatal violence against herself. Evadne's situation is caused partially by the inappropriate relationship with praise speech already associated with her husband, Capaneus, who has apparently been involved in self-praise in the form of boasting to such an extent that he has been blasted by Zeus in punishment (496–9).[22] Evadne, like Capaneus, boasts of her intention to gain great glory regardless of others' wishes. In her case, the wishes of her father, rather than those of the gods, are dismissed (1069–71). Evadne too takes this desire for glory to a fiery death, establishing the comparisons between her and Capaneus.[23] However, as Capaneus is not himself quoted or staged in the *Suppliant Women*, Evadne's problematic language is highlighted, and the problematic elements of *her* character are strengthened by comparison with him.[24]

When Evadne arrives on stage, it becomes clear that she is motivated primarily by her reputation and by the things which others will say about her (ideally in the form of praise). While her father asks her to avoid displaying her behaviour to the chorus of women for their comment (1066),[25] Evadne declares that she is seeking public talk:

> τοῦτ' αὐτὸ χρῄζω, πάντας Ἀργείους μαθεῖν.
>
> But this is exactly what I want, for all the Argives to learn about it.
>
> 1067

Chong-Gossard has rightly noted Evadne's public-facing concern as one connected to women's gossip networks and their power for developing a woman's reputation.[26] However, there is a further aspect to the type of speech she expects to spread about her that is significant given the roles and discourse of women in the *Suppliant Women*.

Throughout her conversation with the chorus and her father, Evadne repeatedly frames the 'glory' she seeks by her suicide in terms of praise poetry. She declares her intention to the chorus as:

> εὐκλεΐας χάριν ἔνθεν ὁρ-
> μάσω τᾶσδ' ἀπὸ πέτρας·
>
> Here I shall rush to the grace of glory, off from these rocks.
>
> 1015–16

Evadne's intention is phrased specifically in terms of εὔκλεια, the glory which has its roots in *kleos*. As she attempts to describe her plan to Iphis, she continues to frame it as attracting fame and glory, particularly the kind which can be established in poetry. Her clothes are described as contributing to a κλεινὸν aim (1055), that is, one which will bring fame, and she even describes herself as coming to the pyre καλλίνικος – glorious in victory (1059). The term is itself redolent of epinician praise poetry,[27] but has a further peculiar resonance in this text, as it was the same description promised to Theseus by Adrastus. Evadne also claims that the victory she will achieve (1060–1) will be one in ἀρετῇ, excellence, a term which is more usually applied to the kind of heroic achievements celebrated in poetic praise for male heroes.[28] In addition, the chorus describe Evadne as κλεινήν (984) as they first see her, and Morwood is likely right to associate this with the anticipated glory she will achieve from her actions, rather than any existing fame.[29]

Evadne, therefore, is persistently concerned with framing deeds in terms of poetic glory and celebration; whereas Adrastus assured Theseus that he could become καλλίνικος if he acted on behalf of the Argives, Evadne claims that through her suicide she will be the one to achieve this epithet. To a far greater and more sustained extent than either of the male leaders, she appears aware of the power of this kind of reputation building through praise, and explicitly seeks after the glory it should result in. It is particularly interesting in this regard that Evadne connects her initial entrance to the stage to a poetic context – the songs celebrating her wedding night:

> ἀνίκ' <ἡδυθρόοις> γάμων
> τῶν ἐμῶν πόλις Ἄργους
> ἀοιδαῖς . . .

> When the city Argos for the sake of <sweet-resounding> songs honouring my marriage-rites. . .
>
> 995–9[30]

Along with this explicit reference to a context of song, Evadne's invocation to her monody draws on a lengthy poetic tradition of light imagery:[31]

> τί φέγγος, τίν' αἴγλαν
> ἐδίφρευε τόθ' ἅλιος
> σελάνα τε κατ' αἰθέρ' ἅ
> λαμπάσιν ὠκὺ θοαῖσι νυμφ-
> φεῖ' ἵππευε δι' ὄρφνας,

> What light, what gleam did the sun and the moon drive across the sky on that day, on horses swiftly accompanying my bridal celebration through the dark with swift torches?
>
> 990–4[32]

The term αἴγλαν has specific connotations of light generally connected to the *paian*,[33] and the use of the Doric ἅλιος (rather than Attic ἥλιος) has a lyric sound.[34] Evadne's first description of her husband, Capaneus, as χαλκεοτευχέος (999), also invokes poetic contexts by the use of the compound verb, and the depiction of the warrior as bronze-wearing.[35] In addition, she sings a hymeneal cry at 1025 (ἴτω φῶς γάμοι), further demonstrating the poetic song context of her remarks and of the glory she is seeking.

Evadne is the most extreme example of a woman seeking poetic praise in the *Suppliant Women*, but there is a further example of a female character's engagement in this discourse. In Athena's unexpected appearance,[36] the goddess promises poetic celebration in song to the sons of the Seven:[37]

> . . . Ἐπίγονοι δ' ἀν' Ἑλλάδα
> κληθέντες **ᾠδὰς** ὑστέροισι θήσετε·

> You will be called the Epigonoi throughout Greece, and you will be established in future **songs**.
>
> 1224–5

Athena addresses the sons for the first time as the Epigonoi, the name associated with the generation in the epic tradition.[38] In her speech describing the war they will wage, she makes repeated use of epic language and terms.[39] Her first address to the sons is in an epic periphrasis: παισὶ Ἀργείων (1213).[40] She describes the army as χαλκοπληθῆ (bronze-clad 1220), using a compound adjective associated with bronze, just as Evadne did. Similarly, Thebes becomes ἑπτάστομον πύργωμα Καδμείων (the seven-towered city of the Cadmeans 1221), evoking both the epic tradition and Aeschylus.[41] The sons themselves are described as σκύμνοι λεόντων (lion cubs 1223), and πόλεος ἐκπορθήτορες (city-sackers 1223), both terms with epic resonance.[42] Athena's promise has resonances of Heracles' in the *Philoctetes*; she ties the sons of the Seven into an epic discourse, and a future of commemoration in praise poetry, using language which itself begins to enact that poetic commemoration.[43] Athena's use of this explicit poetic language and promises of future song in the *Suppliant Women* associates her with the use of the same language by other female characters in the play. There is also an association drawn between Athena's appearance here and the earlier language of female characters, through the only apparent preparation for Athena's involvement in the action. When seeking to understand Evadne's behaviour, Iphis asks whether she intends to be victorious:

> ἔργοις Ἀθάνας ἢ φρενῶν εὐβουλίᾳ;
>
> In the works of Athena or some soundness of thoughts?
>
> 1062

Despite Evadne's rejection of this suggestion, this mention of Athena is the only comment connecting her to the action of the play, before her unexpected appearance *ex machina*. Its connection with Evadne's seeking after poetic glory has the effect of associating the two figures and their shared discourse, especially as Athena will herself later take up a similar approach to glory.[44]

Choral poetics and praise

Athena's final words set the seal on a pattern developed across the *Suppliant Women*. Rather than the male, heroic figures such as Adrastus and Theseus, it is the female characters Aethra, Evadne and Athena, who express the most explicit awareness of the value of poetic praise speech in establishing heroic behaviour. Not only do the female characters participate in this kind of rhetoric, but they are joined by the female chorus, who demonstrate a persistent concern with fame and reputation, and a frequently poetic turn of phrase or tone. Increased lyricism from a chorus is not entirely unexpected, as the tragic chorus is typically found making use of other poetic traditions and lyrical styles in its odes.[45] Given the role of the mothers in this play, it is also not surprising to find a certain amount of lament in the mourning of the chorus, although this role is itself unique.[46] However, it is significant that the chorus draw repeatedly not only on mourning language and poetic lament genres, but also on terms and vocabulary from epic. They make repeated reference to the fame and glory of their dead sons, demonstrating the same awareness of this aspect of heroic life as Aethra and Evadne. In grieving for their sons immediately after Adrastus' funeral speeches, they describe the Seven as κλεινοτάτους ἐν Ἀργείοις, 'most glorious among the Argives' (965). The superlative language associated with fame, as well as the description of their sons as best among the Argives, carry allusive echoes to the epic praise language of 'best of the Achaeans,' especially given the other epic echoes in the choral lament.[47] Coming immediately after Adrastus' problematic reclamation of the Seven's glory in his civic funeral speeches, this epic comment has the effect of beginning to reframe the chorus' sons as glorious in poetic terms, undercutting Adrastus' remarks. Similarly, the chorus describe their sons as εὐδοκίμων δή ποτ' ἐν Μυκήναις, 'once glorious in Mycenae' (1130) in their shared lament with the grandsons. Like Aethra, they demonstrate a concern for and desire to celebrate their sons' public reputations.

The speech of the chorus is marked both in terms of explicit awareness of the importance of reputation, and in relation to its self-referential poeticity. The chorus demonstrate concern for their own reputations, and for attracting blame speech when they fear that if Theseus is unsuccessful in battle:

> τίνα λόγον, τίν' ἄν τῶνδ'
> αἰτίαν λάβοιμι;
>
> What speech and what reputation will I gain?
>
> 606–7

Their comment is similar to Aethra's concern for attracting blame (from herself) if she does not advise Theseus to help the suppliants (297). Like Aethra, Evadne and Athena, the chorus recognize the importance of what is said about them, and the value of praise and blame speech. It is therefore not surprising that they make use of this valuable speech, both in their persuasion of Theseus and in their remembrances of their sons.

The chorus, despite their relatively short choral odes, maintain a particularly poetic and self-reflexive quality to their performances which is unusual.[48] They also make use of a great deal of language associated with non-tragic lyric, specifically epic and lament.[49] The chorus perform two significant laments, first a *kommos* with Adrastus (798–836) and then a *kommos* with the secondary chorus of their grandsons (1114–64). The chorus persistently demonstrate a concern not solely with lament, but also with the wider poetic properties of their performance, *qua* chorus. The chorus invoke this self-referential element early on, as they begin a lament as part of their attempt to persuade Aethra, and describe themselves:

> ἀγὼν ὅδ' ἄλλος ἔρχεται
> γόων γόοις διάδοχος· . . .
> . . .
> ἴτ' ὦ ξυνῳδοὶ κακοῖς,
> ἴτ' ὦ ξυναλγηδόνες
> χορὸν τὸν Ἅιδας σέβει·
>
> Another contest follows and takes up the lament with lament... come o fellow-singers in evils, come o fellow-mourners, the chorus which Hades honours.
>
> 71–5

The chorus label their lament as a γόος, one of the two types of lament familiar from epic onwards.[50] In calling themselves a chorus associated with Hades, they participate in a frequent tragic pattern of imagery surrounding corrupted song.[51] They describe themselves self-reflexively as singers and as a chorus, which draws significant attention to their performance of lament, a genre of song, here and throughout the play.[52] This self-identification is also acknowledged by the characters who come into contact with the chorus, as Theseus recognises the sound of their γόους (87) and θρήνους (88). The association between the chorus and the performance of poetic lament is therefore strong enough to leave an impression on Theseus even before he appreciates the full situation. Once the bodies have been returned, the chorus again refer to themselves as singers, when they claim that their future contains only:

> ἀοιδαί θ' ἅς χρυσοκόμας
> Ἀπόλλων οὐκ ἐνδέχεται·

Songs which golden-haired Apollo does not welcome.

975–6

Loraux sees in this reference not only a moment of self-referentiality, but also a reflexiveness that becomes metatheatrical; in performing a lament unwelcome to Apollo in tragedy, the genre overseen *by* Apollo, the chorus force a reflection on the genre's own conflicting demands.[53] The contrast between Apollo and Hades and songs performed for either god is an idea found elsewhere in poetry, with examples in Stesichorus, Sophocles and Euripides.[54] This metatheatrical degree of choral referentiality, especially given the earlier reference to their performance as a chorus, is striking, drawing attention to their voice and its poetic, performative qualities.

The chorus' independence in performance is also remarkable, especially in their determination to perform laments despite the efforts of Theseus and Adrastus to introduce other kinds of speech.[55] Easterling has identified lament in poetry, beginning with epic, as providing a genre in which female characters may pass comment on events, beyond their own personal loss, and often in conflict with the male speech that generates *kleos*.[56] As a result, the chorus of the *Suppliant Women* repeatedly perform a genre which comes into conflict both with male genres of speech and with the poetic generation of *kleos*.[57] This conflict can be seen in the disagreement between the chorus of mothers and Theseus as to how best to respond to the loss of their sons: with lament, or with Adrastus' *epitaphios*-inspired speech.[58] However, female lament can enact a kind of *kleos,* even if it presents a contrast with the kind represented in other commemorations, by establishing the significance of the loss being endured,[59] so that the lamenting chorus' interest in the reputation of themselves and their sons represents a competing claim to the same aspect of their identity. Both Adrastus and the chorus wish to establish the reputations of the Seven in their commemorations, and to generate their *kleos*, but while Adrastus seeks to commemorate them with the civic praise speeches, the chorus seek the same aim via a contrasting discourse of lament. Dué has shown that it is the female characters' personal stake in the events of epic that can make the same events both a source of lament for them and a generation of *kleos* for the wider audience.[60] In this regard, it is particularly significant that the chorus of the *Suppliant Women* are the mothers of the Seven; their stake in the expedition against Thebes is intensely personal.[61] This personal stake also applies to the other female characters participating in this *kleos*-driven speech: Aethra is Theseus' mother, and Evadne Capaneus' wife. *Suppliant Women* therefore provides a unique set of characters and a chorus with a personal, emotional stake in the *kleos* of their male relatives, and a particularly poetically inspired approach to speaking about those relatives.[62]

Diminishing the male voice

The prominence of these female speakers is made especially stark for the audience by the *Suppliant Women*'s corresponding shift away from authoritative male speech, a traditional feature of the myth. The myth of Athens and Theseus aiding in the burial of the Seven was not new, and had even appeared in tragedy before, in Aeschylus' *Eleusinioi*. However, Euripides made several changes in his handling of the myth, including locating the burial at Argos rather than Eleusis.[63] Two adjustments in the treatments of Theseus and Adrastus also allow the female speakers to become more prominent. In Aeschylus' account of the retrieval of the Seven, Theseus managed to persuade the Thebans to return the bodies through words, rather than violence.[64] In contrast, in the *Suppliant Women*, Theseus must go to war, persuaded by the promise of poetic praise from his mother. Despite the lengthy *agon* with the Herald (399–584), Theseus is not able to achieve his goals through persuasive speech in this play, whereas in at least Aeschylus' account, he could.[65] Given Theseus' own comment that speech is a major distinction between beasts and gods, and a sign that the gods have enabled men to enjoy more good than bad (201–4), this failure to achieve success through speech is pointed.[66]

Adrastus too is affected by the play's limiting presentation of persuasive male speech. In the poetic tradition, Adrastus is a persuasive speaker. His epic epithet, μελίγηρυς, 'honey-voiced', indicates a tradition of attractive speech, and in the context of the fragment in which this description is conveyed, he is associated with effective speaking in relation to the invention of funeral orations.[67] This epithet also has poetic connotations; in Pindar's works it is used to describe the sweetness of poetry, and the value of these 'honey-sweet' songs for confirming fame.[68] In Tyrtaeus, Adrastus' skill in speaking is highlighted in comparison with the man Tyrtaeus would not praise,

> γλῶσσαν δ' Ἀδρήστου μειλιχόγηρυν ἔχοι
>
> [even if] he had the soft-voiced tongue of Adrastus.
>
> fr. 12.8 West

In Pindar's own account of the burial of the Seven, Adrastus appears as an influential speaker, credited with giving an oration in praise of the dead which enables them to be remembered, part of which is quoted.[69] A strong association is created between praise and memory of the dead in Pindar's comment (*Ol.* 6.11–13), and as the poet associates Adrastus' praise with the praise which Pindar is about to award to a victor, there is a poetic tone to the praise envisaged.

In contrast with this tradition, in the *Suppliant Women* Adrastus is portrayed as ineffective in his speech.[70] At the start he fails to persuade Theseus, whereas the chorus and Theseus' mother Aethra succeed in affecting Theseus' concern for the Argives.[71] He fails to respond to the insults of the Argive Herald, he is even interrupted and cut off by Theseus (513),[72] and is later criticized by the messenger for his comments to the chorus of Argive mothers and for encouraging their lamenting (770). Adrastus does, however, embark upon one lengthy example of prominent speech, in the funeral oration. This oration is concerned with praising the Seven (858, 901), and so has a function close to that of the Pindaric tradition. However, Adrastus' speech comes only at the invitation of Theseus, who asks him:

νῦν δ', Ἄδραστ' ἀνιστορῶ·
πόθεν ποθ' οἵδε διαπρεπεῖς εὐψυχίᾳ
θνητῶν ἔφυσαν; εἰπὲ δ' ὡς σοφώτερος
νέοισιν ἀστῶν τῶνδ'· ἐπιστήμων γὰρ εἶ.

And now Adrastus I ask you:[73] From where did these men, distinguished in courage among mortals, spring? Tell it to the young among these citizens, as you are wiser, and understand the issue.

840–4

The invitation is peculiar, as the terms he uses to describe Adrastus are problematized in the context of the play. In their earlier debate, it was precisely the quality of wisdom which Theseus denied to Adrastus:

ἧς καὶ σὺ φαίνῃ δεκάδος **οὐ σοφῆς** γεγώς,

And you too clearly became part of this **unwise** group.

219

In the same criticism of Adrastus' behaviour, Theseus complains that the young's desire to be honoured is what has led them to support the war without reason:[74]

νέοις παραχθεὶς οἵτινες τιμώμενοι
χαίρουσι πολέμους τ' αὐξάνουσ' ἄνευ δίκης

You were led astray by young men, who rejoice at being honoured and increase wars without justice.

232–3

His request for Adrastus to praise the Seven in relation to their warlike deeds (841–2), which Adrastus then emphasizes in his response (844–5, 909–17), is therefore particularly inconsistent.[75]

Theseus' apparent self-contradiction in the introduction to Adrastus' speech is not its only strange aspect. The funeral speech itself has long been identified as deeply problematic in both form and content.[76] The speech is framed as being an *epitaphios logos*, the relatively new Athenian genre of prose praise speeches for their war dead.[77] However, the *epitaphios* focuses on communal good rather than individual glory, while Adrastus' speech does precisely the opposite, discussing each of the Seven and his individual virtues in turn.[78] The 'truthfulness' of the speech is called into question by scholars who object to the apparent differences between the mythical tradition and Adrastus' account.[79] Even if these are judged not to be inconsistent, there remains a distinct contradiction in the handling of Capaneus within the internal realm of the *Suppliant Women* itself. Capaneus' arrogance, boasting, and distinctive death as punishment are highlighted multiple times in the play, by the Herald (495–9), Messenger (638–40), Theseus and Adrastus (934–5), and chorus (984). Yet Adrastus describes him as having no more pride than a poor man (862–3: φρόνημα δὲ / οὐδέν τι μεῖζον εἶχεν ἢ πένης ἀνήρ), and having an 'approachable' manner of speech (869: εὐπροσήγορον στόμα) and shunning those who 'boast' (864: ὅστις ἐξογκοῖτ').

In addition, Adrastus does not successfully praise all of the Seven, as originally requested. Theseus must complete the oration by speaking of Amphiaraus and Polyneices (925–31). Once more, internal contradiction arises as a result, particularly in the case of Amphiaraus. Theseus claims that his method of death can itself be connected to the purpose of praise:

> καὶ μὴν τὸν Οἰκλέους γε γενναῖον τόκον
> θεοὶ ζῶντ' ἀφαρπάσαντες ἐς μυχοὺς χθονὸς
> αὐτοῖς τεθρίπποις εὐλογοῦσιν ἐμφανῶς·
>
> And as for the noble son of Oecleus, the gods snatched him away to the depths of the earth while he was still alive and his chariot too, so clearly they speak well of him.
>
> 925–7

Earlier speakers in the play have already implicitly or directly contradicted the suggestion that Amphiaraus' death should be seen as a mark of divine favour. When Theseus criticized Adrastus for going against the gods' will in his expedition he expressly connected this to disrespect for seers (229–30), as

Adrastus admitted that Amphiaraus had advised against the expedition (158). The Theban Herald also connects the death of Amphiaraus with divine disfavour (500–1). Theseus' sudden claim that this death therefore equates to the gods 'speaking well' of Amphiaraus seems, at least, problematic.[80]

Adrastus' speech is not only problematic in itself: throughout the play, the degree of choral influence over his speech is shown to be a major feature of some of its most problematic aspects. When the messenger brings the news of the successful retrieval of the bodies of the Seven, he complains that Adrastus' outcry of sorrow is inappropriate, as it is unproductive and makes the mothers weep (770). Adrastus responds:

> δοκῶ μέν, αὐταί γ' εἰσὶν αἱ διδάσκαλοι.
> ἀλλ' εἶμ' ἵν' αἴρω χεῖρ' ἀπαντήσας νεκροῖς
> Ἅιδου τε μολπὰς ἐκχέω δακρυρρόους,
>
> It seems to me that they are the teachers here. But I will go and meet the dead, raise my hand in farewell and pour out the tearful songs of Hades.
>
> 771–3

Adrastus acknowledges the chorus' influence by describing them as 'teachers', before making it clear precisely what they have taught him: the songs of Hades. The chorus' self-referential description of themselves as a chorus of Hades at the start of the play is significant; in their function as Hades' chorus they have taught Adrastus the songs he will turn to as his first response to the retrieval of the dead, before Theseus corrects him.[81] Adrastus' delivery of a rather problematic oration, only at the request of Theseus, is a result of this early lesson. Adrastus needs to be additionally corrected by Theseus in his handling of the mothers' approach to the dead sons (941–8), suggesting that Theseus' instruction is ongoing, rather than fully learnt.[82] Even at the end of the play, the chorus continue to demonstrate influence over the kind of speech Adrastus develops, when they instruct him to do as Athena has requested as regards the oath (1232–4). It is striking here that the chorus declare their judgement that the oath is appropriate because:

> ἄξια δ' ἡμῖν
> προμεμοχθήκασι σέβεσθαι.
>
> Their previous work on our behalf is worthy of honouring.
>
> 1233–4

Terms from the same root as σέβεσθαι are elsewhere in tragedy connected to speech celebrating or praising an individual,[83] so that once again the chorus take an influential role in deciding what kind of speech – here, an oath – is appropriate for praising Theseus and Athens. Their earlier assurance that the city's labour would be rewarded is thus confirmed by these closing lines of the play. Yet it remains somewhat surprising that the chorus encourage an oath, not a song of celebration, and that their words refer to the work of the whole city, not to Theseus alone.[84]

The secondary chorus of the sons of the Seven also seem to learn their speech from the main chorus. The chorus of boys are on stage for the majority of the *Suppliant Women*; they are silent until their lament begins, but clearly indicated by Theseus as surrounding Adrastus at 106–7.[85] They seem to form part of the audience for Adrastus' 'educational' praise speech in recognition of the Seven.[86] After this, they are led off the stage to participate in the funeral pyres (954–1113), and return with the urns of their fathers (1114–26), at which point they begin their only vocal portion of the play (1123–64). However, what this secondary chorus seem to have learnt over the course of the play is not civic rhetoric of the kind somewhat unsuccessfully essayed by Adrastus, but rather lament, specifically in the form of a *kommos*.[87] Their lament is full of typical poetic features, such as the direct address to their fathers at 1142 and 1153, and the repeated utterances of 1138–9, shared with the chorus (1113–45, 1147–8, 1163–4).[88] The sons also connect themselves to the poetic tradition with reference to their determination that:

ἔτ' Ἀσωποῦ με δέξεται γάνος
χαλκέοις <ἐν> ὅπλοις Δαναϊδᾶν στρατηλάταν

One day the gleaming Asopus will receive me as general of the Argives in bronze weaponry.

1149–50

As with the examples discussed above, the reference to the boys' bronze armour connects them to archaic, generally epic poetry involving heroic feats of arms. The lament the sons sing takes up one of the most traditionally frightening aspects of female lament, in that it is aimed explicitly at revenge.[89] The chorus of mothers are not entirely enthusiastic about joining their grandsons in the full extent of this revenge-focused song, as indicated by their response to the proposed vengeance:

οὔπω κακὸν τόδ' εὕδει.
ἅλις γόων (αἰαῖ τύχας)
ἅλις <δ'> ἀλγέων ἐμοὶ πάρεστιν.

This trouble does not yet sleep. There are plenty of laments (alas for our fortune), plenty of sufferings still here for me.

1147–50

However, they are also not so reluctant as to reject the proposed revenge as is sometimes argued;[90] they expressly join in the wish for the grandsons to avenge the deaths of the Seven:

Π: πάτερ, σῶν μὲν κλύεις τέκνων γόους;
ἆρ' ἀσπιδοῦχος ἔτι ποτ' ἀντιτείσομαι ...
Χ: ... σὸν φόνον; εἰ γὰρ γένοιτο, τέκνον.

Boys: Father, do you hear the lamenting of your sons? May I some day become a shield-bearer set to revenge...
Chorus: Your death? Oh would that it could happen so, my son.

1143–5[91]

They further finish the sons' wish to become a τοῦ φθιμένου πατρὸς ἐκδικαστάν ('an avenger of your dead father' 1151). The sons' initial promises of vengeance are expressly connected by the sons to their laments, their γόος (1142), and the mothers too connect their comment on this assurance to ongoing lament (1147). The main chorus thus contribute towards what is a traditional role for mourning women; they both lament the dead and create a spur for revenge, effectively taken up by the secondary chorus.

However, Adrastus has been mourning the potential for violence in warfare throughout the play, so that the chorus' revenge-focused laments and their successful transmission demonstrate another contrast between their female speech and the types of speech employed by Adrastus. On hearing the results of the battle for the bodies, he exclaims about the perils of violence and the contrasting benefits of persuasion, and the misfortunes for mortals and cities who are persuaded only by violence (744–9). Upon leaving the stage to join Theseus, he exclaims that the loss of a man's life is the only thing which cannot be recovered (775–7), and immediately after his delivery of the funeral oration gives another generalized warning against war:

... ὦ ταλαίπωροι βροτῶν,
τί κτᾶσθε λόγχας καὶ κατ' ἀλλήλων φόνους
τίθεσθε; παύσασθ', ἀλλὰ λήξαντες πόνων
ἄστη φυλάσσεθ' ἥσυχοι μεθ' ἡσύχων.

O wretched mortals, why do you get spear-heads and use them against one another in murder? Stop it, stay your labours and guard your city instead, and rest along with resting people!

949–52

Adrastus here explicitly rejects πόνους (950), shunning the same discourse which Aethra had used to persuade Theseus to fulfil his supplication in the first place.[92] Adrastus, far more than the grieving mothers, wishes to convey the futility of war and blessings of peace. He frames these comments as a kind of gnomic wisdom, or didactic statement to mortals in general, and in doing so explicitly rejects the persuasive phrasing used by the female characters before him. Yet this peaceful lesson is not successfully conveyed to the chorus of boys. Instead, the encouragement to future revenge which is conveyed in female lament is the only message they 'learn' from the two competing discourses.[93]

Conclusion

Adrastus' advice, both in the types of praise speech suitable for commemorating the dead, and in the desire to encourage peace instead of warfare, seems to have been ineffectual. Conversely, the chorus have educated the sons beyond even their intentions, since the sons' taking up of female lament in its most dangerous function is destined to lead to a further round of poeticized violence. As with the encouragements to seek praise found in Aethra's speech, and the praise-focused language of Evadne, the female usurpation of poetic praise speech has therefore led to violent consequences for their male listeners, while the ineffectual education of the male speakers has not.

The female usurpation of praise and blame speech has an additional negative consequence for Theseus himself. As noted at the start of this chapter, Theseus in the *Suppliant Women* receives an unusually small amount of praise and celebration in this play, and almost all of it is deployed as persuasion rather than as genuine praise in celebration for his deeds. As the play goes on, even the praise which was originally promised to him as part of that persuasion is usurped and reaches targets other than Theseus himself. In this regard, the messenger's comment that Theseus' actions in the war should be praised (707, above) is particularly striking, as when the opportunity arises upon his return to the stage, Theseus receives no such celebration. Instead, all of the language which had been pledged to him previously is taken instead to refer to the Argives, particularly via the speech of the Argive women. As discussed above, Evadne will publicly declare herself to be καλλίνικος, rather than Theseus earning this term after his victory. In the same way, while Adrastus describes Theseus as uniquely qualified to help them since he is a young, vigorous στρατηλάτης (190–2), and the messenger uses the same term to describe Theseus as deserving of praise (707), by the end of the play it is the grandsons, rather than Theseus, who are being described in such terms. The grandsons first claim that they will be:

χαλκέοις <ἐν> ὅπλοις Δαναΐδᾶν στρατηλάταν

A general of the Argives in bronze weapons.

1150

Their claim is then reinforced by Athena, who predicts that Aegialeus will be a στρατηλάτης νέος (1216–17), an echo of Theseus' own intention of being a στρατηλατήσω καινός (593) before the battle. Language which was initially used as a promise of praise for Theseus is subverted and becomes a description only applied to the Argive sons of the Seven. Similarly, the language of having achieved a great πόνος which Aethra suggests could have been Theseus' (317–18, 323) becomes a description of the mothers' (now apparently fruitless) work in bearing and raising their own sons (1133–4) in their lament. Accordingly, a promise made by one mother to her son is transformed into a mourning remembrance by another set of mothers for their sons. The description of their role as mothers as πόνος is not itself as problematic as the usurpation of terms such as καλλίνικος, since it is a term regularly applied to childbirth in Greek.[94] However, given the earlier use of the same description to apply to Theseus' labours, its removal from that context and application instead to the female chorus' grief represents another example of how their poetic manipulation of speech has transferred praise away from Theseus, and into their own sphere. Even the στέφανος which Theseus was to have gained by his actions has ominous echoes in the female mourning which follows the return of the bodies, when the chorus refer to their κουραὶ κἀστέφανοι (973).

As well as this redirection of praise from Theseus to the Argives, there is a further negative consequence of the female involvement in poetic praise which is demonstrated throughout the *Suppliant Women*. This language frequently leads to violence, even in the case of the boys despite Adrastus' clear and explicit preference otherwise. Although Theseus' violence is described as restrained (723–30), and more moderate than it could have been, there is also some graphic description of the violence which he enacts as part of his battle with Thebes:

αὐτός θ' ὅπλισμα τοὐπιδαύριον λαβὼν
δεινῆς κορύνης διαφέρων ἐσφενδόνα
ὁμοῦ τραχήλους κἀπικειμένας κάρᾳ
κυνέας θερίζων κἀποκαυλίζων ξύλῳ.

He, taking up the Epidaurian weapon, a terrible club, hurled it about on either side of him, snapping necks and reaping helmeted heads with the club.

714–17

This description comes soon after the messenger's claim that Theseus did a deed to be praised, αἰνέσαι, (707), so that Theseus' martial prowess is part of his apparently praiseworthy behaviour, in the comment that comes closest to praise awarded without an ulterior motive in the *Suppliant Women*. Even so, the description of Theseus' actions here is strikingly violent, and bears a strange similarity to the description of the violence of tyrants by Theseus himself, as reaping young men (447–9).[95] As a result, just as with Neoptolemus in the *Philoctetes*, promises made of future praise poetry come with unsettling results for the young men involved: violence that will continue a cycle of grief for the Argives, and a worryingly tyrannical moment for the Athenian king Theseus.

Evadne's praise speech too is connected to violence – in this case, violence against herself. Her speech is further marked as explicitly disturbing to the chorus (1032–3) and incomprehensible to her father (1060, 1062, 1064). Chong-Gossard explores in detail how this incomprehension results from her speech being 'out of place,' and the impossibility of women's speech to communicate ideas of seeking after heroic glory successfully.[96] There is a further complication in the case of Evadne. Although she makes use of the same type of language, Evadne seeks glory for herself, rather than for her male relatives; she shares priorities and apparently language with her husband Capaneus, but in the *Suppliant Women* her concern is with her own *kleos* rather than his.

The *Suppliant Women*, therefore, is part of a pattern in tragedy that we shall see in more extreme forms in the following chapters. Where female characters and choruses take advantage of their prominence as tragic speakers to involve themselves in praise and blame speech, particularly where they make use of poetic forms and language to do so, the already fraught relationship between poetic praise and tragedy breaks down further. Poetic praise is subverted by this female involvement; they turn it against the male characters, and use it to manipulate and persuade, or apply it to themselves. The results are often violent, and even Theseus, idealized king of Athens, does not escape the negative results. As a result, this 'encomium of Athens', far from developing a straightforward relationship between poetic praise and Athens or Athens' hero, demonstrates the dangerous effects of female involvement in encomium in general, and how these effects may contaminate even Athens herself, and her greatest hero.

5

Unpraised and Unpraiseworthy: Deianira and the Destruction of Heracles in Sophocles' *Trachiniae*

Like the *Suppliant Women*, Sophocles' *Trachiniae* presents an example of a tragedy in which women become involved with the processes of praise and blame, and in doing so have a significant effect on how the tragedy presents its central hero. In this instance, the hero is one we have seen in Chapter 3 – Heracles – and the woman involved is his second wife, Deianira.[1] In the *Trachiniae*, the robe sent to Heracles on his return home by Deianira ruins his physical strength, the heroic quality for which he is most praised, making him physically unpraiseworthy. Deianira's influence over the speech spoken on stage around her simultaneously causes the world of the *Trachiniae* to be one in which praise of Heracles becomes unsustainable. As a result, the destruction enacted by Deianira is doubled; it consists of a destruction both of his physical capacity for praiseworthiness, and of praise spoken about him within the world of the *Trachiniae*. Greater attention to Deianira's influence in this area, and the effect it has on the poetically significant use of praise, enables us to better appreciate the extent of Deianira's active role in establishing this destruction. Deianira herself can be seen as a figure akin to Philoctetes or Amphitryon, whose awareness of poetic praise and blame speech and its value have a significant influence on those around them, including Heracles.

Deianira, speech and information

One of the most unusual aspects of Deianira's attitude towards speech in the *Trachiniae* is her persistent focus on how information may be conveyed. Deianira frequently shows awareness that messages passed via speech may be inaccurate or incomplete, and is concerned with verifying their source and details before accepting it. Deianira's hostility to 'unprovable' speech, and her desire to seek after what is 'true', therefore has a markedly different effect on the praise and blame context in which this Trachinian Heracles appears, in contrast with Euripides' play, in which the other characters on stage with Heracles were concerned with promoting and maintaining the kind of speech which established his praiseworthiness. Since the roots of *kleos* are in what is heard about an individual, Deianira's concern that what is 'heard' about an individual may not be true creates an environment which is significantly less hospitable for praise for Heracles.

In Deianira's first speech in the *Trachiniae*, there is a clear indication of her approach to spoken information. Deianira demonstrates a desire to de-emphasize what is commonly held as truth in favour of what she herself knows, in saying:

Λόγος μὲν ἔστ᾽ ἀρχαῖος ἀνθρώπων φανεὶς
ὡς οὐκ ἂν αἰῶν᾽ ἐκμάθοις βροτῶν, πρὶν ἂν
θάνῃ τις, οὔτ᾽ εἰ χρηστὸς οὔτ᾽ εἴ τῳ κακός·
ἐγὼ δὲ τὸν ἐμόν, καὶ πρὶν εἰς Ἅιδου μολεῖν,
ἔξοιδ᾽ ἔχουσα δυστυχῆ τε καὶ βαρύν

There is an ancient, revealed saying of men, that you cannot understand a man's life before he dies, whether he had a good one or a bad. But as for me, even before going to Hades, I know well that I have an unfortunate and grievous life.

1–5

The emphatic positioning and repetition of her ἐγὼ δὲ τὸν ἐμόν make clear that she prioritizes her own experience above what 'men' believe to be true.[2] The devaluing of Λόγος, speech, in particular is also accentuated by its positioning. She clarifies that her distinction lies on the respective value of the two sources of information, the ancient proverbial wisdom being judged less valuable a source than her experience. The distinction is one which is maintained throughout the play, as Deianira repeatedly prioritises information gained via direct experience over report.[3]

In her first conversation with Hyllus, when she attempts to gain information about Heracles, Deianira again indicates her judgement of the differing values of his sources of information. This conversation begins to demonstrate Deianira's influence in making those around her accept this distinction in their own speech. Hyllus appears willing to accept the hearsay available on Heracles' location,

ἀλλ᾽ οἶδα, μύθοις γ᾽ εἴ τι πιστεύειν χρεών.

But I know, if we can trust what people are saying!

67[4]

whereas she appears more doubtful, remarking:

> πᾶν τοίνυν, εἰ καὶ τοῦτ᾽ ἔτλη, κλύοι τις ἄν.
>
> Then one might hear anything, if he endured even that!
>
> 71

She does not say that Heracles might be doing anything, if he put up with being a slave, rather that one might *hear* any report of him. As such, the phrasing subtly questions the value of the report. The explicit reference to what is heard, in vocabulary focused around the roots of κλύω, begins to establish a distinction between what may be heard and what is true, creating an uneasy relationship with the kind of praise speech heard by others which makes up *kleos*. From this point, Hyllus follows her lead, demonstrating without being asked that his knowledge is all gained by report: ὡς ἐγὼ κλύω ('As I hear' 72) and φασίν ('They say' 74).[5] Once the source of his information is revealed, Deianira rejects it and turns the conversation to the prophecies left to her, which she calls πιστὰ ('trusted'). Deianira values the prophecies she can see herself above the things she hears from others, again demonstrating a privileging of these sources.[6]

Deianira's attitude to how trustworthy information can be gained has a clear influence on the chorus as well as Hyllus, in what is part of a persistent pattern of influence over their speech. At the key moment of Deianira's action, when she explains to the chorus that she wishes to send the love potion to Heracles, the chorus mirror her own earlier attitude to her, arguing that it is doing which can convey faith (πίστις ἐν τοῖς δρωμένοις, 588). They then follow her comment that she believes in the charm but has not tried it (590–1) with the suggestion that she can only get knowledge by testing it:

> ἀλλ᾽ εἰδέναι χρὴ δρῶσαν· ὡς οὐδ᾽ εἰ δοκεῖς
> ἔχειν, ἔχοις ἂν γνῶμα, μὴ πειρωμένη.
>
> So you need to do it to know: since even if you think you have, you won't have knowledge without trying it.
>
> 593–4

Deianira's earlier indications that she could not be sure of information gained simply through speech are repeated here by the chorus, who accordingly reaffirm her decision to act.[7] Although Deianira will turn out to be disastrously wrong, the attitude to knowledge which she displays here is one which is consistent.

In the same way, Deianira's reception of the messengers who bring news about Heracles involves interrogation as to the sources of their information.

When the first messenger arrives, she has him repeat his information and clarify it (180–6). Once she has clearly ascertained the message, Deianira asks for the source of the information:

> καὶ τοῦ τόδ᾽ ἀστῶν ἢ ξένων μαθὼν λέγεις;
>
> And from which one of the citizens or strangers have you learned this information that you tell me?
>
> 187

Her question differentiates between citizens and strangers, specifying the answer she receives beyond that the messenger heard it from 'someone' and confirming how trustworthy the source should be. It is only after she has confirmed these aspects that she is willing to believe and celebrate the information given (200–4). She also asks Lichas specific questions for his first few moments on stage (232–3, 236, 239, 242–3), quickly gaining the exact information she seeks. She does not ask a more general question until she has obtained this information (246–7), and then finally invites Lichas to give a fuller answer, leading him directly into the story he has come to bring. When attempting to question Lichas about Iole, Deianira similarly begins with a more focused set of questions, asking about her lineage and name (316, 318). Her second question on that occasion resurrects her interest in how information may be gained, as she suggests to Lichas a source from whom he might have gained information about Iole even if his first claim, that he has not asked any questions, might still be true.

Even at her most emotionally charged moment on stage, when Hyllus accuses her of murdering Heracles, Deianira demonstrates this precise, interrogative nature, refusing to accept Hyllus' accusations until she understands their cause:

> τί δ᾽ ἔστιν, ὦ παῖ, πρός γ᾽ ἐμοῦ στυγούμενον;
>
> And what is the hateful thing that I have done, my son?
>
> 738

Her question, in contrast to Hyllus' emotional statements (734–7, 739–40), is brief and precise, seeking information rather than dramatic declarations. Again she seeks to confirm the source of Hyllus' information, asking:

> τοῦ παρ᾽ ἀνθρώπων μαθὼν
> ἄζηλον οὕτως ἔργον εἰργάσθαι με φής;
>
> You say that I have done a terrible thing, but from which man did you learn this?
>
> 744–5

Deianira's next question seeks to clarify the source of Hyllus' information even further; when he claims that it is not a report, but that he has seen the deed, she asks:

ποῦ δ' ἐμπελάζεις τἀνδρὶ καὶ παρίστασαι;

Where did you approach the man, and stand by him?

748

Deianira aims to find out whether Hyllus saw from a distance, or whether he was close enough to know exactly what has happened. As with her questioning of the messengers, Deianira prevents Hyllus from immediately launching into his story until she has ascertained to her satisfaction the source of his information, and the narrative he wishes to tell.[8]

While Deianira does manage to find out that much of the information brought to her is conveyed by eyewitnesses, and is thus potentially reliable, throughout the *Trachiniae* she demonstrates a persistent problem with judging the reliability of her sources of information. The 'trusted' prophecies Deianira relates to Hyllus (76–81) confusingly do not match the oracle as described by Heracles (1168–73), suggesting that one of the sources for this prophecy must be wrong, or that a misinterpretation has intruded between the source and the two characters who later relate the prophecy.[9] When it comes to Lichas, Deianira has no evidence that the messenger's information may be better than Lichas', and moreover, she erroneously suggests that Heracles is the source of Lichas' lie (449–50), a suggestion which he denies (479–83). Finally, she takes as trusted the assurance from Nessus that the philtre will contain a love potion (569–81),[10] and only later realizes that information from this source is bound to be maliciously motivated, and incorrect (707–10).

Deianira's behaviour is, nonetheless, distinctive in comparison to the other characters in the *Trachiniae* itself, none of whom display the same care for identifying the sources from which information comes, and several of whom are therefore led to errors. Hyllus, for example, seems willing to believe reports of Heracles' location without significant doubt (77). Perhaps the most important examples of other characters failing to follow Deianira's example come in the situation that arises between the Messenger and Lichas' alternate accounts of Iole's capture, and Heracles' reaction to the poisoned robe. The information that Lichas brings to Deianira is rejected by the Messenger:

ἀνὴρ ὅδ' οὐδὲν ὧν ἔλεξεν ἀρτίως
φωνεῖ δίκης ἐς ὀρθόν, ἀλλ' ἢ νῦν κακός

ἢ πρόσθεν οὐ δίκαιος ἄγγελος παρῆν.

This man has just told you nothing which is spoken truthfully or justly, but either now he is base, or before he was present as an untruthful messenger.

346–8

But the Messenger bases this accusation only on another version of the message which he has heard, with no evidence as to which version is more truthful.[11] The chorus then suggest that Deianira may be able to get the truth from Lichas by questioning him again (385–6), but there is no obvious reason why his willingness to lie to her previously should be changed by a second questioning. Lichas does change the version of the tale he tells Deianira, so that it matches the version which the Messenger shares, but he does not say what his source is for the second, passion-driven narrative, only that Heracles has not asked him to conceal it (479–80). Neither messenger has any better information than hearsay. Lichas mentions that at least part of his story comes from what Heracles has told him (253), but unusually for this play does not mention witnessing any of the events that he describes. Both the messenger and Lichas are therefore relying on a source of information which Deianira has previously dismissed as unreliable.

This relative carelessness in gathering information is demonstrated most strongly by Heracles, both in his time off stage and once he arrives before the audience, especially in his treatment of Lichas. Hyllus makes it clear that Heracles' original interrogation of his herald is made under the assumption that he is the guilty party (772–4). Even when he has established the truth, Heracles' behaviour is apparently unchanged, as he kills Lichas regardless of the information he gives, in direct contrast with Deianira, who only thinks of her strategy after she has discovered the truth about Iole. Hyllus is later forced to make ten attempts at revealing the truth to Heracles, who is repeatedly resistant to his son's speech. Heracles is so convinced that he already has the truth that he makes no effort to question Hyllus, instead attempting to reject his words:

ὦ παγκάκιστε, καὶ παρεμνήσω γὰρ αὖ
τῆς πατροφόντου μητρός, ὡς κλύειν ἐμέ;

O most base man, have you again mentioned your father-killing mother, so that I can hear it?

1124–5

and following it with a recommendation that, contrary to Hyllus' statement, silence would be best (1127). From then, he repeatedly cuts Hyllus off in his attempts to reveal the full information (esp. 1131, 1133, 1135, 1137). In the final example, Hyllus claims about his mother:

> ἅπαν τὸ χρῆμ᾽ ἥμαρτε χρηστὰ μωμένη
>
> Everything she got wrong, she did with good intention.
>
> 1136

Demonstrating the full extent of their failure to communicate, Heracles responds, objecting to her act itself:

> χρήστ᾽, ὦ κάκιστε, πατέρα σὸν κτείνασα δρᾷ;
>
> Does she do a good thing, wicked one, killing your father?
>
> 1137

Heracles completely misses the significance of Hyllus' statement about intention, and the information contained within. While Hyllus does manage to reveal some truth to his father, it is not the truth he wished to convey – i.e., that of his mother's innocence; rather Heracles seizes on the involvement of the centaur, and when his name is revealed claims that he understands (1145).[12] He never speaks of Deianira again. The scene between Heracles and Hyllus is influenced heavily by the overwhelming emotion of both characters, which makes rational exchange harder. Yet at a similarly emotional moment, when Hyllus tells her what effect her potion has had, Deianira maintains her ability to ask repeated questions about the sources of his information (745, 748), and to hear his responses accurately, something neither Hyllus nor Heracles can manage. Heracles shows even less interest in identifying the source of Hyllus' information than in what that information may be, and the interaction between the two is unsuccessful, as limited useful communication is achieved.

Deianira's preoccupation with attempting to verify the value of information by considering its source, is therefore not shared by anyone else in the play. Most significantly, Deianira particularly does not value information which is simply passed on by speech, preferring information which can be verified via an informant's direct witnessing, or a material source such as the tablets on which the prophecies are written. This resistance to spoken and heard information means that she is frequently resistant to accept praise of Heracles when it comes from other characters.

Influence over speech and silence

On several occasions in the *Trachiniae*, Deianira successfully commands characters to speak or remain silent, effectively exerting influence over the speech which takes place around her. Deianira, as discussed above, directs a great deal of her interaction with Lichas. It is also only on the urging of Deianira that Lichas gives in and reveals his supposedly true version of Heracles' capturing Iole (468–9, and 472–4).[13] In answer to the messenger, Lichas resists and even attempts to refuse the conversation (434–5). Deianira's message to Heracles via Lichas demonstrates a similar attempt to influence the exact words that should be spoken by Lichas. Having told him in detail what he is to say to Heracles (600–15), she outlines to him that he must be careful to pass on her message exactly:

> ἀλλ' ἕρπε, καὶ φύλασσε πρῶτα μὲν νόμον,
> τὸ μὴ 'πιθυμεῖν πομπὸς ὢν περισσὰ δρᾶν·
>
> But go, and first keep your eye on the rule, that a messenger should not want to be over-involved beyond the scope of his message.
>
> 616–17

Lichas agrees, but when he says φράσω σεσωσμένα ('I will explain that all is well' 626), Deianira does not accept this general suggestion. She specifies instead exactly what he will speak of, first pointing him to the fact that she has welcomed Iole φίλως (628), and then adding the rhetorical question:

> τί δῆτ' ἂν ἄλλο γ' ἐννέποις;
>
> Then what else could you tell him?
>
> 630

She makes it clear to Lichas that there is nothing else he *should* say to Heracles, and Lichas goes away agreeably without adding anything else to his proposed message – at least not in front of Deianira.[14]

Deianira's influence is particularly evident in her interactions with the chorus, whose speech she commands or forbids to pronounced effect. The earliest example of this instruction is when she has heard the news of Heracles' return, and addresses those around her, with particular reference to the chorus,

> φωνήσατ', ὦ γυναῖκες, αἵ τ' εἴσω στέγης
> αἵ τ' ἐκτὸς αὐλῆς, . . .
>
> Speak out, women, both those inside the house and outside the court
>
> 202–3

The command has an immediate effect, and the chorus break into song, but their own song includes injunctions for the house, and men to join in:

ἀνολολυξάτω δόμος
ἐφεστίοις ἀλαλαγαῖς
ὁ μελλόνυμφος· ἐν δὲ κοινὸς ἀρσένων
ἴτω κλαγγὰ τὸν εὐφαρέτραν
Ἀπόλλω προστάταν,
ὁμοῦ δὲ παιᾶνα παι-
ᾶν' ἀνάγετ', ὦ παρθένοι,
βοᾶτε . . .

Let the house which is about to be a married household cry out with shouting at the hearth: let the shouts of the men go forth together with them to our protector, Apollo of the bright quiver, and with them, lift up the Paean, maidens, the Paean, shout aloud . . .

205–12

It is as though Deianira's command to speak out has such force that the chorus take it and apply it to others not addressed, including the inanimate force of the house itself.[15]

The most definite example of Deianira's control over the chorus' speech comes with her instruction to them regarding her plan with the robe:

μόνον παρ' ὑμῶν εὖ στεγοίμεθ'·

I only hope that I will be well concealed by you.

596

The silence she enjoins upon them here is maintained beyond the length of the play: the chorus pick up her request for silence and reflect it back in their own speech, when they suggest that Deianira should be silent (σιγᾶν ἂν ἁρμόζοι) when Hyllus is arriving (731–2).[16] Even when Deianira's act has come to light, the chorus never discuss it or reveal its roots to Hyllus, the Nurse or Heracles; they talk of her death, and in their lament they talk of the centaur's blood and his cunning (831–48), but they do not reveal the methods or intentions of Deianira even after she is dead. There is a strong similarity here with the chorus in Euripides' *Hippolytus*, who upon Phaedra's urging to σιγῇ καλύπτειν ἀνθάδ' εἰσηκούσατε ('Keep hidden in silence what you have heard here' 712), agree not to speak of it, and even lie to Theseus, claiming that they do not know why she has died (804–5).[17] However, Phaedra's chorus do indicate their knowledge when they tell Theseus that he has made a mistake in his understanding of the situation (891–2), and describe Hippolytus' innocence (1148–50). They remark much more clearly and decisively on the events that have happened outside Theseus' knowledge, than the chorus of the *Trachiniae* do once Deianira has given her command. It becomes clear that the chorus of the *Trachiniae* recognize the full force of her command when they cry at her exit,

> τί σῖγ' ἀφέρπεις; οὐ κάτοισθ' ὁθούνεκα
> ξυνηγορεῖς σιγῶσα τῷ κατηγόρῳ;
>
> Why do you steal silently away? Do you not understand that your keeping silent seconds your accuser?
>
> 813–14

They acknowledge that both Deianira's silence and their own bind them to an untenable situation. Hyllus cannot be persuaded of the truth if no one will speak, but they are powerless to prevent her choice, or to break their own enforced quiet. Nor are they able to warn Hyllus of Deianira's intention to die (revealed to them at 719), or to hint at it as Sophoclean choruses in similar situations elsewhere do.[18] Their emphatic repetition, σῖγ' . . . σιγῶσα highlights the strength of the idea; both Deianira's silence and their own are too strong to be overcome, and she goes to her death without anyone being able to correct Hyllus.[19]

In her injunction to silence, Deianira demonstrates not just a concern for what she might say if questioned by Hyllus and Heracles. Her command and suicide are also placed within the context of her concern for what others say about her: her reputation. While the characters of the *Trachiniae* do not generally demonstrate the same extent of concern for reputation and renown as the characters of the *Heracles*, it is a topic which recurs more often in connection with Deianira than anyone else: both in her own language and in the chorus' comments about her. Crucially, Deianira's concern is with her own reputation, not with preserving Heracles', as was both Amphitryon's and Megara's overriding concern in the *Heracles*.[20] Deianira refers to her reputation as part of the context for her command of silence made to the chorus:

> μόνον παρ' ὑμῶν εὖ στεγοίμεθ'· ὡς σκότῳ
> κἂν αἰσχρὰ πράσσῃς, οὔποτ' αἰσχύνῃ πεσῇ.
>
> I only hope that I will be well concealed by you: since if you commit shamelessness in darkness, you will never fall into shame.
>
> 596–7

Upon the realization that the charm was a poison rather than a love spell, it is again her reputation to which she returns, since her fear is that she will be shown (φανήσομαι 666) to have done wrong in the hope of doing good. She is not concerned solely with the possibility of having done wrong, but with its revelation to others. She connects her planned death, and the avoidance of such a revelation, to the idea of protecting her reputation:

> ζῆν γὰρ κακῶς κλύουσαν οὐκ ἀνασχετόν,
> ἥτις προτιμᾷ μὴ κακὴ πεφυκέναι.
>
> For it is unendurable to live and be called evil, for any woman who takes care to be good.
>
> 721–2

In this regard, Deianira's act is successful. Not only does she prevent the chorus from discussing her acts, and any further questioning from Hyllus and Heracles, but her death also has the effect of rehabilitating her reputation, such that Hyllus, previously her greatest accuser (749–812), is willing to attempt to defend her virtue to his father (1114–42). Hyllus' recognition of Deianira's innocence is itself connected to the sight of her death:

> ἰδὼν δ' ὁ παῖς ᾤμωξεν· ἔγνω γὰρ τάλας
> τοὔργον κατ' ὀργὴν ὡς ἐφάψειεν τόδε,
>
> Seeing this, her son cried out; for the wretched man realized that he had charged her with that crime in anger.
>
> 932–3

While not sufficient to preserve her marriage (or her life), Deianira's command of silence does prove to be successful in achieving its more focused goals in the preservation of her reputation. The chorus too reflect some of this concern briefly in her discussion with Lichas, since they add the curious comment that if he answers Deianira, he shall never have cause to blame her (κοὐ μέμψῃ χρόνῳ / γυναικὶ τῇδε (470–1)). As with her silence, the chorus reflect in their language a particular concern of Deianira's: her own reputation and the things which others say of her.

Deianira's influence on silence and its active, deliberate aspects are further highlighted in the *Trachiniae* through comparison with the other characters. Several commentators have drawn parallels between Deianira and Iole, emphasizing their shared statuses as prizes won or exchanged by men, specifically Heracles, and the link between them created by the empathy Deianira has for Iole.[21] In fact, however, the presence of Iole highlights the unusual nature of Deianira's position in the tragedy, and the change between the position she held as a young woman, and the one she claims now. The only strongly defined characteristic Iole is awarded is her silence. Lichas comments that even beyond her presence on stage, she has wept but never spoken (322–8), with emphasis on her persistent silence (322–3). Moreover, unlike Cassandra in the *Agamemnon*, to whom she is frequently compared, Iole does not speak at all on stage in the *Trachiniae*.[22]

However, this characteristic could hardly be further from Deianira's position in the tragedy. It is certainly the case that Deianira's story of her past courting by Achelous places her in a position similar to Iole's, particularly as regards her passivity (21–5, 523–30) and self-enforced silence about the fight (21–3). Yet Deianira takes deliberate pains to distance the woman she is at the time of the *Trachiniae* from that earlier self. Even in her early conversation with the chorus, she draws a distinction between the types of woman they are, young, unmarried and untroubled by fear (143–8), as she was before the Achelous incident, and the type of woman she now is, in her married, fearful position (148–52).[23] The fear and suffering which Deianira claims the chorus have not experienced is clearly indicated to have begun as part of her own transition to marriage, rather than in relation to the river god (6–8).[24] In her attempt at conversation with Iole, Deianira makes clear that she considers Iole to be counted among young girls, νεανίδων (307), rather than among married women such as herself.[25] Her prayer that Zeus never be turned against her offspring the way he has turned against these young women (303–6) makes the distinction stronger; Deianira aligns herself with Iole's parents in her fears, not Iole. Even as Deianira discovers the truth (535), her initial expression indicates doubt. As her speech continues, she returns specifically to the youth which separates Iole from her, noting particularly her ἥβην ἕρπουσαν (547), and describing her pointedly as τῆς νεωτέρας (551). She even distinguishes between the relationships she and Iole will have with Heracles: he is to be her πόσις (550), but Iole's ἀνήρ (551), making a distinction between her as Heracles' married wife, but Iole as Heracles' lover.[26]

The difference between Iole and Deianira is also highlighted by the dynamics of the drama itself. Unlike some tragic women, Deianira does not problematize her presence in the semi-public arena of the open stage outside the house.[27] However, her position outside the house does contrast with Iole's, who is described in terms which associate her with being inside, not with the external space occupied by Deianira. Deianira first associates Iole with the inside space when she invites Iole to go in οὕτως ὅπως ἥδιστα (330), suggesting that Iole will be more comfortable inside. When Deianira begins to follow her, she is delayed by the messenger (335–8), so that she maintains her position outside of the house while Iole goes in. Deianira expresses awareness of Iole as being positioned 'inside' when she exclaims:

> τίν' **ἐσ**δέδεγμαι πημονὴν ὑπόστεγον
> λαθραῖον;
>
> What secret enemy have I taken **in** under my roof?
>
> 376–7

Once she knows the truth, Deianira goes inside the house with Lichas, but immediately returns, announcing her return to the 'outdoors' of the stage and contrasting that with Lichas and Iole, who are still inside (531–3). She repeats this idea of Lichas and Iole being inside while she is outside in her comment to him before he leaves (601). It is only finally on the destruction of Heracles, and the effective ending of the status Deianira had claimed as older, married woman, that she removes herself from the stage and goes inside in silence, like Iole. Deianira's silence here also maintains a very different function to that displayed by Iole. As Rabinowitz has argued, Iole's silence makes her a passive object, passed between Heracles and Hyllus.[28] In contrast, Deianira's silence serves the two active, controlling purposes she seeks from it: the preservation of her reputation and the prevention of the chorus from speaking about what she has done. Deianira's influence over the speech and silence of others, rather than simply her own silence, therefore demonstrates that she has moved beyond the position Iole holds in this play, and established herself successfully in a more influential position.[29]

There are few others in the *Trachiniae* able to command speech or silence in the same way Deianira does. Lichas makes it very clear that Heracles has not been so careful in his message to Deianira, as he is able to change its content apparently without fearing any repercussions from Heracles (479–83). Perhaps the most striking example of lack of influence and inability to command speech is found in the scene which ends in interaction between Hyllus and Heracles at the end of the play, just as the same scene demonstrates Heracles' and Hyllus' comparative unwillingness to seek truthful information. In his extremity of pain, Heracles is originally silent and sleeping, and three times the accompanying old man warns Hyllus that he must be quiet, and avoid waking his father (974–7, 978–81, 988–91), but his commands and urgings have no affect at all. First Hyllus answers the old man's command with a question urging the old man to more speech rather than less (977), then he rejects (rather abruptly, ἀλλ᾽ ἐπί μοι) the other's command to lament his own misery (982–3), and when the old man remonstrates with him a third time, he rejects his instructions again, commenting on his own feelings (992–3). The old man has no influence on Hyllus' speech, and is unable to keep him silent even to protect his beloved father.

Once Heracles awakens, his pain is poured out in a great flood of speech, with the old man and Hyllus interjecting once, but unable to interrupt him again. He ends his speech with a desire to have Deianira near, not to punish her physically (recognizing this as impossible, 1107–8), but claims:

> προσμόλοι μόνον,
> ἵν' ἐκδιδαχθῇ πᾶσιν ἀγγέλλειν ὅτι
> καὶ ζῶν κακούς γε καὶ θανὼν ἐτεισάμην.

> Let her only come close, so that she may be taught to announce to everyone that both living and dead I have punished the wicked.
>
> 1109–11

His wish to have her ἀγγέλλειν his message suggests that his focus is on exerting control over Deianira's speech, particularly as this statement is combined with his recognition of his inability to punish her physically. However, Deianira's silence has been made permanent by her death, and so his wish to control her speech is ineffectual. He then begins his conversation with his son and they repeatedly talk at cross purposes. Heracles attempts to interrupt or stop his son from talking several times, and Hyllus continues determinedly, uncontrolled by his father's words. But similarly, Hyllus is not able to influence his father to accept his speech; the frequent interruptions and objections prevent his reaching the crucial point for over twenty lines. Despite Heracles' insistence that Hyllus should pity him (1034, 1070–1) Hyllus does not address him while he is awake with any direct pity, instead choosing to focus on his mother (1122–3) and on Heracles' commands (1151–1278).[30] Neither speaker is strong enough to assert control over the conversation or affect the speech of the other.

Hyllus' failure to control his own speech, and the failure of the old man's imprecations, are the result of an emotional response to his father's desperate situation. Similarly, the ineffectual speech of both Heracles' and Hyllus' in their shared scene is undoubtedly driven by emotion rather than reason. However, at similarly heightened points of emotion (on discovering the effects of sunlight on Nessus' potion, 678–80, and on hearing its effects from Hyllus along with his accusations, 734–813), Deianira's care and control over speech continue to be maintained. The confusion and contradictions of her husband and son contrast strongly with Deianira's control, and leave a powerful impression of her care in this area.

An unpraiseworthy Heracles

Deianira's influence on speech may have only a limited positive result when it comes to the information she gains, or even the content of the speech she influences, but it does have a substantial effect on the genre of praise discourses, as is the case with the other figures discussed throughout this volume. Deianira's influence and control over speech undermines the presentation of her husband as praiseworthy throughout the play, until his physical state ends up mirroring Deianira's presentation of him: through her influence he is unpraised, and by the end of the play, he becomes unpraiseworthy.

The return of Heracles is initially portrayed in the *Trachiniae* so as to establish it within the poetic context of the return of the victor, as envisaged in the epinician odes of Pindar and Bacchylides.[31] The announcement of Heracles' return represents the messenger as similar to the epinician herald; wearing the traditional garland (καταστεφῆ 178), he declares Heracles' return by reference to his family, as found in the victory statements of the herald at the games, and describes him as νικηφόρῳ, a word commonly found in Pindar.[32] He is described by the chorus as ἀρετᾶς λάφυρ' ἔχων ('bearing trophies of valour' 645). As scholars have previously discussed, the contest described at the start of the play between Achelous and Heracles is also suggestively framed by the chorus as an athletic contest, one worthy of epinician description.[33] Heracles' return is framed by language associated with praise poetry, setting up a context which will be of central importance throughout the rest of the play.

Despite the messenger's or chorus' attempts to establish this epinician praise-poetry context for talking about Heracles, Deianira demonstrates a clear unwillingness to accept the praiseworthiness of her husband, and to contribute to the praise culture surrounding him. She declines ever to praise him directly; the closest she comes to such an action is when she calls him κλεινός ('famous' 19), evoking the praise that others have given him in the past, but adding none of her own. Given the doubt she expresses throughout the play about reports 'heard' of Heracles, there is potential for this doubt to be implied in her description of Heracles solely as 'famous', especially when it appears without the addition of any direct praise resulting from her own experience. It is also significant that κλεινός shares roots with *kleos*; someone κλεινός is heard of in a positive fashion, and yet it is precisely what can be 'heard' of Heracles to which Deianira will object in the immediately following conversation with Hyllus. Deianira contributes none of her own praise for the feat which Heracles performed upon their first meeting. Heracles' rescuing her from Achelous, the event which she is nominally describing, is in fact left pointedly unnarrated or celebrated. Her rescue is described as a πόνος for Heracles (21), thus evoking the labours for which he is traditionally celebrated.[34] However, rather than contributing her own praise to this extra πόνος of Heracles, Deianira claims that she cannot talk of it:

καὶ τρόπων μὲν ἄν πόνων
οὐκ ἂν διείποιμ'· οὐ γὰρ οἶδ·

And I could not tell you fully about the manner of this labour, for I do not know it.

21–2

Thus at a key moment when Deianira *could* have provided her own account of a praiseworthy labour accomplished by Heracles, she is revealed as having been too afraid to witness it (24–5) and so cannot speak of it.[35] She confesses herself even unsure whether it ended well (εἰ δὴ καλῶς 27), providing a very doubtful account of what could have been a triumph for Heracles.[36] Instead, she is forced to rely only on the accounts of others to consider Heracles as praiseworthy, which, as we have seen, she is reluctant to trust.

This potential for distinction between what others may say of Heracles, and what Deianira herself might say becomes actual once she begins to discuss him at greater length, upon the announcement of his return. In Deianira's descriptions of Heracles, the same care over words is seen as in her phrasing of the message to him. She is careful to avoid direct praise, and even implies that he should be blamed rather than praised. This careful approach to begins as soon as his return is announced. While the messenger, as noted above, frames his return in terms of the celebration of an epinician victor, Deianira does not take up his invitation to praise her husband, saying instead, rather doubtfully:

πῶς δ' οὐκ ἐγὼ χαίροιμ' ἄν, ἀνδρὸς εὐτυχῆ
κλύουσα πρᾶξιν τήνδε, πανδίκῳ φρενί;
πολλή 'στ' ἀνάγκη τῇδε τοῦτο συντρέχειν.

How then should I not rejoice with an entirely righteous heart, in hearing about this successful business of my husband? My rejoicing should match up to this success.

293–5

This is the closest she comes to sharing in the celebration, but she immediately turns away from it, focusing on her pity for the captured women. Her questioning tone to begin,[37] use of the potential optative (χαίροιμ' ἄν) rather than more definite 'I shall rejoice', discussion of the triumph in terms of obligation (πολλὴ ἀνάγκη) and her focus on what is fitting or right (πανδίκῳ φρενί) all suggest obligation rather than any spontaneous joy. As a result, she declines the messenger's epinician framing of the return, and avoids praising Heracles, instead casting doubt on the process before she fails to participate in it and turns to pity instead.[38]

Once she has heard the full story of Iole, she takes this line of thought to its bitter end, calling Heracles sarcastically,

> ὁ πιστὸς ἡμῖν κἀγαθὸς καλούμενος
>
> He who is called both trustworthy and noble.
>
> 541

Rather than directly describing her husband positively here, Deianira highlights the fact that this is what he is called by others, raising a dissenting voice against the praise given to him and disassociating it from anything she might say. In the context of her caution over the value of oral reports, this distinction is striking. Her message to Lichas similarly contains none of the praise or welcome found from other wives to their returning husbands, focusing instead on the idea that she has welcomed Iole, and warning Lichas against expanding further.[39]

Deianira is not only involved in denying Heracles praise, she is also responsible for implying deserved blame for her husband, in her response to what the chorus and messenger see as his triumphant victories. Even early on, while the other characters on stage are celebrating her husband's return, she warns that she must fear for Heracles:

> ὅμως δ᾽ ἔνεστι τοῖσιν εὖ σκοπουμένοις
> ταρβεῖν τὸν εὖ πράσσοντα, μὴ σφαλῇ ποτε.
>
> Nevertheless, it is for those who consider things well to be terrified for the man who is doing well, lest one day he is thrown down.
>
> 296–7

While her words mirror a trope often found in Greek thought, and particularly in disclaimers such as those found in Pindar's poetry,[40] they are still an unexpected negative note from someone who claims that she 'should' rejoice at hearing of her husband's return. This is particularly the case as Deianira expresses the sentiment in strong terms, by describing it as right to ταρβεῖν.[41] As the tragedy progresses, she takes this negative note further, and while she never moves into outright blame, she makes several comments which invite those around her to consider whether Heracles' actions might be at least unworthy of praise, if not outright blameworthy. When she interrogates Lichas, she comments:

εἰ μὲν ἐκ κείνου μαθὼν
ψεύδῃ, μάθησιν οὐ καλὴν ἐκμανθάνεις·
εἰ δ' αὐτὸς αὑτὸν ὧδε παιδεύεις, ὅταν
θέλῃς λέγεσθαι χρηστός, ὀφθήσῃ κακός.

If you lie because you have learnt it from him [Heracles], you are not learning a fine lesson well: but if you yourself have educated yourself in this fashion, whenever you want to be said to be honest, you will in fact be seen as base.

449–52

Deianira's focus is on what others will say about Lichas, implying blame from others rather than solely mistrust. The strength of her language to Lichas, and the description of him she provides as acting in such a way as to prevent his ever being spoken of as honest, is damning.[42] Its potential extension to Heracles is also significant: there has in fact been no indication from Lichas that he might be repeating a message he has been schooled in by Heracles. Deianira's suggestion of her husband as a cause for the blameworthy actions she sees in Lichas is unfounded, as Lichas himself will reveal (479–83). Yet Deianira introduces Heracles into the issue, thus introducing potential criticism and censure against Heracles himself, representing him as the teacher of lessons which can only earn blame from others.

Similarly, Deianira manages to indicate reproach for Heracles' actions in discussing Iole, without directly blaming him. She remarks:

πλείστας ἀνὴρ εἷς Ἡρακλῆς ἔγημε δή;
κοὔπω τις αὐτῶν ἔκ γ' ἐμοῦ λόγον κακὸν
ἠνέγκατ' οὐδ' ὄνειδος·

Did not one man, Heracles, sleep with very many women? But not one of these has yet borne a bad word from me, nor any blame.

460–2

Although Deianira rhetorically claims that she has never spoken evilly or reproached any of the women Heracles has slept with, the very fact that she denies having done so raises the possibility, and invites her hearers, the chorus and Lichas, to consider that she would not have been entirely unreasonable to do so. The 'yet' in κοὔπω similarly leaves the implication open as to the possibility of this as a source of future blame, even if Deianira claims not to have blamed them so far. She also makes Heracles distinctly the agent in the situation, while stating only that she does not blame the women involved, leaving rather obviously unspoken her opinion of his behaviour. The strength of her opening sentence, contrasting the singled-out εἷς Heracles with not simply other women, but πλείστας, 'very many' women, emphasizes the potential for blame. When Deianira decides to act to change the situation, it is also Heracles' behaviour which becomes her target; she does not seem to consider acting against Iole.[43]

It is not only the crisis of infidelity that Deianira hints at blaming in the *Trachiniae*. The undertaking that became synonymous with Heracles' identity, his labours, also becomes a target for her disapproval. At the beginning of the play, she describes her married life in negative terms,

τέλος δ' ἔθηκε Ζεὺς ἀγώνιος καλῶς,
εἰ δὴ καλῶς. λέχος γὰρ Ἡρακλεῖ κριτὸν
ξυστᾶσ' ἀεί τιν' ἐκ φόβου φόβον τρέφω,
κείνου προκηραίνουσα. . . .
. . . .
κἀφύσαμεν δὴ παῖδας, οὓς κεῖνός ποτε,
γήτης ὅπως ἄρουραν ἔκτοπον λαβών,
σπείρων μόνον προσεῖδε κἀξαμῶν ἅπαξ·
τοιοῦτος αἰὼν εἰς δόμους τε κἀκ δόμων
ἀεὶ τὸν ἄνδρ' ἔπεμπε λατρεύοντά τῳ.

Finally Zeus god of contests settled it well, if indeed it *was* well. For, won as the chosen bride for Heracles, I always foster some fear after another, anxious for him . . . indeed we had children together, who he, just like a farmer who has taken a distant piece of ploughland, only looks at when he is sowing or reaping: such is the life which sends my husband, working in service to someone, always to and from home.

27–9, 31–5

Her description is unflattering; she reveals no joy in her marriage to Heracles, or any feeling greater than 'anxiety' for him (which, given her later musings on the difficult state of women when their husbands/male protectors are defeated (298–306), may in fact be closer to anxiety for herself). Her description of his role as a father again stops short of actual blame; she does not clearly indicate that she holds him responsible for his attitude, or even that such an attitude is necessarily reprehensible; the farmer, after all, is not doing anything obviously wrong. However, her language is critical, particularly the description of him as λατρεύοντα, 'working for hire', along with the careful omission of the mythical context of Heracles' service to Eurystheus which the audience must recognize. The context in which the image is presented also makes it clear that even if Deianira does not blame Heracles directly, she invites those around her to share in recognizing how her marriage to him has been negative. She indicates scepticism about whether her marriage to Heracles *was* a better result than being married to Achelous, despite her fear of him, in the qualification that Zeus' decision may or may not have been made καλῶς.[44] In raising these doubts she is successful, for both the Nurse and the chorus on their entries to the stage comment on her misery (49–50 and 103–31), and neither reproach her for it; the chorus even suggest that they sympathize with her, although they urge her to hold on to hope, ὧν ἐπιμεμφομένας (122). Athough Deianira has not directly blamed her husband for her unhappiness, the chorus in responding use the verb ἐπιμέμφομαι, often used with a dative object to mean 'cast blame upon'. The chorus therefore read an implication of blame from Deianira's words and acknowledge in their response the blameworthy aspects of her marriage.

Deianira's refusal to praise Heracles has its strongest effect on the group most affected by her influence over speech, and otherwise most concerned with praise for Heracles: the chorus. Deianira's early indication to the chorus that Heracles may be worthy of *blame*, not praise (122), presents a sharp contrast with the attitude of Megara in the *Heracles*, and suggests to the chorus that praise songs may not be appropriate. The chorus of the *Trachiniae*'s identity as a group of Trachinian women is also interesting: unlike the elder men of Thebes who form the chorus of the *Heracles*, they have more limited public authority, and may be more vulnerable to influence from Deianira. In the *Heracles*, the chorus and Amphitryon also had a shared purpose in praising Heracles and maintaining his *kleos*. Deianira's influence, in contrast, is skewed towards highlighting more negative aspects of Heracles' reputation, and even towards encouraging blame for the hero.

Following Deianira's criticisms, the chorus' ostensibly praise-focused songs throughout the play become corrupted with elements which are jarring and unsuitable, and which demonstrate the effects of Deianira's influence on their speech. In their lyric interlude celebrating the return of Heracles (205–24) the chorus are responding to a command from Deianira to speak out. Therefore, they act to celebrate Heracles with less of the authoritative, independent stance than the chorus of Euripides' *Heracles*.[45] In their celebration, the chorus struggle to settle on an appropriate genre for their song, mixing elements of multiple genres.[46] The ode begins with strong elements of the *hymenaios*, welcoming Heracles to the house as if he were a bridegroom, describing him as μελλόνυμφος

(207), and emphasizing his coming into the house and hearth (205–6) in the style of a wedding song. However, this genre will have ominous implications given the new 'bride' Heracles is bringing back to the house,[47] and given Deianira's criticism of marriage, it is also not as celebratory a genre as it might be in another context. It is also a genre which Deianira has, herself, suggested to the chorus. In her early conversation with the chorus (141–52), Deianira expresses her belief that they cannot fully understand her position due to their unwedded status, with an image of the chorus as young plants, found in imagery of wedding songs.[48] Deianira's dwelling on marriage has clearly influenced the chorus' song.[49] The chorus do not settle in this genre, however, instead beginning a *paian* at line 208, initiated by a shout to Apollo (209–10) and featuring the explicit παιᾶνα παιᾶν call (210–11), following invocations to Artemis (214).[50] Again, however, this genre proves unfruitful for the chorus, who lapse quickly into the 'generic mutation' Rutherford identifies, and find themselves singing a bacchic song, excited by ivy (219), and describing themselves as Βακχίαν / ὑποστρέφων ἅμιλλαν ('whirling around in the Bacchic race' 219–20).[51] They finish with a return to the *paian*, complete with ritual cry, ἰὼ ἰὼ Παιάν (221), and a conclusion which focuses on Deianira (222–5).

Deianira's influence has a similar effect on the chorus' second attempt to celebrate Heracles, particularly in connection to her own inability to speak praise of Heracles' πόνος, her rescue. Again, the chorus sings a song which appears partially triggered by Deianira's own words, since alongside her claim that she could not herself speak of that rescue, she suggests:

ἀλλ' ὅστις ἦν
θακῶν ἀταρβὴς τῆς θέας, ὅδ' ἂν λέγοι.

Whoever was sitting there unafraid of the sight, he could tell you about it.

23–4

Apparently in response, the chorus take up the suggestion of this topic of song in their first stasimon,[52] perhaps even describing themselves as οἷα θάτηρ (525), reflecting Deianira's instruction that someone who saw the contest should tell of the events.[53] Their song makes an attempt to reframe Deianira's negative tale of the clash between Achelous and Heracles, so that they turn it into a praise song, focused ostensibly on Heracles' victory, with a strong Pindaric opening.[54] However, the *laudandus* here becomes Aphrodite rather than Heracles, diverting praise away from Heracles in an epinician context.[55] The emphasis on the power and influence of love, in the form of Aphrodite, itself reflects a comment of Deianira's, when she indicated that no one could stand up to Eros in her persuasion of Lichas (441–4). In making Aphrodite both the umpire (515) and implicitly the *laudanda* and victor in the contest, the chorus echo Deianira's description of someone standing up to Eros πύκτης ὅπως (441), involved in precisely the kind of athletic contest which the chorus now seem to be celebrating.[56] The epinician qualities of the poem are tainted with erotic language which connects Achelous and Heracles around Aphrodite, displacing Deianira from their relationship.[57] Its structure also mixes together elements of the epinician and the narrative qualities of a dithyramb.[58]

Some of Deianira's language and poetic influence around wedding song has again come into the chorus' framing, beyond simply her instruction that it should be told by a spectator. It is striking that when the chorus take up the suggestion to tell of Heracles and Achelous' contest, they describe Deianira's εὐῶπις ἁβρά ('fair-eyed beauty' 523), using a tragic hapax in εὐῶπις, which in epic describes the potential of Nausicaa as a bride.[59] They also describe Deianira as a πόρτις ἐρήμα (a 'bereft calf' 530), another image from wedding songs.[60] The chorus have again taken on Deianira's own language in their efforts to understand and represent her position. In doing so, they allow the language from a separate genre, wedding songs, to corrupt the attempt at epinician which they perform in celebration of Heracles, just as the wedding song became mixed into their earlier celebration of his anticipated return. Deianira's negative emotions around the contest have a further impact on the song, since the chorus describe her as waiting ἐλεινόν (528), hardly a celebratory position.[61] Again the chorus' gender may be particularly significant here; as a female chorus (at least, in character), they struggle to sing the kind of epinician praises with which the male chorus of the *Heracles* were more at home, instead mixing in the more female-oriented genre of wedding songs.[62] In particular, wedding songs which are associated with the negative aspects of wedding, such as the bereft nature of the girl leaving her home, are a female-oriented genre, so the chorus' introduction of these into other types of song is influenced by the use of the female chorus in this tragedy.[63]

In the second stasimon, their celebration of Heracles' return (634–62), the Trachinian chorus begin again to frame their praise for Heracles in epinician terms, referring to the 'trophies' that he brings (645) and virtues celebrated in the earlier odes, such as his physical prowess and ἀρετή (640–2).[64] They develop a geographical focus on Heracles' community and 'home' (634–9), which may evoke the chorus' earlier mention of the 'competitors' in the epinician in relation to their cities (510–11).[65] Once more, however, there are troubling elements, since, as Janka has discussed, the 'encomiastic topography' is focused around Mt. Oeta, the place of Heracles' death.[66] There is also a mistake in the chorus' celebration of Trachis as Heracles' home. The chorus promise further epinician songs celebrating the return of Heracles, just as the return of an athletic victory was celebrated (640–2),[67] connecting them to the kind of extended, explicitly musical celebration that we see in the *Heracles*. However, the future songs they offer are unusual too: they will apparently make use of an aulos (640) that is *like* a lyre (θείας ἀντίλυρον μούσας 642–3), and they include the somewhat ominous disclaimer that those songs will be οὐκ ἀναρσίαν ἀχῶν καναχὰν ('not in a hostile noise of sorrows' 640–1). Loraux has connected tragedy's 'songs without a lyre', accompanied by an *aulos*, to the inherent negativity of tragic musicality.[68] The chorus' promises of future songs, therefore, are marked not by the signs of praise songs, but by tragedy: the chorus' celebration is infected by the 'negative sign' of tragedy,[69] and points to precisely the kind of sorrows they will sing for Heracles in their final ode.[70] Bagordo has also identified a potential allusion here to the lyric fragments 947 a and b *PMG*, but with these negative elements which, in contrast with the original, add to the ambiguity of the language here.[71] There is also a further reference to Deianira's grief in Heracles' absence (650–2) in their celebration, in a pleonastic form which emphasizes its strength, so that once again the chorus are unable to ignore Deianira's more negative experience, even in what purports to be a celebratory song.[72]

By their final song, the chorus have moved fully into the strain of sorrows which they had claimed to be avoiding; they describe themselves 'lamenting' (947), and προὔκλαιον, ὀξύφωνος ὡς ἀηδών (lamenting 'like a shrill-voiced nightingale' 961–2). The earlier suggestion of epinician has been left unfulfilled as the play progresses, and replaced by the nightingale's lament. Once again, there is an intrusive element of Deianira's concerns upon this song ostensibly connected to Heracles. Despite seeming to present their song as connected to the end of Heracles' labours (825), they move in their lament to focus upon Deianira once more, particularly her ignorance, which is again connected to the wedding she intimated, and which influenced their earlier attitudes to Heracles (841–4). Upon seeing Heracles' arrival, they further describe him as **ἄσπετον** θέαμα, 'an **unspeakable** sight' (961),[73] and their emphasis on Heracles' 'silent' approach and the silence of those bringing him (967, 968) strengthens this contrast between the praise songs they hoped for, and the unspeakable, silent reality. This focus on silence could be seen to reflect Deianira's strongest injunction to them, that of silence. Finally, Aphrodite's appearance as the πράκτωρ of what has happened, in the final lines of the ode (861) returns to the theme of their earlier celebrations, Aphrodite's power, and thus again sounds a note which was originally indicated to them by Deianira.[74]

The chorus of the *Trachiniae*, faced with Deianira's refusal to encourage epinician description of Heracles, and encouraged by her to blame him instead, struggle to maintain praise songs for Heracles throughout the play. The influence exerted on their songs by Deianira, both in their occasion and the genres and content they sing on, is repeatedly negative. As a result, they attempt an epinician which conveys limited praise for Heracles, since they celebrate Aphrodite rather than the hero, and they introduce unsuitable elements into both this and their paian, with the influence of Deianira's negative feelings about weddings appearing throughout the choral stasima. Finally, when Heracles' destruction is revealed, they become unable to speak of him at all, instead taking refuge in silence: the same silence which Deianira had previously successfully mandated from them. In this regard they are similar to the chorus of Euripides' *Heracles*, who also find their hero straying into 'unsingable' sorrows.[75] However, unlike the chorus of the *Heracles*, the Trachinian women are joined by no one who will reconstruct a positive discourse of praise for Heracles; Hyllus is concerned with his mother's situation (1122–3 and following) instead, and this concern itself is the result of Deianira's influence exerted through her death by suicide.

Deianira has an instrumental role in not only rejecting the praise tradition for Heracles, but also in inviting blame from others, even if she never speaks such blame aloud herself. Her destruction of the very qualities for which he was previously praised, his strength and vitality, is simultaneously the final overturning of any possibility of praise for Heracles. Nearly all the praise which Heracles does receive in the *Trachiniae* is focused on his physical strength, and often his vitality. The messenger announces his return by specifically mentioning his κράτει νικηφόρῳ ('victorious might' 186). Lichas emphasizes the same points when giving a report of Heracles' condition,

ἔγωγέ τοί σφ᾽ ἔλειπον ἰσχύοντά τε
καὶ ζῶντα καὶ θάλλοντα κοὐ νόσῳ βαρύν

For myself, I left him strong, alive, and flourishing, and not weighed down by any illness.

234–5

Deianira has no reason to suspect illness in Heracles (perhaps she might fear that he would be wounded or dead), but Lichas' focus on health highlights this as one of his most-praised characteristics. Later, he will similarly describe Heracles as ἀριστεύων χεροῖν ('best in strength' 488), repeating the same focus. The chorus imagine his πάσας ἀρετᾶς λάφυρ᾽ ('trophies of all valour' 645) and later describe him as ἄλκιμον ('mighty' 956). Heracles himself focuses on his many feats in relation to the physical parts of his body which have brought them about, talking of the καὶ χερσὶ καὶ νώτοισι μοχθήσας ἐγώ· ('labours of my arms and my back' 1047).

These praiseworthy attributes are then described as ruined by the robe Deianira sends. Heracles himself recognizes the robe's effect as a devastation of the body, focusing on it when he cries

πλευραῖσι γὰρ προσμαχθὲν ἐκ μὲν ἐσχάτας
βέβρωκε σάρκας, πλεύμονός τ' ἀρτηρίας
ῥοφεῖ ξυνοικοῦν· ἐκ δὲ χλωρὸν αἷμά μου
πέπωκεν ἤδη, καὶ διέφθαρμαι δέμας
τὸ πᾶν, ἀφράστῳ τῇδε χειρωθεὶς πέδῃ

It has stuck to my sides and eaten into my innermost flesh, and it lies within me and devours the pipes of my lungs: already it has drunk my fresh blood from me, and my whole body is utterly destroyed, as I have been mastered by these unspeakable fetters.

1053–7

The focus on the physical effects is accentuated by his insistence that the entirety (τὸ πᾶν) of his body is ruined.[76] Heracles stresses this point further in his cry,

ὦ χέρες χέρες,
ὦ νῶτα καὶ στέρν', ὦ φίλοι βραχίονες,
ὑμεῖς ἐκεῖνοι δὴ καθέσταθ' ....

O my hands, my hands, O my back and shoulders, O my beloved arms, are you the same ones which once subdued [the Nemean lion].

1089–91

Similarly, a little later he complains, immediately after a description of his successful labours (1101–3):

νῦν δ' ὧδ' ἄναρθρος καὶ κατερρακωμένος
τυφλῆς ὑπ' ἄτης ἐκπεπόρθημαι τάλας,

But now, unjointed and torn to rags, I, wretched, am undone by blind ruin.

1103–4

Heracles contrasts the descriptions of his past glories with his physical devastation through his close juxtaposition of both. As a result, the undoing of his physical strength is presented as simultaneously the destruction of his glorious, praiseworthy self, mirroring the undermining of this praise that Deianira had caused earlier in the play.[77] His recognition that this ruin of his strength has been effected by a woman φασγάνου δίχα ('without a sword' 1063) emphasizes the incongruity of Deianira's strength. Without recourse to 'manly' might (1062), she has destroyed his strength and made of him something unworthy of praise.[78]

Conclusion

Heracles' surprise at Deianira's involvement, however, is mistaken. In ruining his physical, praise-earning form, even by accident, she has merely enacted more fully the undoing of his praiseworthiness that had already begun in her language. Thus Deianira's destruction of her husband has a double impact. Through her speech, she prevents or limits the celebration of him with praise, leaving him unpraised. In the sending of the robe, she causes the physical destruction that will leave him an unpraiseworthy, even unspeakable figure. Deianira shows that she doubts the praiseworthiness of her husband from the start of the play. By the end, other characters, particularly the chorus, have been both encouraged by her speech and forced by her action to share her opinion. This destruction is the result of the unusual attitude to speech and information which is a key part of Deianira's behaviour in the play. Throughout the *Trachiniae*, Deianira demonstrates a persistent concern with the sources of information and with controlling the speech spoken around her, a concern which is not matched by any other character in the play. While this concern has very limited efficacy when it comes to her understanding of events, where it *does* have a substantial effect is on undermining and rejecting the praise spoken for Heracles. Heracles, therefore, repeatedly unpraised by Deianira in the *Trachiniae*, eventually becomes both unpraised and unpraiseworthy.

As with the *Suppliant Women*, Sophocles' *Trachiniae* demonstrates the potential risks and dangers of women's involvement with *kleos* and praise speech. Here, it is not the chorus themselves, but rather the female influence on the chorus of a resistant, reluctant woman, which has such a dramatic effect on the hero concerned. As we shall see in the following chapter, however, this effect can also be found in tragedy manipulated even more effectively by one of tragedy's most famously destructive wives: Euripides' *Medea*.

6

Medea and the Mastery of Blame

The distribution of praise and blame, especially in the form of blame, is central to Euripides' *Medea*. Both Jason and Medea face an exceptionally high level of blame from one another, often addressed directly. The focus on poetry and song as a way of establishing reputations from the chorus, Jason and Medea demonstrates the importance of this concept within the tragedy, as in the plays discussed so far. In this context, the chorus express a wish for the reputations of men and women to be exchanged, so that women become better thought of while men receive the condemnations for faithlessness which they deserve. However, what the chorus do not recognize is that Euripides' *Medea* represents a world where their anticipated reversal has already happened, based on the manipulations of blame achieved by Medea.

Medea demonstrates a similar awareness to Philoctetes or Deianira of the functioning of praise and blame in constructing identity. Unlike Deianira, Medea does not simply resist the discourses of praise established by others about her husband.[1] Instead, she propagates her own discourse of blame within which Jason is positioned both by her, but also by the chorus and other characters in response to her complaints. This blame is unusually and explicitly gendered. Medea, and even Jason himself, both express awareness of how this blame is gendered, assigning it to a generalized discourse of blame traditionally applied to women. Medea's recognition of this aspect indicates a high level of self-awareness in her use of this tactic. By repeatedly positioning Jason within discourses of blame marked as suitable for positioning women, not men, Medea's blame has the effect of positioning Jason not simply as blameworthy, but specifically as a blameworthy woman, according to the terms of the discourse.[2]

The process of establishing *kleos* has an inherent risk as it is discursive, requiring others to sing of or spread the reputation being established. As demonstrated in earlier chapters, it is possible for others to refuse to accept praise discourses or to attempt to establish competing discourses in a dialogic genre such as tragedy, where multiple voices may be contributing to the generation of *kleos* on stage. In the *Medea,* Medea and the chorus engage in precisely this type of activity, since she leads the chorus in considering the importance of what is said in establishing reputation, and in the production of specific discourses of blame. Medea's approach makes destructive use of her understanding, since she chooses to draw on discourses of blame which Jason has identified and named as gendered feminine, and positions him in these rather than discourses of blame which would be marked more normally as applying to masculine values.

As more recognizable discourses are more likely to be successfully perpetuated, it is not surprising that Medea makes use of blame discourses which are indicated within the world of the play to be those already established to effectively position Jason, even if these are not discourses within which men could normally be positioned. The chorus, after all, recognise that poets have not previously said enough about men's weaknesses (429–30), indicating a lack of any recognizable discourse along these lines which Medea could appropriate. It has long been acknowledged that an awareness of poetry's role in establishing discourses of praise and blame is placed centre-stage in the *Medea* by the chorus' famous lines:

ἄνω ποταμῶν ἱερῶν χωροῦσι παγαί,
καὶ δίκα καὶ πάντα πάλιν στρέφεται·
ἀνδράσι μὲν δόλιαι βουλαί, θεῶν δ'
οὐκέτι πίστις ἄραρεν.
τὰν δ' ἐμὰν εὔκλειαν ἔχειν βιοτὰν στρέψουσι φᾶμαι·
ἔρχεται τιμὰ γυναικείῳ γένει·
οὐκέτι δυσκέλαδος φάμα γυναῖκας ἕξει.

μοῦσαι δὲ παλαιγενέων λήξουσ' ἀοιδῶν
τὰν ἐμὰν ὑμνεῦσαι ἀπιστοσύναν.
οὐ γὰρ ἐν ἁμετέρᾳ γνώμᾳ λύρας
ὤπασε θέσπιν ἀοιδὰν
Φοῖβος ἁγήτωρ μελέων· ἐπεὶ ἀντάχησ' ἂν ὕμνον
ἀρσένων γέννᾳ. μακρὸς δ' αἰὼν ἔχει
πολλὰ μὲν ἁμετέραν ἀνδρῶν τε μοῖραν εἰπεῖν.

The streams of sacred rivers flow upwards, and order and everything is reversed; for the thoughts of men are deceptive, and their pledges by the gods no longer hold fast. Rumour will overturn my life and bring it good repute; honour is coming to the race of women: no longer will slanderous rumour come to women. The songs of ancient poets will stop singing our faithlessness. For Phoebus lord of songs did not grant to our minds the inspired songs of the lyre: or I could sing a hymn in answer to the race of men. For great time could say many things about the fate of men as well as ours.

410–30

The chorus' ode is sung in a decorative style and its highly poetic nature, with specific reference to Phoebus and the lyre, emphasizes the unusually metapoetic style.[3] Their references to song, the dactylo-epitrite metre, the lyre and the vocabulary, indicate particularly epinician and epic as their targets,[4] songs commonly associated with the construction of heroic identities through praise.[5] There may be an indication of archaic blame poetry in the use of Ionian dialect, which presents an unusual combination with the metre.[6] The ode's focus on poetry as a vehicle also for transmitting discourses of blame against women further demonstrates an unusual level of self-awareness of this feature within the world of tragedy, itself a poetic vehicle.[7] The description of poetry as θέσπιν ἀοιδὰν has strong epic resonances, and the implication of lyric poetry in μελέων establish lyric and epic as two genres against which the chorus' tragic song, with its aulos accompaniment, is performed.[8] The ode has the effect therefore of highlighting the importance of this element in interpreting the play. The audience is presented with a chorus who, along with many of the characters, demonstrate awareness of the functioning of poetry to transmit and authorise discourses of praise and blame.

Interpretation of this ode has tended to fall into two camps. The first suggests that the song indicates the confusion of the chorus, who have been taken in by Medea's speech, leading to their own inability to correctly pass moral judgements on her behaviour as the play goes on.[9] The second focuses more on the awareness of genre and literature displayed by the chorus, leading to a reading which argues that the play itself is attempting to do what the chorus sing of, with limited success. One of the first to suggest this reading was Knox (1977), who claimed: '"Legends now shall change direction; woman's life have glory" sings the chorus, but the future tense is unnecessary. Euripides' play itself is the change of direction.'[10] Later readers added some very necessary caveats, with Rabinowitz rightly pointing out that the chorus of male voices singing a male author's words, might not be able to represent the full reversal the chorus anticipate in women's position,[11] and Boedecker positioning the play as a conflict between literary genres: tragedy and epic, with tragedy overtaking and negating the old-fashioned heroics of epic.[12] Rehm argued similarly to Boedecker, although with a rather more gendered perspective, that the *Medea* represents Medea's failed attempt to break out of a male, heroics-based method of discourse and replace it with a new female λόγος.[13] The latter argument is similar to those of scholars such as Foley, who see the *Medea* as demonstrating a conflict of values and characteristics as embodied in the figure of Medea: male, heroic, traditional morals contrasted with female 'virtues' such as maternal feeling.[14] However, close examination of the deployment of praise and blame discourses in the play itself reveals that far from expressing only a wish for the future, the chorus effectively describe the action engendered across the play: a complete reversal in the types of gendered praise and blame given to the central male/female pair, Jason and Medea.

This reversal is not the result of Medea's violence, however, which in itself has no obvious effect on reversing poetic discourses of blame against women. Rather, it is found in how the others on stage around Medea speak of why the violence was carried out, specifically, the terms which they choose to blame Jason. Medea's awareness of discourses of gendered blame, traditionally used to position women as lustful, crafty, faithless and over-emotional, allows her to draw on these discourses for blame which positions Jason in precisely the same way.[15] This construction of Jason is largely accepted by those around her, so that combined with the reversal in their respective fates enacted by her violence, her blame succeeds in leaving Jason positioned as blameworthy, and feminine.

Renown and reputation

The characters of the *Medea* display a keen awareness of the importance of praise or blame in forming their reputations, and their public presentations of themselves. This awareness is thus not only to be found in the chorus' ode, quoted above. In fact, the chorus there are responding to an attitude which Medea has already demonstrated in her time on stage. Medea establishes the importance of this idea explicitly as part of her concern for self-construction and self-presentation to those around her.[16] She frames her entry on to the stage as due to concerns for her reputation and that she might earn blame:

> ἐξῆλθον δόμων
> μή μοί τι **μέμψησθ'**· οἶδα γὰρ πολλοὺς βροτῶν
> σεμνοὺς γεγῶτας, τοὺς μὲν ὀμμάτων ἄπο,
> τοὺς δ' ἐν θυραίοις· οἱ δ' ἀφ' ἡσύχου ποδὸς
> δύσκλειαν ἐκτήσαντο καὶ ῥᾳθυμίαν.

> I have come out of the house lest **you blame me:** for I know that many mortals are haughty, both in private and in public: but others from their retiring way of life get a bad reputation and one for indifference.
>
> 214–18

She carries on talking about potential risks to a reputation for a further four lines, including an additional mention of praise and blame speech through her discussion of the type of citizen she does not praise (οὐδ' ᾔνεσ' 223). She finally turns to discuss her own situation twelve lines into her opening speech (225), so that the concern for reputation and blame is more prominent.[17] Upon Creon's entry, there is a recurring emphasis on reputation and blame. First, Creon claims that he is relying partly on the reports of others against Medea to make his decision (287–9). However, Medea claims in her refutation that the whole matter is one of an unfairly bad reputation, crying:

> οὐ νῦν με πρῶτον ἀλλὰ πολλάκις, Κρέον,
> ἔβλαψε δόξα μεγάλα τ' εἴργασται κακά.
>
> Not for the first time now, but often, Creon, has my reputation greatly harmed me and caused trouble.
>
> 292–3

She develops at length a discussion of the harm a particular reputation can cause, dwelling on the perils of being thought clever. Given the way she speaks about the others around her, and the way they view her cleverness (303), it might be expected to see some evidence of more widespread hostility among the Corinthians, perhaps represented by the chorus. However, it seems that, despite her argument here, Medea has been able to preserve her reputation with everyone except for Creon.[18]

Medea attempts to set up an alternate identity for herself to that established by any negative reputation, as she argues:

> οὐχ ὧδ' ἔχει μοι, μὴ τρέσῃς ἡμᾶς, Κρέον,
> ὥστ' ἐς τυράννους ἄνδρας ἐξαμαρτάνειν.
>
> Do not fear me, this is not in me, Creon, to be able to harm the royal family.
>
> 307–8

However, even if the audience had not heard the same threats for themselves, the Nurse's words at the very start of the play make it impossible for this alternative identity to stand as the 'true' Medea, as she wishes it to. The Nurse has expressed fears that Medea is precisely this kind of person (39–42), backing it up with the assertion ἐγᾦδα τήνδε (39), and revealed that she has already committed crimes against the leaders of two lands: Pelias (9) and her father (1–6), as Medea herself later confirms (31–4, 166–7). Medea's attempt to create a new identity for herself with Creon, rejecting the one at the root of her unfavourable reputation, is unsurprisingly unsuccessful; it forces her to turn instead to formal supplication, which does not rely on her being a particular kind of person to succeed.[19] Medea's awareness of the potential distinctions between a reputation and 'actual' identity, shown in her first statements to the chorus, leads to her understanding that this gap can be manipulated in order for her to influence Creon. Even if her attempt is unsuccessful, it shows a subtle degree of recognition of how reputation and blame can be turned against her and thus, at her hands, against Jason.

Medea is not the only character to demonstrate awareness of the importance of a reputation. Aegeus, despite his brief time on stage, expresses his desire to remain blameless, ἀναίτιος, in the eyes of his hosts (730). It is also a focus for the other main character of the play: Jason. After the chorus have introduced the idea of poetry as conveying praise and blame and establishing negative reputations for women, Jason takes up the same idea in his argument against Medea. He claims:

> πάντες δέ σ' ᾔσθοντ' οὖσαν Ἕλληνες σοφὴν
> καὶ δόξαν ἔσχες· εἰ δὲ γῆς ἐπ' ἐσχάτοις
> ὅροισιν ᾤκεις, οὐκ ἂν ἦν λόγος σέθεν.
> εἴη δ' ἔμοιγε μήτε χρυσὸς ἐν δόμοις
> μήτ' Ὀρφέως κάλλιον ὑμνῆσαι μέλος,
> εἰ μὴ 'πίσημος ἡ τύχη γένοιτό μοι.

> All the Greeks know that you are clever and you have a reputation: if you were still living on the farthest boundaries of the land, there would be no story about you. Let there be neither gold in my house nor the power to sing songs more beautiful than those of Orpheus, if fame does not become my lot.
>
> 539–44

Not only does Jason acknowledge Medea's own desire for a good reputation and fame, but he also makes it clear that such considerations are important to him, more so even than gold, which has partly spurred him on to his new marriage (559–65). He connects this expression of the value of reputation with song. This revelation of Jason's key motivation, however, makes him particularly vulnerable to Medea's approach. Jason, as Luschnig has identified, wishes to be the subject of a song rather than its singer, but as the chorus have indicated (410–30) and will confirm (1089) Medea's activities will reverse the subjects of song. As a subject rather than singer, Jason cannot resist such a technique.[20]

As with many of the plays focused on reputation and renown discussed in this volume, there is also a repeated focus from the chorus and characters in the *Medea* on poetry and music, including poetry as a vehicle for praise, blame, and reputation, which Jason's own language reflects. As discussed above, the first stasimon (410–30) provides a striking, programmatic example of this language. However, this is not the only instance of characters reflecting on the role of poetry and its importance for Medea's own production of blame. Medea herself introduces one musical genre into the play, through her opening laments, identified explicitly as such by the Tutor (γόων 59), Nurse (ἀποιμώξῃ 31, νέφος οἰμωγῆς 107), and chorus (γόον 135, γόων 206),[21] who also describe Medea as μέλπει (150), further emphasizing the musical qualities of her offstage laments. The impact of Medea's lament is so great that the Nurse complains about the unsuitability of song as an invention, in a surprisingly extensive tirade:

> σκαιοὺς δὲ λέγων κοὐδέν τι σοφοὺς
> τοὺς πρόσθε βροτοὺς οὐκ ἂν ἁμάρτοις,
> οἵτινες ὕμνους ἐπὶ μὲν θαλίαις
> ἐπί τ' εἰλαπίναις καὶ παρὰ δείπνοις
> ηὕροντο βίῳ τερπνὰς ἀκοάς·
> στυγίους δὲ βροτῶν οὐδεὶς λύπας
> ηὕρετο μούσῃ καὶ πολυχόρδοις
> ᾠδαῖς παύειν, ἐξ ὧν θάνατοι
> δειναί τε τύχαι σφάλλουσι δόμους.
> καίτοι τάδε μὲν κέρδος ἀκεῖσθαι
> μολπαῖσι βροτούς· ἵνα δ' εὔδειπνοι
> δαῖτες, τί μάτην τείνουσι βοήν;
> τὸ παρὸν γὰρ ἔχει τέρψιν ἀφ' αὑτοῦ
> δαιτὸς πλήρωμα βροτοῖσιν.
>
> You would not be wrong to describe men of old as foolish and not at all wise, since they invented songs for our life as delightful things to hear, for celebrations and feasts along with banquets, while no one has discovered how to stop the bitter griefs of mortals with music and songs sung to the lyre; from these griefs deaths and terrible disasters overthrow their houses. So there would have been a profit for mortals in healing through song; whereas wherever there are banquets with well-stocked feasts, why do they pointlessly raise their shout? For the fullness of the feast at hand provides its own pleasure for mortals.
>
> 190–203

Like the choral statement which will follow, the Nurse's generalizing comments on the limits of music's capacity to engage with human suffering, coming so early and extensively, have a metapoetic quality which indicates the importance of the issue to the play. This is particularly the case given their appearance within a genre of poetry – that is, tragedy – which engages almost exclusively with human suffering.[22] Yet, the Nurse's dismissal of song when someone is grieving will promptly be shown to underestimate its impact when that song appears in Medea's hands. The strength of Medea's lamenting is such that she causes the Nurse herself to abandon her iambic trimeters and chant in response (99–203).[23] Similarly, the chorus' references to hearing Medea's lament (131–2, 205–6) make it clear that Medea's lamenting has drawn the chorus in and will begin the process of making them allies through sympathy.[24] Medea's lamentation also enables her to introduce the powerful speech which will be most efficacious against Jason: blame speech. As McClure has identified, Medea's early laments include both blame and cursing, powerful elements of women's laments in Ancient Greece, and thus make it clear that Medea's speech draws on the most powerful genres open to her from the earliest stages of the play.[25]

The chorus similarly participate in discourse on the role of song, beyond their early programmatic statement. Athens, Medea's planned haven, is signalled as a land of song (533–4) through the chorus' references to Harmonia born of the nine Muses.[26] There is a strongly gendered element to this connection with song, as the chorus envisage a daughter born entirely to mothers (the Muses) here,[27] and draw on the female-oriented lyric style of Sappho to create the scene.[28] The chorus' final recognition that they have engaged in inappropriate μύθων as part of their support for Medea (1082) is connected to a Muse, to whom they claim some women have access (1089). The kind of μύθος which the chorus seem to regret involvement with, is explicitly connected to the Muses' arts, song, dance and poetry, and reflects back to their initial programmatic claim that women have not previously had command over song. Now that they have enjoyed such a command, the chorus recognise the destructive power of these arts and express regret, claiming that these engagements have taken the chorus beyond their usual limits as women (1083–4).[29] Throughout the play, therefore, the audience are invited to reflect on the roles of song and music both in Medea's society and in their own, through the reference to Athens.[30] Their gendered aspect is also brought out particularly in the changing pattern of engagement from the female chorus across the play.

This repeated emphasis on the issues of praise, blame and reputations makes it clear that these are central to any interpretation of the play, as is poetry's use as a vehicle for their construction. Medea's subtle understanding of how reputation, blame speech and identity can be manipulated to cause harm, is a central facet of her success in destroying Jason. This understanding enables her to appropriate traditional, particularly poetic, blame discourses to position him in such a damaging way.

Blaming Jason

Medea's introduction to the audience, while she remains off stage, is framed in terms more usual for describing a male, heroic figure than a woman. Her off-stage cries of grief parallel those of Sophocles' Ajax,[31] and the images the Nurse uses to describe her of a rock and then a wave (28), present her as masculine in her hardness.[32] The repeated allusions to her wrath (93–4, 99, 107–8, 172) and references to her potential for violence are unusual in descriptions of a woman. The word χόλος used repeatedly of her anger (94, 99, 126, 172, 590, 898, 1150) is applied more commonly in tragedy to male figures, and associates her with the Iliadic Achilles.[33] The famous comparison between childbirth and battle which she makes in describing women's fate (241–58) insistently brings the heroic, masculine world of war into the female realm, assimilating them.[34]

Her reversal of traditionally gendered discourses is not limited to the way she herself is presented. Medea is not alone in tragedy in being a female character described in language more usually applied to men, since such descriptions are also applied to characters such as Clytemnestra.[35] What makes Medea particularly unusual is her active participation in continuing the process of gender reversal in the discourses of blame which she directs against Jason, and which are taken up and propagated by the chorus and other characters. Each of these discourses is marked by Jason, Creon or Medea herself as being properly applicable within the world of the play to women, not men. This approach is indicated by Medea's first direct criticism to Jason of his behaviour:

ὦ παγκάκιστε, τοῦτο γάρ σ' εἰπεῖν ἔχω,
γλώσσῃ μέγιστον εἰς **ἀνανδρίαν** κακόν,

O most vile man, for I have this to say to you, the worst thing from a tongue against such base **unmanliness**.

465–6

Medea connects her blame with his 'unmanliness', closely intertwining her blame and the feminization of Jason that these discourses produce.

One of the discourses of blame most obviously marked by the tragedy's characters as gendered feminine, is one which positions women as lustful, and over-invested in sex. This type of blame is modelled on a traditional discourse of blame regarding women as excessively sexual which is found throughout Greek literature.[36] Discussion of this issue in the *Medea* is unusually common for a tragedy, which is filled with terms for Jason and Medea's relationships which evoke a sexual context in their use of words for 'bed', so that the words λέχος, λέκτρον, εὐνή and κοίτη occur thirty-two separate times in the play.[37] Medea first identifies this discourse as being marked for use against women, when she argues:

> ὅταν δ' ἐς εὐνὴν ἠδικημένη κυρῇ,
> οὐκ ἔστιν ἄλλη φρὴν μιαιφονωτέρα.
>
> Whenever she turns out to have been wronged in matters to do with the bed, her mind is more murderous than any other.
>
> 265–6

Jason makes a similar generalized statement of blame, positioning women as excessively concerned with sex, to Medea in their *agon*:

> ἀλλ' ἐς τοσοῦτον ἥκεθ' ὥστ' ὀρθουμένης
> εὐνῆς γυναῖκες πάντ' ἔχειν νομίζετε,
> ἢν δ' αὖ γένηται ξυμφορά τις ἐς λέχος,
> τὰ λῷστα καὶ κάλλιστα πολεμιώτατα
> τίθεσθε.
>
> But you women have come to such a point, that you think if the bed has been set straight then you have everything, but if some disaster occurs to your bed, you hold your most agreeable and finest things to be most hostile.
>
> 569–73

Both Jason and Medea in their use of generalizations mark this blame as explicitly gendered, to be applied to women as a class, not just Medea.[38] In Jason's case this is unexpected: his conflict is with Medea, not women generally. Moreover, Jason is already engaged in a relationship with a different woman, Creon's daughter, making his generalization hypocritical and rather jarring.

Medea's use of this generalization is also unusual, since it suggests a self-loathing willingness to draw on traditional blame discourses to criticize herself. However, rather than acknowledging this discourse as applicable to her, Medea instead persists in drawing on it to blame her husband. A great deal of her blame for Jason attempts to position him within this same discourse, as destructively lustful and over-concerned with his bed. Medea is significantly more successful in this attempt than Jason is in his own efforts to blame her in the same terms, since while Medea and the chorus never accept that such criticism might be applied to her, the chorus and even Aegeus do accept (and even perpetuate) her criticisms of Jason connected to his sexual conduct.[39]

Medea often expresses her blame for Jason's behaviour in terms which establish the sexual nature of his transgression. In her conversation with Creon, she attributes her troubles to ἔρωτες, loving (330), in a complaint that will return in the chorus' words later (627–44). At this point the reference to the perils of love is likely to apply to her own feelings as much as Jason's, but once Jason has arrived on stage, he is faced with her direct accusation:

> καινὰ δ' ἐκτήσω λέχη,
> παίδων γεγώτων·
>
> You have taken a new bed although we already had children.
>
> 489–90

She also describes him as 'longing for' or 'desiring' the marriage (bed), ἐρασθῆναι λέχους (491), a description which makes clear the sexual desire she believes Jason is operating under. In contrast to her earlier statements, which described his union to the chorus and Creon simply as a marriage (313, 405), here she makes explicit reference to the marriage bed twice, once as a source of children. Significantly it is this aspect of the accusation which Jason attempts to refute, claiming:

> οὐχ, ᾗ σὺ κνίζῃ, σὸν μὲν ἐχθαίρων λέχος
> καινῆς δὲ νύμφης ἱμέρῳ πεπληγμένος
>
> It was not the thing which provokes you so, that after hating your bed I was struck with longing for the bed of the maiden.
>
> 555–6

He complains again a few lines later that Medea is galled by the issue of sex specifically (568), before making the generalization noted above, that this is a typically blameworthy quality of women.[40] Yet despite his complaints that this is Medea's preoccupation, not his, in referring to his new bride a few lines on, he calls her λέκτρα βασιλέων (594), a term more literally translated as 'bedfellow'.[41] His expression here even echoes Medea's own framing of their divorce as his rejecting a βάρβαρον λέχος (591), suggesting the influence of her words on his.[42] It is therefore perhaps in response to Jason's lingering on these terms that Medea accuses him:

> χώρει· πόθῳ γὰρ τῆς νεοδμήτου κόρης
> αἱρῇ χρονίζων δωμάτων ἐξώπιος.
> νύμφευ'·
>
> Go away: for you are seized with desire for your newly tamed maiden, having spent so much time outside of your house. Go off and be married.
>
> 623–5

Her focus on Jason's desire, πόθος, often sexual in meaning, suggests a more erotic approach to his new bride than Jason has previously admitted (555–66).[43] Jason makes no further response to this accusation, but simply leaves, so that Medea's interpretation of departure is the only motivation suggested.

This comment by Medea is followed by the chorus' ode about Aphrodite's power which takes up her earlier complaint about love, featuring the prayer:

> μηδέ ποτ' ἀμφιλόγους ὀργὰς ἀκόρεστά τε νείκη
> θυμὸν ἐκπλήξασ' ἑτέροις ἐπὶ λέκτροις
> προσβάλοι δεινὰ Κύπρις,
>
> Never, terrible Cypris, dash disputatious anger and unending strife against me,
> when you've struck my heart with desire for another's bed.
>
> 639–41

As Buchan has argued, this ode's fear of excessive lust is likely aimed not at Medea, but Jason, and thus supports the construction of Jason which Medea has put forward, as causing disaster as a result of his sexual desire.[44] The chorus had earlier suggested tentative willingness to accept this idea with their comment, phrased as a conditional but with rather a strong verb chosen:

> εἰ δὲ σὸς πόσις καινὰ λέχη σεβί-
> ζει,
>
> If your husband reveres a new bed[45]
>
> 155–6

Now, no trace of that conditional remains, and the impression is conveyed that in their time on stage together the chorus have come to believe Medea's blame to be an appropriate way to criticize Jason. The chorus also explicitly connect this excessive desire with blame on their own part, since they begin their ode:

> ἔρωτες ὑπὲρ μὲν ἄγαν ἐλθόντες οὐκ **εὐδοξίαν**
> οὐδ' ἀρετὰν παρέδωκαν ἄνδρασιν·
>
> Loves coming in great excess provide to men neither **glory** nor excellence.
>
> 629–30

Their inclusion of the poor reputation which men may earn through 'excessive' love, echoing Medea's earlier complaint to Creon, represents a direct confirmation of the success of Medea's attempted blame. The term ἔρωτες, which they repeat from her earlier usage, carries with it implications of sexual love.[46] The chorus therefore demonstrate how this kind of blame can be effective for damaging a reputation, revealing the success of Medea's methods. In their final ode the chorus demonstrates again how successful these terms of Medea's blame have been, when they claim that Jason has abandoned the marriage bed (λεχέων 999) and instead has another "bedmate" (συνεύνῳ 1001).

Once she has apparently convinced the chorus, Medea next turns to Aegeus, and in her conversation with him draws upon the same discourse of blame. When Aegeus asks why Medea has been set aside, the conversation proceeds:

> Α: πότερον ἐρασθεὶς ἢ σὸν ἐχθαίρων λέχος;
> Μ: μέγαν γ' ἔρωτα· πιστὸς οὐκ ἔφυ φίλοις.
> Α: ἴτω νυν, εἴπερ, ὡς λέγεις, ἐστὶν κακός.
>
> Aegeus: Was it some passion or was he starting to hate your bed?
> Medea: A great passion: he has become unfaithful to his loved ones.
> Aegeus: Well then, if that's the case, as you say, he is wicked!
>
> 697–9

Aegeus introduces the idea that Jason may have developed a new love, and his vocabulary, while more dispassionate than Medea's, discusses Jason's actions in terms of ἐρασθείς and the bed. Medea agrees by blaming Jason for developing a great ἔρωτα, again eschewing the more neutral talk of a marriage for talk of erotic passion. Aegeus immediately accepts Medea's claim and agrees that Jason is therefore base. He directly connects this blameworthy character of Jason's to what Medea has said, marking the success of her criticisms.

The Nurse provides further evidence that this type of blame by Medea has been successful by talking of Jason's new match in explicitly sexual terms:

> γάμοις Ἰάσων βασιλικοῖς εὐνάζεται,
>
> Jason is lying down in a royal marriage.
>
> 18

The use of the verb εὐνάζεται in combination with the more neutral γάμοις draws attention to the sexual side of his relationship, since it refers specifically to Jason and Creon's daughter lying down together. It is also a rather unusual verb in the context of marriage.[47] The tutor too describes Jason as acting 'for the sake of his new marriage [bed]' (εὐνῆς οὕνεκ' 88).[48] In the Nurse's later description of the situation to the chorus, she claims:

> τὸν μὲν γὰρ ἔχει λέκτρα τυράννων
>
> The bed of the royals holds on to him.
>
> 140

The Nurse again describes Jason's interest as being specifically the royal 'bed'. Her use of this blame is not quite the same as the chorus' or Aegeus', since these take their cue from Medea's words on stage, whereas the Nurse speaks before Medea at the start of the play. Nonetheless, given Medea's ability to convince the supportive characters around her that this is the appropriate way to blame Jason, it is reasonable to suggest that the Nurse, as a subordinate if supportive character, also imitates this language from Medea's attitude.

The discourse of women as blameworthy in lust is not the only blame directed at women that Medea draws upon in her criticisms of Jason. She identifies early on a traditional discourse of blame for women as tricky and deceptive, and suited to planning harmful acts in secret:[49]

> . . . πρὸς δὲ καὶ πεφύκαμεν
> γυναῖκες, ἐς μὲν ἔσθλ' ἀμηχανώταται,
> κακῶν δὲ πάντων τέκτονες σοφώταται.
>
> And furthermore we are women by nature, totally resourceless in noble things, but most clever in crafting all kinds of harm.
>
> 407–10

Her contrast between 'noble' deeds and the evils which women can work reflects the decision she has made not to take the 'noble' route and stab Jason and his new wife (378–80), but instead to use poison and stealth (384–5) and is thus intimately bound up with the type of trickery she anticipates for her course of action. Creon makes a similar complaint about a dangerous type of woman which draws upon the same discourse of blame:

> γυνὴ γὰρ ὀξύθυμος, ὡς δ' αὔτως ἀνήρ,
> ῥᾴων φυλάσσειν ἢ σιωπηλὸς σοφή.
>
> For a hot-tempered woman, or a man like that even, is guarded against more easily than a silent, clever woman.
>
> 319–20

Although Medea does attract the description 'clever' (303–5, 539) it is predominantly Jason in the *Medea* who is blamed for having acted in secret, and for being deceptive and unfaithful. Once again Medea establishes this as an appropriate type of blame for him, since the Nurse describes her crying out about his broken oaths (20–3) and his deception, and the audience is shortly treated to the same type of outburst (160–3), with the Nurse's and chorus' acknowledgement (168–70, 206–10). She labels his behaviour in terms of deceit and trickery, describing:

τοῖς Σισυφείοις τοῖσδ' Ἰάσονος γάμοις,

This Sisyphean marriage of Jason.

405

In their *agon* Medea first objects at length to his having broken his oath to her (492–5), then directly argues against his long justification of his actions:

χρῆν σ', εἴπερ ἦσθα μὴ κακός, πείσαντά με
γαμεῖν γάμον τόνδ', ἀλλὰ μὴ σιγῇ φίλων.

It was necessary for you, if you were not to be wicked, to have persuaded me about making this marriage, but not secreted it away from your loved ones.

586–7

Jason ignores her comments about his oaths entirely and dismisses her argument about his acting in secret (588–90). However, in doing so he simultaneously admits that her accusation is valid, since he confirms that he has acted without having told her, and even describes himself as doing so cleverly (548). As a result, Medea's positioning of Jason within this type of blame is effective; she demonstrates that he is the type of person that Creon had warned against, and she herself had identified as generally a dangerous type of woman. Once Aegeus arrives, Medea again makes a similar criticism to Aegeus, although this time more subtly, when Aegeus asks whether Jason approves her exile (707):

λόγῳ μὲν οὐχί, καρτερεῖν δὲ βούλεται.

In what he says, he does not, but he is willing to put up with it!

708

Medea blames Jason for acting deceptively, contrary to what he says, and Aegeus accepts this without comment.

Aegeus is not the only person to accept Medea's blame of Jason as deceptive; he is joined by the chorus. The crisis in poetic blame which the chorus envisage is, after all, triggered by their dismay at Jason's failure to keep a sworn oath (413–14), and they claim:

ἀνδράσι μὲν δόλιαι βουλαί

The thoughts of men are deceptive.

413

Here the chorus take Medea's construction and, just as she and Creon had indicated it as a discourse of blame suitable for women generally, insist on expanding it outwards beyond Jason so that it becomes a discourse of blame that is given authority by its analogy to the established poetic discourses they refer to, and rendered suitable for criticizing men in general.

An overlapping discourse of poetic blame is also indicated by the chorus' complaints about poets:

> μοῦσαι δὲ παλαιγενέων λήξουσ' ἀοιδῶν
> τὰν ἐμὰν ὑμνεῦσαι ἀπιστοσύναν.
>
> The songs of ancient poets will stop singing our faithlessness.
>
> 421–2

The chorus identifies a discourse of blame found in poetry which positions women as faithless, even as they avow that it will no longer be applied to women at all. This avowal is triggered by Medea's fury at and blame for Jason's corresponding faithlessness in his inability to keep to his oaths. The audience's first experience of Medea involves hearing her cries about Jason's oaths:

> ὦ μεγάλα Θέμι καὶ πότνι' Ἄρτεμι,
> λεύσσεθ' ἃ πάσχω, μεγάλοις ὅρκοις
> ἐνδησαμένα τὸν κατάρατον
> πόσιν;
>
> O great Themis and mistress Artemis, do you see the things I suffer, I who have bound my abominable husband with great oaths.
>
> 160–3

The Nurse claims that Medea has been making such statements for some time (20–3, 168–70), and the chorus support this point by echoing what she is saying. Medea's blame for Jason's failure to keep his oath is not only highlighted by her own cries, but also taken up and passed on, primarily in the form of a reported statement, by both the chorus and the Nurse.

Once they confront one another, Medea emphasises his faithless conduct:

> ὅρκων δὲ φρούδη πίστις, οὐδ' ἔχω μαθεῖν
> εἰ θεοὺς νομίζεις τοὺς τότ' οὐκ ἄρχειν ἔτι
> ἢ καινὰ κεῖσθαι θέσμι' ἀνθρώποις τὰ νῦν,
> ἐπεὶ σύνοισθά γ' εἰς ἔμ' οὐκ εὔορκος ὤν.
>
> Trust in your oaths is gone, and I do not understand if you think the gods no longer rule or that now there are new rules laid down for men, since you know that you have not been faithful to your oath to me.
>
> 492–5

Jason's faithlessness is here raised up as so heinous that it can even run counter to established theology, echoing her earlier complaints to the gods that his offence is against them as much as her. She similarly accuses him sarcastically:

θαυμαστὸν δέ σε
ἔχω πόσιν καὶ **πιστὸν** ἡ τάλαιν' ἐγώ,
εἰ φεύξομαί γε γαῖαν ἐκβεβλημένη,

I have in you a wonderful and **faithful** husband, wretched me, if I am to flee the land, thrown out of it!

510–11

In his response, Jason does not even refer to Medea's accusations about oath-breaking, much less successfully refute them. Even when the children are dead, he does not attempt to refute Medea's calling him ψευδόρκου (1392). Medea again uses this type of blame to persuade Aegeus of the identity he should ascribe to Jason, claiming:

πιστὸς οὐκ ἔφυ φίλοις.

He has not been faithful to his loved-ones.

688

Medea here describes Jason's failure to be faithful as something he *is*, rather than a way he has behaved, and Aegeus follows this cue in his response, by claiming that Jason therefore *is* base (699), just as Medea says. His faithlessness, along with his lust, is therefore accepted by Aegeus as being a quality of Jason's identity, established successfully through Medea's blame. Much has been made of the following scene with Aegeus and the oath he swears to protect Medea (731–55), with scholars arguing both that it is meant to demonstrate the oath that took place between Medea and Jason, and that it is meant to contrast with an oath which did not properly take place.[50] However, whether the oaths Jason swore were legitimate to an Athenian audience or not, the preceding discussion between Medea and Aegeus shows that Aegeus accepts her construction of Jason as faithless, in a way that Aegeus proves himself not to be. The effectiveness of this construction once again lies partly on the fact that Medea draws on a traditional discourse of blame for women, to establish it as part of Jason's identity.

A further discourse of blame marked as appropriate for women yet used primarily against Jason in the *Medea* is one directed against women as 'over-emotional'.[51] Medea's use of this discourse in her construction of Jason as blameworthy in these terms is also reflected in their relative statuses as the play progresses. At the start, Medea laments, and Jason argues coolly,[52] whereas by the end of the play, the situation is reversed, and Jason laments while Medea responds coolly. While this type of blame receives less acknowledgement from the characters who interact with Medea, it is demonstrated to be a reasonable criticism of Jason by his own behaviour. Again Medea marks out this type of blame as being appropriate for women, when she comments:

> γυνὴ δὲ θῆλυ κἀπὶ δακρύοις ἔφυ.
>
> A woman is by nature female and prone to tears.
>
> 928

The statement occurs as part of what scholars have called Medea's 'performance' of femininity to persuade Jason, and he accepts it as a legitimate argument immediately.[53]

Yet Medea explicitly ensures that this blame cannot apply to her, by several times connecting her emotion for her children to the idea that she will be laughed at and her reputation damaged, and rejecting it as therefore inappropriate to the identity she wishes to establish.[54] The chorus first suggest that her emotion will prevent her plans, when they ask:

> πῶς δ' ὄμματα προσβαλοῦσα
> τέκνοις ἄδακρυν μοῖραν
> σχήσεις φόνου;
>
> Having turned your eyes to your children how will you bear their fate of murder tearlessly?
>
> 860–2

Medea overcomes that emotional response in her lengthy monologue (1019–80), so that by the time she has heard of the fate of Creon's daughter and is fully resolved on infanticide, she no longer speaks emotionally (1236–50). Once the children are dead, it is not Medea who gives way to grief and proves 'prone to tears', but Jason. He claims ἐμοὶ δὲ τὸν ἐμὸν δαίμον' αἰάζειν πάρα ('mine is a fate to bewail' 1347), and Medea recognizes that she has 'touched his heart' (1360). As the scene goes on, Jason attempts to make her take a greater share in their joint grief (1361), but she does not accept it. He moves from anger into a wish to κλαῦσαι ('mourn' 1377) his children, calls them φίλτατα (1397) and longs to touch them (1399–1400), before begging Medea directly that he might touch them (1402–3). He also cries:

> ἀλλ' ὁπόσον γοῦν πάρα καὶ δύναμαι
> τάδε καὶ **θρηνῶ** κἀπιθεάζω

But groaning as much as I can I call the gods against you and **lament**.

1408–9

His use of the formal word for a lament emphasizes the emotional nature of his appeals. In response Medea remains calm, choosing to insult Jason rather than express any similar mourning,[55] and making her previous claim that women are inclined towards tears more apt for Jason's behaviour than her own.

Thus in her blame against Jason, Medea repeatedly draws on discourses of blame against women as lustful, purveyors of secret tricks, unfaithful and overly emotional. Both she and Jason explicitly acknowledge the usual appropriateness of this blame for positioning women, thus marking the gendered aspects of the blame discourses. As a result, Medea's persuasive blame successfully constructs an identity for Jason which is blameworthy, but also feminized.

Self-praise and identity

The most significant difference between the cases of Jason in the *Medea* and Heracles in the *Trachiniae*, or even Ajax and Heracles in the *Ajax* and *Heracles*, is that none of the characters or chorus around him participate in establishing even briefly any competing discourse of praise for him. There are, however, some attempts by Jason himself to create a competing discourse of praise which establishes a contrasting identity to the blameworthy, female-indexing one which Medea propagates. In fact, Jason attempts to convert the discourse surrounding both Medea's main accusations, that he has betrayed his oaths and marriage to her, and that he has done wrong in marrying again at all, into discourses which position him as the heroic, reasonable male leader of the household.

In his longest speech in answer to Medea's accusation, Jason manages to praise himself for the speech itself, claiming that he will have to be a good speaker to counter her (522–4), and creating an image of himself as captain of a ship, which has Argonautic echoes.[56] Then, rather than allowing Medea's help (476–89) as being the key factor of his success, Jason instead argues that he was helped by a god:

ἐγὼ δ᾽, ἐπειδὴ καὶ λίαν πυργοῖς χάριν,
Κύπριν νομίζω τῆς ἐμῆς ναυκληρίας
σώτειραν εἶναι θεῶν τε κἀνθρώπων μόνην.

> But I, since you exaggerate your kindness so much, I think that Cypris alone of gods and men was my saviour on the voyage.
>
> 526–8

The image is intended to raise Jason's profile as a heroic figure, through divine association rather than the association Medea had claimed with herself.[57] Given Medea's blame for Jason's passions, the association with Aphrodite may, however, be somewhat unfortunate for him. At the same time, Jason attempts to re-narrate his major heroic achievements, although, as Mossman has pointed out, he fails to strike an epic tone in doing so, making use instead of sophistic-style rhetoric.[58] Finally, in speaking of their earlier history, Jason adds a curious detail of praise for his own treatment of Medea:

> πάντες δέ σ' ᾔσθοντ' οὖσαν Ἕλληνες σοφὴν
> καὶ δόξαν ἔσχες· εἰ δὲ γῆς ἐπ' ἐσχάτοις
> ὅροισιν ᾤκεις, οὐκ ἂν ἦν λόγος σέθεν.
>
> All the Greeks know that you are clever and you have a reputation: if you were still living on the farthest boundaries of the land, there would be no story about you.
>
> 539–41

The comment is followed immediately by Jason's own statement placing fame and a good reputation beyond wealth or talent in his estimation (542–4). Jason's statement is somewhat undermined by the claim Medea has already made that her reputation for cleverness does not benefit her, but rather leads to suspicion:

> οὐ νῦν με πρῶτον ἀλλὰ πολλάκις, Κρέον,
> ἔβλαψε δόξα μεγάλα τ' εἴργασται κακά
> ...
> σοφὴ γὰρ οὖσα, τοῖς μέν εἰμ' ἐπίφθονος
> ...
> σὺ δ' αὖ φοβῇ με·
>
> Not for me for the first time but often, Creon, has my reputation hit me greatly and made harm for me ... for being clever, I am envied by some ... and you fear me.
>
> 293–4, 303, 309

Medea has thus already argued that the conclusion Jason draws is incorrect. While he may have had a major part in the exploits which formed her wider reputation, given the harmful effects of that reputation, this is hardly to his credit. Medea has undermined Jason's discourse of self-praise before he even gives it, making it significantly less effective as an alternative to her own discourse of blame.

In the same way, Jason attempts to defend himself from her blame about the new marriage by instead arguing that he deserves praise as an ideal husband and father:

> ἃ δ' ἐς γάμους μοι βασιλικοὺς ὠνείδισας,
> ἐν τῷδε δείξω πρῶτα μὲν σοφὸς γεγώς,
> ἔπειτα σώφρων, εἶτα σοὶ μέγας φίλος
> καὶ παισὶ τοῖς ἐμοῖσιν
>
> But for the things about which you blamed me for my royal marriage, in this thing I shall show first that I have been clever, then sensible, since I have been a great friend to you and the children.
>
> 547–50

Alongside the claims to have been demonstrably σοφὸς and σώφρων, his assertion that he has been a 'great friend' to Medea and his children taps into the heroic code of values found throughout tragedy.[59] The praise he awards himself covers a range of positive descriptions, including some of those (e.g. cleverness) which Medea has also included among her own self-praise, in her confrontation with Creon. But Jason's attempt to position himself within this discourse, against Medea's blame, proves flatly unsuccessful. The chorus acknowledge his skilful speaking, but refuse to concede any other point, instead arguing that he has acted οὐ δίκαια (578), and no one else accepts any aspect of Jason's self-praise. The contrast with the success of Medea's discourses of blame is distinct. Medea's blame was readily accepted as reasonable and as establishing a consistent identity for Jason not only by the supportive chorus and Nurse, but also by the disinterested Aegeus. In his own comment, Jason correctly identifies Medea's speech against him as blame (ὠνείδισας), implicitly recognizing the technique which will prove so successful against him, even while he fails to counteract it.

The failure of Jason's self-praise to convince described above, and his failure to establish a credible alternative identity, is intrinsically bound up in one of the events he attempts to praise himself for: his introduction of Medea into a land where she can establish a praiseworthy reputation (539–44). This introduction of Medea into a context where renown and discourses of praise and blame are influential has in fact been Jason's own undoing since it is precisely these discourses which Medea deploys against him. Medea's speech and song, such as her early laments, are shown throughout the play to be persuasive,[60] and her constructions of Jason's identity through female-indexed discourses of blame are the ones that endure, against his own attempts to position himself instead through self-praise.[61] Faced with Jason's attempts to position Medea herself as a blameworthy woman, Medea not only appropriates traditional blame discourses to position him within them but simultaneously makes use of her awareness of these traditional praise and blame discourses to construct a heroic, masculine identity for herself, in her descriptions of their shared past.[62] She claims multiple times to have saved Jason (476, 482), and more specifically, that she was the one who killed the dragon that Jason had to defeat to get the golden fleece (480–2).[63] Her descriptions, unlike Jason's, are fully epic in tone.[64] Once Medea has received sanctuary from Aegeus and confirmed her plans, she also claims that she will be:

> νῦν καλλίνικοι τῶν ἐμῶν ἐχθρῶν
>
> Now glorious in victory over my enemies.
>
> 765

The use of the term καλλίνικος positions her within a discourse of praise usually appropriate to male heroes (primarily Heracles), and is a particularly unusual term to be claimed by a woman.[65] Moreover, the Nurse has already signalled that Medea has been aiming to identify herself in such a way since before the play began (45), suggesting a long association with the concept as part of her self-identity.[66] Significantly, the Nurse has indicated that no one else will be able to sing a victory *song* if they clash with Medea, signalling the term's epinician echoes.[67] Medea's self-praise therefore does not only involve praise for her own exploits in helping Jason, she also invokes a term which has a masculine poetic praise context associated.

Medea's concern with reputation and mockery from her enemies is itself perhaps part of constructing a masculine, heroic identity.[68] It also demonstrates a further problem with Jason's attempt to praise himself for bringing her a good reputation, since she now is angry with the likelihood of his harming that reputation.[69] Just as Medea begins to reveal her plot (364–409), she expresses the importance to her of avoiding the 'laughter of enemies', a 'heroic' spur to action in tragedy, and one which is clearly focused outward. She recognizes the chance of being laughed at as a risk to her first plan (384), so that it is instrumental in the choice she makes to proceed with drugs. The situation she envisages is self-generated, and the mockery she expects does not materialize, but she nonetheless treats it as an essential aspect of judging how she should act:[70]

> ὁρᾷς ἃ πάσχεις; οὐ γέλωτα δεῖ σ' ὀφλεῖν
>
> Do you see what you are suffering? It is necessary for you not to incur mockery.
>
> 404

She spurs herself on to killing her children by imagining the laughter of her enemies (797), and famously expressing the desire to be thought:

> βαρεῖαν ἐχθροῖς καὶ φίλοισιν εὐμενῆ·
> τῶν γὰρ τοιούτων εὐκλεέστατος βίος.
>
> Hurtful to enemies, and kind to friends: for such people have the most glorious lives.
>
> 809–10

Her desired image has been identified as coming extremely close to the code of ethics identified by Blundell as central to the Sophoclean hero.[71] Medea also invokes the poetic praise discourses which result in awarded *kleos*, itself a heroic spur to action, by claiming that people who behave as she intends to have εὐκλεέστατος lives. The statement almost becomes a form of pre-emptive self-praise, since she anticipates joining the ranks of these praiseworthy individuals. However, the discourse she appropriates is one which is usually applied not to women, but to men, so that Medea is again attempting to position herself within masculine praise discourses.[72] Medea returns to the same spur on the very point of the infanticide, crying,

> βούλομαι γέλωτ' ὀφλεῖν
> ἐχθροὺς μεθεῖσα τοὺς ἐμοὺς ἀζημίους;
> τολμητέον τάδ';
>
> Do I want to incur mockery, and let my enemies go unpunished? Must I endure that?
>
> 1049–50

This reiteration of the importance of reputation to her is enough to drive her to the deed. As is often the case with this type of statement, Medea's behaviour is therefore driven by the type of blame she fears to attract.[73] However, it is also part of a sustained approach to praise and blame which she develops to construct her identity as one which is masculine, heroic and fears blame in the same way a male hero might, and seeks praise in the same terms.[74]

Medea's self-praise is therefore significantly more effective than Jason's, partly as it is combined with the awareness of her attempts to establish her masculine, heroic identity. As a result, she strengthens her powerful presence on stage. Her success in constructing an unfavourable and diminished identity for Jason can thus be seen not only as a result of his failure to maintain an alternative subject position, but also as due to her successful construction of herself as someone who belongs in this context of masculine praise and blame. It is striking that when Jason does attempt to enter into praising and blaming Medea's actions, in rather formal and explicitly gendered terms, he ends up incorrectly praising what will turn out to be an entirely deceptive attitude from her when she feigns a wish for reconciliation, and claiming not to blame her earlier anger, when in fact precisely that anger will prove his undoing:

> αἰνῶ, γύναι, τάδ', οὐδ' ἐκεῖνα μέμφομαι·
>
> I approve this, woman, and I do not blame that [previous attitude].
>
> 908

Unlike Medea, Jason is incapable of identifying what should be persuasively praised or blamed, and so is unable to use either discourse against Medea just as he is unable to prevent her using them against himself.

Conclusion

Medea succeeds in her destructive positioning of Jason within discourses of blame typically marked as female not only through her facility in drawing on these discourses, but also through her skill at constructing a powerful identity for herself where he fails. Just as in the situations of Ajax and Heracles (twice), where praiseworthy, masculine identities come under siege from competing discourses of praise or blame, the deployment of these discourses of blame against Jason is also combined with an end result of physical violence. This violence simultaneously has an effect on Jason's identity which mirrors the effect caused by Medea's use of blame discourses. Medea's blame does not focus on Jason as a father, nor does she position him solely as a 'bad husband'; instead by drawing on discourses of blame traditionally used for women she avoids constructing him as a husband at all. It is partly these roles that he therefore attempts to reconstruct in his competing discourse of self-praise, as discussed above, when he claims that he has acted as a good husband and father. Not only does Jason prove discursively unable to establish himself as father and husband, but by acting violently against her children, Medea destroys any possibility of these roles.[75] Jason is removed not only linguistically but physically through her violence into the subject position Medea held at the start of the play. Where she was separated from friends and family, from her spouse, and facing potential separation from her children, now Jason has experienced the same, through the deaths of his father-in-law and new wife, and Medea's refusal even to enable him to perform the role of father in burying his dead children (1377).[76] Medea retains her hold over their (dead) children and, with her journey to Athens already arranged, has secured future connections with a new Greek ruler, just as Jason had at the start of the play.[77] Jason's acceptance of Medea's repeated refusal to allow him to touch the children (1399–1404), is signalled by Jason's declaration of an even more substantial linguistic distancing from his identity as father, since he cries:

οὓς μήποτ' ἐγὼ φύσας ὄφελον
πρὸς σοῦ φθιμένους ἐπιδέσθαι.

I really wish I had never begotten them, to see them destroyed by you.

1413–14

Jason's wish to have never been a father is the final thing he says on stage, and represents the pinnacle of Medea's successful transformation of his identity. Jason makes a further unsuccessful attempt to disassociate Medea from the identity she has chosen to use throughout the play to engage the chorus, that of 'woman like them':

οὐκ ἔστιν ἥτις τοῦτ' ἂν Ἑλληνὶς γυνὴ
ἔτλη ποθ' . . .
λέαιναν, οὐ γυναῖκα, τῆς Τυρσηνίδος
Σκύλλης ἔχουσαν ἀγριωτέραν φύσιν.

There is no Greek woman who would have dared this . . . you are a lioness, not a woman, and have a nature more savage than that of Tuscan Skylla.

1339–43

However, Greek women in the stories known to both the chorus and the audience *do* sometimes kill their children.[78] The description of Medea as a lioness also sets up a problematic association, since it was precisely Medea's being like a lioness which led the Nurse to fear violence in the first scene of the play (187–9) As a result, while the identification may be right, the use Jason attempts to make of it in his accusation fails, partly because its premise is incorrectly founded on a claim to tradition. Unlike Medea's successful understanding of how and when to manipulate existing discourses to cast blame, Jason makes an attempt to cast blame on Medea which only points to its inaccuracy. Conversely, Medea demonstrates one final return to many of her previously successful discourses, leaving these firmly embedded in the story told about Jason: he is again motivated by the bed (1367) and an oath-breaker, making use of a term ψευδόρκου (1392) which is found only here in tragedy, and likely to be striking to the audience's ear.[79]

Medea's destruction of Jason therefore contains two major elements. The first, and the one which scholarship and audiences have reasonably been focused on as the most dramatic, is the violence which physically destroys his identities as father, bridegroom and new son-in-law. However, this is combined with the effect enabled through her blaming speech, in which she draws repeatedly on discourses of blame marked by her and Jason himself as more appropriate to women, to construct an unflattering identity for him. Jason's praiseworthy, masculine identities are undermined by her effective use of this blame, to the extent that the chorus, Nurse, and Aegeus all accept Medea's construction of his blameworthy, feminised identity. Jason's own attempts to counteract this by self-praise fail, partly due to Medea's faculty in the same area, and he is left by the end of the play only with the blameworthy, feminized identity Medea has created for him, while she – having successfully constructed herself as a heroic, masculine worthy opponent to him – triumphs.

Medea's manipulation of praise and blame discourses is in some ways the most successful of the cases discussed in terms of active power for the individual characters involved in transmitting praise or blame, beyond its persuasive effects. Even if it comes at the cost of her children, her technique does not result in her own death, as Deianira's actions do. Unlike Deianira, Medea chooses to go beyond simple rejection of discourses of praise or blame constructed for Jason and herself, and participates in establishing alternative discourses for them both, ensuring that her own identity is established securely and successfully as Jason's is destroyed.

Of course even if such destruction is intentional, the results achieved are not generally positive; the loss of her children for herself, and the wider social destruction caused prevent any triumphalist reading of the *Medea.* As a result, it can be argued that the tragedy persistently represents the participation of female characters in generating praise and blame discourses as dangerous, troubling, and problematic for society, just as the *Suppliant Women* did, although in this play that danger has a much more directly destructive effect. Simultaneously, the *Medea* presents an explicit recognition of the power which poetry has in this regard; with the characters' metapoetic comments on poetry's influence here, their own situation is marked as increasingly problematic for an audience experiencing their participation in precisely such poetry.

Conclusion

We began with Clytemnestra's (insincere) claim that to praise or blame her would be 'all the same'. However, as this study has shown, Clytemnestra's avowed bravado in the *Agamemnon* clearly does not represent the attitude of many of the other characters of Greek tragedy, even if we were to take it seriously as an expression of her own view. Instead, time and time again, the characters and choruses of tragedy are represented as keenly interested in discourses of praise and blame. Heroic figures such as Neoptolemus, Philoctetes, Heracles, Ajax and Jason appear in this new dramatic genre and immediately begin repeating patterns of behaviour from their earlier poetic traditions: seeking after poetic praise and to avoid blame, to gain *kleos*. Characters and choruses across tragedy, from a wide spectrum of social groups and identities, also find themselves implicated as the new poets, generating these discourses of praise and blame. Often, in the process of producing these discourses, characters and choruses draw on existing genres of poetry, including epinician, epic and the laments or *threnoi* which are a core component of tragedy. As such, tragedy takes on and redevelops not only the lyric and epic genres in which such discourses appear, but the production of poetic praise and blame itself, defining itself as a genre which continues this socially significant role.

However, tragedy does not provide a safe home for the production of these discourses of praise and blame. The lack of a single authorial or narratorial voice, along with tragedy's multivocality, means that when praise and blame discourses are produced in this genre, they are open to challenge by another speaker, including other speakers with access to their own discourses of poetic praise and blame, as a result of tragedy's capacity to absorb multiple genres. Tragedy sets up a situation ripe with conflict for the context of its production of praise and blame discourses, and it is that conflict which we see played out across the plays considered in this study.

For some of the examples considered, this conflict is between expectations, including traditional poetic expectations, and the reality of the discourse being produced. Ajax and Heracles, in their attempts to reframe the praise discourses around them, come into conflict with wider expectations of suitable praise. This issue is not limited to figures in the middle of their heroic careers, but is shown also to be key in influencing Neoptolemus into taking what will eventually be a destructive path. Even more significant for tragedy's exploration of how praise and blame could (or could not) be managed is the prominent role of women as speakers in tragedy. As this discussion has shown, where women become involved in the generation or denial of discourses of praise and blame, this can have just as significant an effect on the heroes whose spouses or relatives they are as those heroes' own behaviour.

In the *Suppliant Women*, the access of both female characters and choruses to poetic praise has the result of perpetuating dangerous discourses which lead to repeated violence, and leaves the Athenian hero Theseus in an unusual position: unpraised. Evadne also demonstrates the some of the most extremely destructive (in this case self-destructive) aspects of tragic wives' involvement in praise and blame discourses. In the *Trachiniae*, again the access of women to these discourses and the resistance of his wife, Deianira, to praising Heracles, become significant negative elements. Deianira's influence over speech and silence, in connection with the female chorus of the play, as in the *Suppliant Women*, amplifies the hostile environment created for praise for Heracles. The female influence, coming from Heracles' wife, is also personal, as in the *Suppliant Women*, adding to its efficacy. Finally, Medea demonstrates how a wife's access to the kind of mastery over praise and blame speech demonstrated by figures such as Philoctetes can be wholly destructive, in her mastery of Jason.

Rather than arguing for itself as the new genre or type of speaker to take on production of democratic praise and blame discourses, therefore, tragedy's multivocal nature demonstrates some of the most dangerous conflicts which can arise from the handling of these discourses. Tragedy's gendered approach to this element also aligns it with the Periclean funeral speech, in demonstrating that women should not be a part of perpetuating such discourses. In appreciating this key element of poetry and how tragedy stages it, we can therefore understand both tragedy's critical contribution to a live poetic and literary question of democratic Athens, how to praise and blame, and how tragedy situates itself in the wider tradition of poetic genres. The new readings that arise from appreciating the significances of this element to individual tragedies shed new light both on tragedy's handling of the heroic figures of tragedy and of its handling of gender, particularly in adding a further destructive element to its depiction of women's speech.

Although this study has focused on a selection of particularly interesting examples, many of the issues explored here are prominent in other tragedies; in Aeschylus' *Agamemnon* itself, for example, or in the fragments of Euripides, where we find the topic of what should or should not be praised brought explicitly to the attention of the audience.[1] Greek tragedy is almost as concerned with what we say about one another, and how we say it, as what we do to one another. As a result, tragedy proves itself once again a unique combination of both a quintessentially fifth-century Athenian genre, and a continuation of the archaic poetic tradition from which it had developed.

Notes

Introduction

1 Texts from the Loeb editions of the tragedies; translations are my own.
2 This sung address, in which the chorus ask how to avoid 'over-shooting' their reverent address to Agamemnon, is reminiscent of the Pindaric technique of comparing the selection of the appropriate extent of praise to the shooting of a projectile, as with the arrow of *Nem.* 6.26–8, or *Ol.* 2.83, 89–90. On the Pindaric resonances of the use of this image in the *Agamemnon*, see Steiner (2010): 25–6.
3 For more on the metapoetic and genre-establishing aspects of Pindar's criticism here, see Farrell (2003): 386–8; Brown (2006).
4 Detienne (1996): 45–8. See similarly on the distribution of praise and blame as a social function of Greek poetry Gentili (1988): 107–14.
5 Pindar himself acknowledges the central role of Homer in establishing *kleos* through his praise (or lack thereof) in *Isthm.* 4.37–42, *Nem.* 7.20–3. Nagy (1979); Nagy (1990), esp. 146–98 where Nagy has argued for praise songs as a basis for the development of epic as a genre. As Lardinois (1995): 180–1 points out, the ancient *Vitae* of Homer represent him as an expert in distributing praise and blame. See also Martin (1989): 102–10 on praise poetics as a central part of the epic narrative, and a key aspect of Nestor's tradition-oriented speech. For more on this aspect of Pindaric poetry see Kurke (1991), esp. 73–95. On the *Homeric Hymns* and especially the *Homeric Hymn to Aphrodite* as participating in this traditional function, see Bergren (1989).
6 On *kleos* and its establishment through praise and blame poetry, see Schmitt (1967): 67–8; Nagy (1979): 174–211; Segal (1989): 336–7; Goldhill (1991): 69–72 on *kleos* and on the developing relationship between poet and *kleos* more generally, 69–166; Segal (1994): 90, 133–5; Detienne (1996): 46–7; Dué (2006): 41.
7 Pind. *Nem.* 7.61–3, *Isthm.* 4.30, 7.17–19, Bacchyl. 3.90–5, 13.199–204. See further on Pindar's opposition of praise and blame as choices for the poet, Race (1983): 105–8, and on the wider poetic opposition of praise and blame, Nagy (1979): 222–42; Detienne: (1996): 47.
8 Herington (1985). See also Bagordo (2003): 23–4 on the indispensability of the lyric tradition to tragedy, Nagy (1990): 400–13; Rodighiero (2012): 7 and Nagy (2020): 98–100 on the likely connections in performance context between epic, lyric and tragedy in classical Athens.

9 Swift (2010). The more tightly focused Rodighiero (2012) is a valuable study of lyric interaction in Sophocles' choruses. Similarly the recent volume by Andújar, Coward and Hadjimichael (2019) explores a wide range of uses of lyric in Greek tragedy. Dué (2006) explores how tragedy draws on older song traditions in presenting the laments of captive women; and Steiner (2010) and Carey (2012) explore examples of use of the epinician in theatre, particularly tragedy. See Rutherford (2001): 108–26 for a discussion of tragedy's use of the paean; Rutherford (2012): 45–7 on tragic appropriation of ritual song, and 48–52 on lyric genres more generally. Nooter (2012a) examines the 'lyricism' of the language of Sophocles' heroes. For a more general overview of this development in the study of tragedy, see Gagné and Hopman (2013): 18–25.

10 On the number of actors in tragedy and its development, see Pickard-Cambridge et al. (1968): 131–49 and for a useful warning against the overschematic account given by ancient sources, Csapo and Slater (2009): 221–4.

11 Segal (1992), esp. 85–92 and on tragedy's lack of the poet's voice in comparison to existing poetic genres, Segal (1989): 347–52. On the multiple voices of tragedy, see McClure (1989): 5–6, and its resulting appeal to the multiple perspectives of its audience, Allan and Kelly (2013). On the strength of the narratorial voice in epinician praise poetry, see Rawles (2011): 147 and in archaic and classical poetry generally, but lack thereof in drama, Morrison (2012): 2, 36–102.

12 Segal (1986): 78.

13 Carey (2013): 159–61, whose focus is the comedic chorus' ability to move between the civic choral voice and the more distanced voice like that of the tragic chorus which results from their persistent fictionalized identities.

14 Calame (2005a): 104–6, 117–18.

15 *Il.* 24.723–75.

16 On the female laments for Hector as opposition to the heroic ethos of the *Iliad*, see Murnaghan (1999), Derderian (2000): 40–3 and Perkell (2008). For how this epic scene provides a model for the alternative voices of later genres such as tragedy, see Easterling (1991).

17 Derderian (2000): 44–51 points to how female lament is subordinated to the poem's narrative of epic *kleos*.

18 *Frogs* 948–9 where Euripides claims specifically to have made the γυνή (wife or married woman), παρθένος (younger, unmarried woman or girl) and γραῦς (old woman) speak.

19 On tragedy's 'plurality of voices' allowing for the possible appearance of the voice of historical women, see Goff (2004): 294–5.

20 On the idea that this speech represents the limited status of women in Athens, see Rusten (1989), esp. 176–7. More recently, scholars have moved away from considering this a generalized statement regarding all women: Hardwick (1993)

discusses their relevance to the necessity of moderating the lament to follow; Tyrrell and Bennett (1999) argue that Pericles' comment is intended to prevent women raising their voices and shaming their husbands or male relatives for Pericles' policy of abandoning the countryside.

21 As in the *Suda* K 2087, which claims that she ἐνίκησε δὲ πεντάκις ὡς λόγος Πίνδαρον – 'defeated Pindar five times, according to the story', or the story in Plut. *glor. Athen.* 4. 347f–348a which presents Corinna as criticizing Pindar's compositions, and Pindar creating a work as a direct response to those criticisms. See similarly on Corinna defeating Pindar in some competition Ael. *V.H.* 13.25, Paus. 9. 22.3. Although these references specify that Corinna was a lyric poet, they do not indicate any genre or context in which these competitions happened. However, fr 664a *PMG*: ἰώνει δ' εἱρώων ἀρετὰς / χεἰρωάδων ('But I for my part sing the excellences of heroes and heroines') is suggestive of glorifying, *kleos*-granting poetry of praise, along with the direct and apparently repeated associations between Corinna and Pindar both in the tradition noted here and in the fragments of her poetry, as at fr. 664a *PMG*. The debate about the date of Corinna's work is ongoing; see Collins (2006): 19–20. Collins (2006), esp. 23–32, argues that Corinna's poetry shows signs of a self-fashioning and deployment of myth which bears comparison to the works of Pindar; and Skinner (1983): 10–12 that fr. 665 *PMG* and its invocation to Terpsichore sets Corinna's poetry within the same genre as Pindar's. Larmour (2005): 39–58 argues that Corinna associates herself with Pindar's epinicians primarily to challenge some of the conventions of the genre with a more female-oriented view, presenting her work as directly competitive with Pindar's.

22 O'Higgins (2003): 90–1. Herodotus (2.135.6) also describes Sappho as producing blame poetry against Rhodopis.

23 As in Alcman fr.1 *PMG*, see McClure (1999a): 55; and Calame (2001): 60–2 on the Daphnephoria at Thebes providing a context for female choral praise both of a male leader and the leading girl of the chorus.

24 In her funeral speech for Hector, Helen will repeat the claim that both the men and women of Troy participate in blaming her for her marriage to Paris *Il.* 24.768–71. Helen's own manipulation of self-blame throughout the *Iliad* is notable from a female speaker; see further Ebbott (1999) and Blondell (2010).

25 Apollod. 1.5.1, Plut. *Vit. Lyc.* 14.3, Hdt. 5.83.3, Apollon. 4.1717–28, Paus. 7.27.10. On festivals featuring female mocking choruses, see McClure (1999a): 47–52, Calame (2001): 138–9 and Kowalzig (2004): 50; on the Spartan context, see Detienne (1996): 45.

26 Tyrrell and Bennett (1999) refer to the Homeric passage (43–4) in relation to precisely what type of speech from women Pericles aims to 'mute'.

27 Goldhill (1991), esp. 109–66. See also Vernant (1979): 1371–4 for the argument that even before this time, the question of how and who to praise had been of central importance in the developing poetic traditions after Homeric epic.

28 Steiner (1999). See also Most (1994) for the argument that Simonides' 'Scopas Ode' also concerns itself with the question of how best to praise in its social context.
29 Diod. Sic. 11.11.6. Rawles (2013): 181.
30 Steiner (1999): 388–91
31 Loraux (2006): 22–3.
32 Loraux (1981): 3 notes the parallel function of the *epitaphios* in preserving the dead and the city in memory, against forgetfulness and oblivion.
33 Loraux (2006): 89.
34 How political or even Athenian a genre was tragedy is debated; Carter (2011) is a comprehensive foray into this subject. For a good overview of the various potential positions involved, see Griffith and Carter (2011): 2–7, 10–11; see also Swift (2010): 43–60 for a discussion of the 'elite' material of older choral genres and relationship to the 'democratic values' of tragedy.
35 Eudoxus apparently made the accusation (DK80 A21).
36 DK82 A25. Aristotle in *Rh.* 1418a32–7 describes Gorgias making use of epideictic oratory for extensive praise of mythological heroes.
37 Isocrates *Encomium of Helen* (Isoc. 10) provides another example of the same practice.
38 On Gorgias' *epitaphios* see Loraux (2006): 284–90.
39 Quoted in Quintilian 3 4.11, in his discussion of the style called *epideictic* rhetoric by Aristotle (*Rh.* 1538b) and framed as suitable for distributing praise and blame.
40 632a. For more on the role of praise and blame and its poetic connections in the *Laws*, see Morgan (2013).
41 On Herodotus, see Nagy (1990) ch.10ff; on Thucydides, Hornblower (2004).
42 Maslov (2015): 44–6.
43 On how lyric poets define their genres through interaction with predecessors, see e.g. Steiner (2005): 347; Spelman (2018): 84–5.
44 Weiss (2020).
45 Cook (2021).
46 This possibility for interaction forms part of Antiphanes' complaint that tragedy is accordingly easier to compose than comedy (fr. 189).
47 Finglass (2011): 42–3 identifies some key problems with use of the word 'hero' to describe the (usually male) protagonists of tragedy.
48 Vernant and Vidal-Naquet (1988): 33–8. Langerwerf and Ryan (2010): 12–16 provide a very good overview of some of the approaches taken to the idea of 'tragic heroes', and of how far the concept maps on to earlier concepts of the hero. Knox (1964) is one of the most influential types of this scholarship, examining what makes a Sophoclean 'hero'. Similarly, although with a very different set of qualities for the 'heroic', Ahrensdorf (2009) examines how far Sophoclean 'heroes' match up to the qualities of rationalism and piety valued in Athenian political philosophy. There is a great deal of

similar work on individual tragedies, such as Kokkini (2010) on the *Alcestis,* or on the *Andromache* Allan (2000): 96–137 (partly responding to Whitman (1974): 124). The view of tragedy as exploring how epic heroes suit later realities is prevalent in scholarship on Sophocles' *Ajax*; see for example Knox (1961): 22–3, Winnington-Ingram (1980): 59 and Segal (1981): 150. This focus on the 'hero' in tragedy often also involves discussion of heroes as those who receive cult, and works such as Garland (1992) and Seaford (1994) have been productive discussions of this kind.

49 On tragedy's use of 'stylised generic markers' to refer to other types of poetry, see Carey (1991): 18. Rodighiero (2012): 7–11 gives a valuable discussion of the difficulties of identifying such generic interaction given the flexibility of lyric genres, but points to formal constants, syntax, linguistic and metric effects as all enabling such comparisons between lyric and tragedy. Bagordo (2003), esp. 23–35, cautions against reading examples of direct allusion between tragedy and individual works of lyric when reflections of more generic poetic styles or ideas may be a better explanation for seeming correspondences: the latter is my focus in this study.

50 Swift (2010): 29–31 describes this type of allusion as medium- or high-level generic interaction, and shows (31) how it is rooted in the widespread familiarity with choral traditions that is a key feature of Greek society. Swift also provides thorough overviews of this kind of allusion for the paean (61–103) and epinician (104–72).

51 See further Rutherford (2001): 111–12. As my focus is primarily on praise and blame awarded or denied to the 'heroic' male mortals of tragedy, this volume does not discuss tragedies such as the *Ion* which develop engagements with the lyric genres suitable for praising gods, such as the paean (on the distinctions between these genres see Färber (1936): 46–66).

52 For the way Greek thought set these two terms in opposition, see Nagy (1979): 222–4. As Carey (2018) notes, however, the two genres are not always quite as distinct as Pindar would like to present in this comparison with Archilochus.

53 Carey (2009): 149–50.

54 Bowie (2001).

55 Carey (2009): 151.

56 A common problem for Greek poetic genres, cf. Swift (2010): 8–11; Foster, Kurke and Weiss (2019). In relation to iambos, see Carey (2009): 149–50.

57 The connection between iambic and comedy which Aristotle makes at *Poetics* 1449a reflects some of their shared content, such as obscenity.

58 Swift (2010): 120.

59 As above.

60 *Andr.* 773, *Hec.* 1225, *El.* 1084, *Tro.* 386, *Or.* 1151, *IA* 357, 567, 1383, 1504, 1531, and *Hel.* 135, 845, 941, 999, 1603, where it is connected explicitly to the questioning of the poetic tradition of the Trojan War which takes place throughout the play, on which see Meltzer (1994).

61 *Phoen.* 576. As the Theban epics are lost it is difficult to trace connections between the *Phoenissae* and epic poetry, although there are at least clear signs of engagement with Stesichorus' *Thebais* – see Mastronarde (1994): 17–30 who sees especially Euripides' treatment of the sons of Oedipus' dispute with their father as demonstrating some close connections with the epic *Thebaid*, or Swift (2020): 347–8.

62 Eur. *Bacch.* 972, *Ion* 1588. There are also appearances in fr. 1051 *TrGF*, and two reconstructed appearances at *Hypsipyle* frs. 12.145 and 286, in connection with the Argonauts, another epic tale.

63 *Aj.* 769, *El.* 60, 985, *Phil.* 251, 1347 – the only non-Trojan appearance is in *Ant.* 502. There is one appearance in fragmentary tragedy (938 *TrGF*) where the play is not identifiable, although *kleos* appears in connection with the *agon* and πόνων language of heroic labours.

64 There are also three uses in fragmentary tragedy, two of which appear in Trojan-focused plays: fr. 99 from the *Europa*, fr. 139 from the *Myrmidons*, and one use whose context cannot be identified: fr. 315 *TrGF*.

65 Winnington-Ingram (1960): 34–5.

66 Lee (1986): 311–12.

67 Twelve out of twenty uses in extant Sophoclean tragedy (*Aj.* 216, 596, 861, *El.* 8, 160, 300, 681, 694, 1086, 1177, *Phil.* 575, 654). In fragmentary tragedy, *kleinos* appears twice (frs. 323, 959 *TrGF*), both times in reference to places.

68 *Pers.* 474, with two appearances in the possibly un-Aeschylean *PV.* 834 and 872.

69 See further McClay (2021): 111 and n23.

70 For the importance of this vocabulary, see Nagy (1979): 222–3; Detienne (1996): 45–9.

71 On this as a fifth-century Athenian attitude, see Gregory (1991): 52–5.

72 Nagy (1979): 223. μῶμος does not appear in extant tragedy, but does feature twice in the Sophoclean fragments, fr. 257 *TrGF* in the generalized claim that 'blame does not attach to justified hurry', and apparently as the title of a Satyr drama featuring Momos, the personification of blame (which is a particularly sad loss for the present study!). The verb form μωμάομαι appears only once, at Aesch. *Ag.* 277.

73 LSJ s.v.

74 See further Chapter 6 on how this tradition of generalized blame directed against women is manipulated by Medea in Euripides' *Medea*.

75 McClure (1999a), Mossman (2001); Griffith (2001); Roisman (2004).

1 Praise and the Construction of a Hero: Neoptolemus in the *Philoctetes*

1 Nagy (1996): 60–3. According to Pindar, epic could also establish insufficient praise for one hero or even blame, by prioritizing celebration for another, as is the case for Ajax who suffers by comparison with Odysseus in Homer: see *Nem.* 7.20–3.

2 According to Proclus, in the *Little Iliad* Odysseus and Diomedes sailed to Lemnos to retrieve Philoctetes. Aeschylus' account may only have featured Odysseus, and Euripides' has Diomedes along with Odysseus sent to retrieve Philoctetes (Dio *Or.* 52§14).

3 Neoptolemus' arrival at Troy and his receipt of the arms of Achilles appeared in the *Little Iliad*; his defeat of Eurypylos is described in the *Odyssey* as well as the *Little Iliad* (11.519–21). His role in the sack is narrated at *Od.* 11.523–32, and Stesichorus seems to have included him among the Greeks in the horse (Eu-*Od.* 11.522, p. 1698). His slaughter of Priam, Agenor and Eioneus were all included in the *Little Iliad* according to Pausanias (10.25–2#7), and fr. 29–30 West also credits him with the death of Astyanax. Neoptolemus' deeds seem to have been repeated in the *Iliou Persis*, although in this account of Astanyax's death, Odysseus is the culprit (fr. 5 *PEG*). Neoptolemus' involvement in the sacrifice of Polyxena appeared in Ibycus (fr. 307 *PMG*), and may have been narrated in the *Little Iliad* or the *Iliou Persis* (or both) – the summary of neither includes this detail, but the summary of the *Iliou Persis* in particular is compressed.

4 *Paean* 6.105–20, in which Neoptolemus is killed by Apollo as revenge for his murder of Priam at the altar, and *Nem.* 7.33–49, which does not mention Priam's death and has been seen by some scholars as an attempt to mitigate the negative impression made by the version that connected Neoptolemus and Priam (Roisman (2005): 38).

5 Sophocles' *Eurypylos* will have had some role for Neoptolemus as Eurypylos' slayer, with the duel between them likely described in fr. 210, although none of the surviving fragments feature Neoptolemus as a character. His *Peleus* did feature Neoptolemus, late in his career, with Neoptolemus likely acting to restore Peleus' kingdom after the Trojan War.

6 The likely dating of the *Andromache* (see Storey (2016): 123–4) to 427–425 puts it earlier than the *Philoctetes*. Sophocles' *Hermione* may have included Neoptolemus' death without the plot by Orestes.

7 There is some debate as to whether Neoptolemus in the *Philoctetes* has been to Troy, been welcomed there, and then come to Lemnos, or whether Odysseus and he are on their way from Skyros having not yet gone to Troy at all; the issue arises based on how much of Neoptolemus' mendacious tale to Philoctetes about the arms of Achilles should be read as a distortion of true events, and how much it is entirely fictional. Calder (1971): 159, claims that the entire course of events laid out by Neoptolemus is a lie, and he has not yet been to Troy. Pucci (2003): 200–1 and Kyriakou (2011): 282–3 argue for some elements of truth in Neoptolemus' story, based partly on the language used. Budelmann (2000): 100–6 suggests that the smoothness in Neoptolemus' language does not necessarily imply truth about aspects of the story, but rather greater facility in bending myth when speaking about himself. Roisman (2001): 43–4 suggests that Neoptolemus' account is reasonably

accurate but adjusted to spare Odysseus. Even if Neoptolemus *has* been to Troy before the *Philoctetes*, the only events there seem to have been a brief welcome and possible transfer of or unresolved quarrel over his father's arms, so that neither acceptance nor rejection of Neoptolemus' story substantially changes the position of the *Philoctetes* – the play remains an account of one of Neoptolemus' first significant deeds or campaigns as part of the war at Troy.

8 In the *Little Iliad* the fetching of Neoptolemus came after that of Philoctetes, and these two events, combined with the stealing of the Palladion, form a series of adventures involving Odysseus and sometimes Diomedes as protagonists.

9 Carden (1974): 94. Fuqua (1976): 43–5 plausibly argues for the *Skyrioi* being performed before the *Philoctetes*, and exerting an influence on its content. Davidson (2001): 38 sees the introduction of Neoptolemus, a young man, as part of a pattern in Sophocles' plays of exploring the conflict of generations – Diomedes would not present the same opportunities.

10 Odysseus calls Neoptolemus παῖ in his speech laying out Neoptolemus' task (79), and the chorus address Neoptolemus as τέκνον in their first address to him (141). Philoctetes calls Neoptolemus either παῖ or τέκνον over fifty times, which Roisman (2005): 90–1 connects to his parental role towards Neoptolemus.

11 Vidal-Naquet (1988) even read the *Philoctetes* as depicting the formal ritual associated with young male Athenians' growing up to adulthood, the *ephebeia*. For problems with this reading, see Gregory (2018b): 168–9. Lada-Richards (1998) demonstrates however that a reading which takes account of the *Philoctetes*' potential ritual context, even if it is not strictly related to the *ephebeia*, can be extremely fruitful.

12 E.g. Craik (1980); Carlevale (2000); Gregory (2018b): 165–90.

13 E.g. Roisman (1997). Goff (2010): 224–6 connects the transmission of arms from father to son in the *Philoctetes* with the establishment of heroic identity, and argues that the alienation of his father's weapons leaves Neoptolemus in this play searching to construct a father figure from the other characters in the play.

14 Kosak (2006), in a persuasive account, represents Neoptolemus' 'choice' as one between contrasting models of masculinity.

15 Roisman (1997): 128.

16 On the *Ajax* and this type of reading, see further Chapter 2: 50 and n20.

17 Roisman (2005): 60. Schein (2006): 132–3 argues that the *Philoctetes* nuances the contrast between 'heroic types', in representing Odysseus' use of persuasion, deception and μῆτις as associated with force or violence, rather than contrasting with it. See also Billings (2021): 132–3 who notes parallels between this play's treatment of the two figures and the sophistic syncrises of mythological heroes.

18 Austin (2011): 168 does briefly point to the growing association between 'reverence' and Neoptolemus in the play as part of his becoming a *cult* hero.

19 See further on *kleos* and poetry, Introduction: 2, 5–8.

20 Buccheri (2016): 3 also demonstrates the connection between living up to paternal identity and developing fame and a glorious reputation for the heroes in Homeric epic, so that the question of how far Neoptolemus is like Achilles is itself connected with the kind of reputation Neoptolemus will establish for himself.

21 Allan (2011) rightly acknowledges the force of *kleos* in motivating Neoptolemus' actions, but does not connect this to the awareness of poetic praise and blame with which this motivation is repeatedly connected throughout the play.

22 On 'best of the Achaeans', see Nagy (1979), and for the concept in Sophocles' *Ajax*, see Chapter 2. In the *Iliad*, κράτιστος is applied as a description only to those heroes reaching the peak of prowess in fighting, and particularly past heroes. Nestor describes the former generation of heroes and their opponents by the term (1.266–7, 7.155), Glaucus attaches it to a battle of Bellerephon (6.185), and Phoenix similarly uses it to describe men in the time of Meleager (9.558). It is more rarely found describing men living at the time of the *Iliad* – Diomedes is described by Helenus as proving himself κράτιστος at the peak of his *aristeia* (6.98), and Achilles when fighting in the river earns the term via a simile (21.253). Other uses of the term apply to Zeus (8.17, 20.243). Odysseus' use of the description for Achilles here therefore immortalizes Achilles as the superlative, now past generation, just as Nestor's and Phoenix's stories in the *Iliad* commemorated men greater than those living now. In Pindar's epinician, κράτιστος appears again as a description of Zeus (*Ol.* 14.14), as a description of Ajax and Achilles in connection with the awarding of the arms of Achilles, in an ode which will be discussed further below (*Nem.* 7.39–40), and twice connected to ideas of inherited excellence and benefits (*Ol.* 9.100, *Pyth.* 11.58). It is not a commonly occurring term, and seems to have maintained some of the significant connotations it bore from the *Iliad*. It is also relatively rare in tragedy, appearing perhaps only once in Aeschylus (*PV.* 216), nine times in Euripides, and ten in Sophocles. (In comparison, forms of μέγιστος appear 130 times in tragedy.)

23 See Wells (2009): 77–8 on naming the father in Pindar's epinician as part of the ἀγγελία, and Rose (1992): 141–84 on the importance of inherited excellence to Pindar's odes. On epic fathers, see further Chapter 2, n18. cf. Phillippo (1995): 358–9 on the significance of the patronymics here.

24 Deicke (1999): 177 notes a persistent theme in the difference between seeming and being which Odysseus' words make use of here, also represented in Neoptolemus looking like Achilles (356–8), yet, given the uncertainties about his φύσις, not *being* like Achilles.

25 Gregory (2018b): 174 connects this to Odysseus' awareness of a 'heroic education'; he expects that Neoptolemus will have been educated to appreciate such an argument. See further 180 for the contemporary, Athenian, and sophistic flavour of

Odysseus' claim that it is 'sweet to gain victory'. Carlevale (2000): 34 also points out how cynical and superficial Odysseus' argument is here. Similarly Segal (1995): 99–100 relates this comment to a persistent cynicism in Odysseus' approach to piety and its language throughout the *Philoctetes*.

26 On the role of deception in the play and its contemporary resonances, see Hesk (2000): 188–201. As Heath (1999): 142–4 points out, Neoptolemus' position on deception here goes further than Achilles' in the *Iliad*. Achilles shows distaste for the deception of friends, but does not object to ambush or the deception of enemies. Neoptolemus' extreme view may therefore be a mark of immaturity. Roisman (1997): 160–1 points to consistent signs of immaturity in the behaviour of Neoptolemus.

27 No such concern about a reputation for violence is expressed. Schein (2006): 135–6 notes that Neoptolemus' choice of violence over deception in proposing how to handle Philoctetes (90–2) originally seems to connect him with Achilles, before his willingness to pursue profit undoes such an identification.

28 On promises of praise as a method of persuasion in tragedy, see also Chapter 4.

29 Achilles is described as ἐσθλός at *Il.* 11.664 and 16.837, where it is treated as an inalienable quality. His undying *kleos* is similarly described at *Od.* 24.94.

30 Conversely in the similar persuasion scene at the start of the *Antigone*, Antigone promises Ismene that she can reveal her **nature** (δείξεις. . . πέφυκας 37–8) as either noble or base by acting as Antigone wants her to, and follows this up with a claim that Ismene is *being* the type of person that suits her (71) by refusing to help. In Sophocles' *Electra*, Electra assures Chrysothemis that if she aids her, Chrysothemis will be called free in terms that match how she is by nature, ὥσπερ ἐξέφυς (969–70), emphasizing the match between the praise she will earn and the reality. Chrysothemis' excellence is also described as a fact which will be proven by their actions (971–2). Odysseus' and Neoptolemus' emphasis on what Neoptolemus will be called, has the verb in this passive form repeated three times in thirty-four lines, more frequently than any other example of the phrase's use in Sophocles, demonstrating the idea's importance to the discussion and to both participants. On the distinction made in Sophocles between the positive things someone may be called in comparison to the reality, see further Chapter 5.

31 See Davidson (2001): 30–1; Roisman (2005): 43; Allan (2011): 3–5; Gregory (2018b): 173–4. Heath (1999): 154–5 notes that Neoptolemus' role as subordinate, with orders to follow, must also be considered as a motivating factor raised by the play in presenting his dilemma, and Vidal-Naquet (1988): 170–1 points to Neoptolemus' responsibility to obey authority as part of his discussion of the ephebic elements of Neoptolemus' task. Blundell (1989): 184–6 demonstrates that Neoptolemus' role is cast by Odysseus as part of the moral imperative to 'help friends' in his society.

32 Podlecki (1966): 238 notes the importance of *kleos* in Neoptolemus' decision, although he rightly points out that Odysseus' simultaneous disavowal of interest in his own reputation makes him an unlikely proponent of this motivation.

33 Loraux (2006): 147 describes γέρας as 'no less important than *kleos*' in the Homeric hero's life. The connection between a γέρας won by difficulty and praise can also be seen in Simonides fr. 582 *PMG* where the *geras* for what is 'danger-free' is only silence, the lack of praise.

34 Pind. *Nem.* 7.61–3, *Pyth.* 52–6. See also Introduction: 1–2 on this opposition in Greek poetry.

35 There is some debate as to the chorus' behaviour throughout this scene, particularly in relation to the ode they sing at 674–29; see Visvardi (2015): 193–5 for a good discussion of the debate, and scholars' attempts to solve the issue through staging of the scene.

36 On ἀρετή as a Homeric quality of heroic valour, see Wróblewski (1972), who also connects it to the capacity to be considered 'ἄριστος', thus suggesting a connection again here between Philoctetes' potential praise for Neoptolemus and the Iliadic praise discourse of 'best'. See similarly Parks (2014): 28. On the connection between songs (ὕμνους) and the endurance of excellence (ἀρετή), see also Pind. *Isthm.* 2.44–5, which associates the reperformance of Pindar's epinician with the capacity of excellence to live on (Clear (2013): 33–4), or *Isthm.* 4.37–40 on the claim that Homer has immortalized Ajax's ἀρετὰν through the 'immortal voice' (40) of ἐπέων (39). Similarly a fragment of Bacchylides claims that it is the poet's 'skill and truth' which confirm ἀρετή, fr. 14 SM.

37 Pucci (1994): 37–8 and Gregory (2018b): 189–90 (although with some reasonable reservations) approve Neoptolemus' apparent willingness to sacrifice such glory when he finally agrees to take Philoctetes home at the end of the play. Allan (2011): 19–20 notes, however, that seeking glory continues to be a persistent concern in Neoptolemus' decision-making, and argues that Neoptolemus does not initially believe that he *would* be sacrificing his glory in reuniting with Philoctetes, since he believes that he can still convince Philoctetes to go to Troy with him.

38 Hose (2009): 30–1 argues that Philoctetes' use of blame against Odysseus and the Greek leaders marks him as a victim of 'peer-rejection' and is a key aspect of understanding his situation and status.

39 In *Nem.* 7.61–3 Pindar indicates that his presence as a praise poet will 'ward off' blame by bringing *kleos*, and in *Pyth.* 2.52–3 he indicates that his poetic activity involves avoiding κακαγοριᾶν, presenting the two as close alternatives. For similar examples, see *Pyth.* 1.82–5, *Nem.* 4.93, 8.32–9, *Ol.* 2.90–8 also Bacchyl. 13.201–2.

40 Detienne (1996): 47–9 ; see further Pind. *Pyth.* 2.53, *Nem.* 7.61–3.

41 Rehm (2006); Austin (2011): 140–1.

42 Rose (1976): 68; Perysinakis (1992): 90–1; Austin (2011): 165; also see Schein (2013) ad loc. for the many Homeric allusions throughout this speech. Kamerbeek

(1980) ad 927–8 connects Philoctetes' description of Neoptolemus as fire to Iliadic descriptions of Achilles, and Schein (2013) ad 927 suggests a particularly Odyssean allusion in the association of πῦρ with πανουργία. Rehm (2006): 95–6 further explores the allusions that tie Neoptolemus to both Achilles and Odysseus in Philoctetes' fire imagery, and in his descriptions of Neoptolemus' deception.

43 On flyting generally, see Martin (1989), Hesk (2006) and Parks (2014). On the poetic qualities of flyting, see Mackie (1996): 66–74 and on flyting as blame poetry 82–3.

44 On the use of rhetorical questions as a regular feature of flyting, see Martin (1989): 69–70 and Hesk (2006): 12. Examples appear at *Il.* 1.122–3, 134–5 and 150–1 in the quarrel between Achilles and Agamemnon, 4.242, 340 and 371 in Agamemnon's reproaches to the Greek commanders, 5.633–4 from Tlepolemus to Sarpedon, 6.145–6 from Glaucus to Diomedes, in an example which averts rather than leading to combat, and 20.178–81 in Achilles' address to Aeneas.

45 Parks (2014); 105 and see examples at *Il.* 2.225, 8.161, 20.200. The combination of this kind of identification with a term of abuse, as here, is also discussed by Parks.

46 On references to past significant speech in flyting, see Martin (1989): 72. Also see Nestor at *Il.* 2.349 or Achilles at 16.200 for significant examples.

47 Minchin (2007): 27–31.

48 Rehm (2006): 104–6. The descriptions of the landscape, and terms used of Neoptolemus by Philoctetes as the invective progresses, such as ἐπαισχύνῃ, are also epic in flavour.

49 Griffin (1986): 40. σχέτλιε is used once in the *Odyssey* by the narrator, at *Od.* 21.28.

50 Parks (2014): 110–12 where he notes the example of Sarpedon to Hector at *Il.* 5.472–92.

51 On the connections between Sophocles' *Philoctetes* and *Electra,* see Schein (1982): 71–8, and for Electra's use of lament aggressively to blame Clytemnestra, see Foley (2001): 151–60. For the connections between lament and blame speech in the *Medea*, see Chapter 6 in this volume. In the *Trojan Women*, Andromache's lament for Astyanax on hearing of his fate features some exceptionally strong blame against the Greeks (esp. 764–5) – see further Dué (2006): 147–8. On the Iliadic laments by Andromache, Hecuba and Helen as indicating reproach both of Hector and blame for the wider 'heroic code' of the *Iliad*, see Perkell (2008), and Minchin (2007): 30–1. For Helen herself as exemplifying the connections between lament and blame speech in the *Iliad*, see Martin (2003): 126 and esp. n25. For the wider connections between lament and blame see McClure (1999a): 46–7, Holst-Warhaft (2002): 61–81 and Alexiou (2002): 182–4; on the connections in Greek poetic thought between lamentation and wrath, see Loraux (1998): 43–56. Lament also has significant capacity for the inclusion of poetic praise of the dead, for which see Swift (2010): 313–14 and Chapter 4.

52 Nooter (2012): 214–15 describes Philoctetes' ability to 'sound like a poet' as a 'strength' in comparison to his physical weakness.

53 Nooter (2012): 136 points out, however, that Philoctetes is *not* alone here, and his speech does have a significant impact on its audience – the chorus and Neoptolemus – despite his lack of direct address.

54 Craik (1980): 248 sees the language of teaching and learning as part of a pattern which establishes a master/pupil relationship between Odysseus and Neoptolemus, connecting Odysseus to the contemporary sophists.

55 See Nooter (2012): 136–7 for an interesting discussion of the increasingly effective 'apostrophic force' of Philoctetes' language at this point in the play.

56 Cairns (1993): 16–17 and esp. 55–60.

57 There may be a specific allusion here to Odysseus' praise of Achilles in the underworld (*Od.*11.482–5); see Schein (2013) ad 1312–13.

58 *Phil.* 112–15.

59 Neoptolemus himself makes this point at 839–42. However, given the apparent confusion over the terms of the oracle in the play, there is some doubt as to how much Neoptolemus knows. Segal (1995): 103–4 argues that Neoptolemus (alone) recognizes the 'divine qualities' of the bow and its importance to fulfilling the oracle. Calder (1971): 162–3 conversely claims that both Neoptolemus and Odysseus see that both the bow and Philoctetes must be brought to Troy, and any apparent difference between their positions is only a matter of the various methods they pursue in trying to deceive Philoctetes. For further views, see Allan (2011): 11–12.

60 Deicke (1999): 174 points to signs that the trust or friendship between them is not fully restored by the return of the bow, making it less likely that Neoptolemus can convince Philoctetes by any means at this stage.

61 Neoptolemus also attempts to blame Philoctetes' for his behaviour, but has no more success there – Minadeo (1993): 103 is right to point to the ironies present in Neoptolemus' attempts at blame, which seem applicable to himself as much as to Philoctetes.

62 Davidson (1995); Schein (2006).

63 Whitby (1996): 38.

64 For similarities between Philoctetes and Odysseus, see Greengard (1987): 64–5, O'Higgins (1991): 47 and Davidson (1995): 26–9. For Philoctetes and Achilles, see Perysinakis (1994): 382, Michelakis (2002): 164 and Roisman (2005): 57; for Philoctetes as similar to both, see Schein (2006): 129–30. For Achilles and Odysseus as exemplars of the epic praise poetry, see Nagy (1979): 26–42, and Perysinakis (1994): 388 for Sophocles combining both traditions in the *Philoctetes.*

65 The story of Philoctetes' exile and suffering *was* extant in poetry for the contemporary Athenian audience (*Il.* 2.716–25, Pind. *Pyth.* 1.50–5, Bacchyl. fr.7 SM), so that his expectation of *kleos* would not be seen by them as unreasonable. Worman

(2000): 22 argues that the vehemence of Neoptolemus' denial of Philoctetes' *kleos* points to its falsity for the audience, but this claim increases Philoctetes' isolation nonetheless.

66 Soph. *OT* 318.

67 Detienne (1996): 47. See Pind. *Ol.* 2.15–22, 10.91–5, *Isthm.* 7.17–19 and fr. 121 SM.

68 For an interesting argument that this risk of oblivion assimilates Philoctetes on Lemnos to the dead, see O'Higgins (1991): 44–6.

69 Schein (2013) ad 575. Hose (2009): 32 points to this moment as Philoctetes' regaining of his heroic identity.

70 Hose (2009): 31–2 notes that Philoctetes' exclusion from the Greek group seems to have caused a loss of identity, which is then regained through the mini-tragedy 'staged' by Neoptolemus. It is notable that it is Philoctetes who remembers and values Neoptolemus' own 'epic tale' (Scodel (2009): 52) about the loss of his arms, and reminds Neoptolemus about it at 1362–7.

71 Allen-Hornblower (2013): 5–19 is a good discussion of the use of sound by Sophocles to depict Philoctetes' pain and suffering. See also Nooter (2012a): 125–7.

72 There may also be a further acknowledgement of Philoctetes' use of lament in line 1401, if Pearson's (1924) reading ἅλις γάρ μοι τεθρήνηται γόοις is preferred to Lloyd-Jones' ἅλις γάρ μοι τεθρύληται λόγος. Given the manuscript issues here, however, it is difficult to be certain of this line, despite its attractions for furthering the presentation of Philoctetes as explicitly self-aware and self-conscious in his use of lament.

73 Nooter (2012): 126–7 also notes the poetic sense of the chorus' description here.

74 Vidal-Naquet (1988): 175.

75 Nooter (2012a): 145–6.

76 E.g. *Nem.* 7.77–9, *Pyth.* 8.57. In *Isthm.* 5.7–8 crowns bring *kleos* to the victor, which is then also associated with sung praises (13). Pindar's fr. 76 SM with its description of Athens as ἰοστέφανοι, violet-crowned and celebrated in song, ἀοίδιμοι, was apparently recognizable enough to be parodied in Arist. *Ach.* 622–40. See further Kurke (1991): 92. In tragedy, this language describes poetic celebration especially associated with epinician-flavoured scenes, e.g. Eur. *HF* 355–6 or Eur. *El.* 860–5. Bacchylides describes 'Eucleia' herself, goddess of good *kleos*, as 'garland-loving' (φιλοστεφ[άνωι 13.184), demonstrating a clear association between *kleos* and garlands, see further Nagy (2011): 198–200.

77 See Finglass (2006): 218 on the bow as a 'special object', worthy of a heroic quest to obtain it, and Mueller (2015): 39–40 on the bow as a 'haptic actor', which reshapes the tragic plot through its own influence. Fletcher (2013): 199–210 explores the 'life' on stage of the bow, with valuable attention to its changing status and functions throughout the play. Buccheri (2016): 2 and n4 connects the bow, as heroic object, to Neoptolemus' attempt to establish his heroic identity as Achilles' son.

78 See Poster (2006): 7–8 for the 'epical' nature of the terms evoked here, and the likely familiarity of this wordplay for a fifth-century audience.

79 The description of Achilles' loss of Briseis as the deprivation of a γέρας occurs throughout his conversation with Agamemnon and thereafter (*Il.* 1.118–87, 1.356, etc). Although the awarding of Achilles' arms to Ajax is not narrated fully in extant epic poetry, Philoctetes in this play describes Achilles' arms as a γέρας which have been taken from Neoptolemus (1365).

80 Mueller (2015): 38–9 notes the epic bow's ability to tie Neoptolemus into a line of succession with Philoctetes and Heracles through its 'mythic biography'. Fletcher (2013), esp. 207–10, describes the bow as a 'haunted' prop, in that it brings Heracles to the stage in the mind of the audience, before apparently inflicting Heracles' life and sufferings on its new owner, Philoctetes, and finally causing the appearance of Heracles himself to redirect the bow's future activity.

81 Pucci (1994): 31–44 demonstrates the epic tone of the epiphany.

82 Heracles' words are described as μῦθοι (1410, 1447), which from Homer onwards denote a more authoritative speech than λόγοι. See Martin (1989): 10–18 and, for the use of the term here, Pucci (1994): 36–7. Easterling (1978): 31 argues for Philoctetes' final acceptance of his fate here as 'the ultimate and paradoxical success of persuasion', whereas Podlecki (1966): 245 argues that Philoctetes 'obeys' the new type of divine speech here, despite not being persuaded.

83 This praise is also often connected to his suffering rather than solely his accomplishments, e.g. Pind. fr. 291 SM, where Heracles' glory is the result of what he has endured from Hera, and *Nem.* 1.69–72. See Galinsky (1972): 23–40.

84 The celebration of Philoctetes' endurance in Pind. *Pyth.* 1 (50–60) suggests that the audience may have been hearing here a promise of forthcoming praise which, for them, existed.

85 Pucci (1994): 36–7; Segal (1995): 105; Schein (2006): 138, who notes also the potentially negative echoes of the *Doloneia* here; Perysinakis (1994): 387.

86 The connection established here is not entirely positive – Heracles' warning about the behaviour to be encouraged at Troy (1440–4) also appears to connect Neoptolemus to a wider poetic tradition about his violence and disgrace. See Goff (2010): 226; Gregory (2018b): 189–90.

87 Ns. 62–4 above. For similarities between Neoptolemus and Telemachus, see Whitby (1996).

88 See further Chapter 2.

89 The *Little Iliad* suggests that it was **praise** which won Odysseus the arms – this tradition may be what Pindar is drawing on. See further Chapter 2: n8.

90 Philoctetes is not mentioned in *Nem.* 7, or connected to this account of Neoptolemus' death, but does appear favourably elsewhere in Pindar, e.g. *Pyth.* 1.50–60.

91 According to the *Aethiopis*, Thersites has died by the time Philoctetes arrives in Troy, and we are aware of no tradition of a dispute or even any contact between them during the gathering of troops or journey to Troy.

92 *Aethiopis* fr. 68 *PEG*. Whether or not Neoptolemus is lying here has caused much distress in scholarship, see especially Calder (1971): 159, who supports Huxley (1967) in arguing that Neoptolemus is lying. Ryzman (1991): 37 n4 cites this tale as evidence for Neoptolemus' enthusiasm for his deception. Kyriakou (2011): 252–3 argues conversely that this claim demonstrates Neoptolemus' ignorance about the heroic (epic) past, and his own past. Roberts (1989): 169 reasonably suggests that the audience should not be expected to have been certain either of Neoptolemus' truth or falsity here, rather they should experience a 'dislocation' and loss of certainty in their own knowledge.

93 Austin (2011): 37 and 94, who sees the reference to Thersites as designed to connect Philoctetes to 'our' *Iliad* as the main source for his epic past. The connection has further ramifications for other characters in the *Philoctetes*: O'Higgins (1991): 43 argues that Philoctetes' suggested parallels between Thersites and Odysseus are supported by Odysseus' behaviour in the play, such that this brief reference adds to his credit.

94 On νεῖκος as blame language rather than just 'quarrelling' in Homer, see Nagy (2021), and compare Nestor at *Il.* 10.114–18.

95 Nagy (1979): 259–64.

96 On this role of Nestor's, see further Martin (1989): 105–9 and on Thersites as a contrasting or opposing figure to Nestor 109–13. On Nestor and *kleos*, see Dickson (1993).

97 See n25 above for comparisons between Odysseus and the sophists. Detienne (1996): 116–20 connects the sophists to a development of a new attitude to speech and effective speech in Greek thought, away from those held among the poets. See also Loraux (2006): 291–2 for prose, including that used by sophists such as Gorgias, as slowly replacing and being held as distinct from poetic speech in classical Athens.

2 The Best of the Rest: Ajax Thwarted

1 See further Introduction: 1–2.

2 As we have already seen (Chapter 1: esp. 21, 31–2), the same discourse also occurs repeatedly as a promised form of praise for Neoptolemus in the *Philoctetes*, in connection with his father.

3 Moore (1994): 66.

4 Moore (1994): 67–9; Wade (1994) noted the tendency of violence to break out among Colombian men as a result of a failure to sustain two competing subject

positions. Niehaus (2012) has also argued that this same process is at the root of narratives of male suicides in the South African Lowveld. It is important to acknowledge the different cultural contexts present between such case studies and the tragic world depicted in the *Ajax*. Nonetheless, the similarities in the pattern of male individuals failing to sustain particular subject positions, undergoing 'thwarting' (as Moore describes it), and turning to external violence and suicide, makes these useful comparative studies.

5 Such as Taplin (1978): 28, Machin (1989): 31–59, Garvie (1998): 12–14, 196–7, Burian (2013): 80–1, Finglass (2011): 62–3 and Carter (2013): 140.

6 The poet's introduction of the leaders of the full Greek set of leaders in the Catalogue of the Ships is capped with a request for the Muses to tell the poet who is ἄριστος among the leaders (760–2), and both these and the best horses (763) are identified. In the *Iliad* Ajax himself is identified as holding this position at the time, but with the caveat that he in fact takes second place to Achilles when the latter is present and fighting: ἀνδρῶν αὖ μέγ' ἄριστος ἔην Τελαμώνιος Αἴας, / ὄφρ' Ἀχιλεὺς μένιεν· ὁ γὰρ πολὺ φέρτατος ἦεν (768–9).

7 Nagy (1979).

8 In the *Little Iliad*, the awarding of the arms is the result of a paean awarded to Odysseus but not Ajax, so that the giving of the prize is tied closely to the awarding of formal praise. See further Detienne (1996): 47 n50.

9 cf. *Il* 2.768. In contrast to those such as Winnington-Ingram (1980): 14–15, who argues that this boast showed Ajax's 'megalomaniac pride', since he makes the claim of being like no other without the Iliadic exception for Achilles, Rose (1995): 68 and n24 and Garvie (1998) ad loc., have both argued that Ajax's boast is not unusual for an epic hero, as it claims that he is 'uniquely great' rather than better than others such as Achilles. Hesk (2003): 59–60 is useful on this debate and adds the interesting caveat that Ajax may still be mad at the point of making this claim.

10 Michelakis (2002): 145–6 argues that by omitting Achilles, Ajax's boasting at 421–6 threatens Achilles with oblivion, as Ajax attempts to replace him. As O'Higgins argues (1989 esp. 49–50), Ajax also insists on representing his relationship with Hector in such a way that he effectively substitutes himself for Achilles in that regard.

11 Nagy (1979): 2§3 notes the centrality of *kleos* (established through praise poetry: and which brings εὔκλεια §3n5) to Achilles' claim to be the 'best' of the Achaeans, so that Ajax's invocation of the same terms in relation to Telamon carries similar connotations.

12 As at *Il.* 1.244, 412, 16.274 – each time Achilles contrasts his identity as 'best' with the lack of honour shown to him by Agamemnon, just as Ajax here brings out the contrast between Telamon's identity as 'best' and the dishonour Ajax faces from the Argives. Nagy (1979): 26–35 discusses the only places where this formulation in the *Iliad*

describes individuals other than Achilles, and points out that several times, individuals called 'best' are themselves substitutes for Achilles during his absence. At *Il.* 11.784 Nestor claims that Achilles himself aims to be 'best' partly due to an instruction from Peleus to Achilles, thus presenting a further parallel with Ajax's concerns here.

13 See further Chapter 1: 35 and n76.

14 Starobinski (1974): 49–50 also notes how Ajax's failure to gain the arms of Achilles has broken the succession of honour from generation to generation.

15 Goff (2010).

16 Goff (2010): 226–7. See also on the significance of the failure to inherit or pass on weapons as 'external markers of glory' for Ajax's sense of disinheritance Mueller (2015): 135.

17 Rosenbloom (2001): 116 recognizes that the arms are a symbol for 'shared essence of Ajax and Achilles as heroes of *kratos* and of *kleos*'.

18 At *Il.* 5.800–13 Athena reproaches Diomedes for not living up to the example of his father, and specifically for not being 'ἐοικότα' to him. Agamemnon berates Diomedes for the same fault at 4.401–2. Similar examples showing a warrior son's concern with living up to his father's standards are found at *Il.* 6.206–11 (Glaucus), 11.683 (Nestor), 6.476–81 (Astyanax, expressed here by the father, Hector), and 11.785–90 (Patroclus, reproached by Nestor). On the father as 'internalized other', see Williams (1993) esp. on Ajax 84–6 and for Ajax specifically Hesk (2003): 61.

19 Campbell (1993). Bowra (2001): 378–80 connects this pair of songs to the Peisistratid era, suggesting that this connection of comparisons between Telamon, Ajax and Achilles is rather older than Sophocles' Ajax's raising of it.

20 Nagy (1979): 45–9.

21 E.g. Segal (1995): 6, 17 and Langerwerf and Ryan (2010): 7. Finglass (2011): 44–5 usefully discusses some problems with this model; see also Hesk (2003): 104–24.

22 Hirsch (2014): 219 connects Homeric epithets to the 'praise names' of heroes in poetic genres from other cultures.

23 It is very similar to an image found in Bacchyl. *Ep.* 4.16–30.

24 Whitman (1958): 138–44; Schein (1984): 128–9, 138.

25 Goff (2010): 228–30.

26 On the Iliadic resonances, see Mueller (2015): 135–8. Finglass (2011): 143 notes the epic resonances of the early description of Ajax in the play as σακεσφόρῳ (19).

27 Goff (2010): 230–1 on Eurysakes' name and the complicated relations between the shield, father and son.

28 Mueller (2015): 140–2.

29 Allan (2005): 1–16. The contest for Achilles' arms featured in the *Ajax* also prevents their ever being passed on to his own heir, Neoptolemus (made the root of his persuasion of Philoctetes in the *Philoctetes,* (359–81) although the claims Neoptolemus makes here are false (Chapter 1)). Thus Ajax's concern with the

transmission of his shield to Eurysakes is antithetical to the situation of Achilles' arms. See Goff (2010): 224–6.

30 Although cf. Sorum (1986): 364 on Achilles elsewhere in the *Iliad* as aggressor, contrasted with Ajax as defender.

31 Griffiths (2020): 125–6 argues that this inheritance is tarnished by Ajax's loss 'of [his] role as a great hero' so that Eurysakes' name and inheritance are empty here.

32 Sorum (1986): 366 on the sailors as victims of Ajax's heroic desire. Blundell (1989): 75–90, esp. 86–8, on how Ajax's suicide not only removes protection from but results in injuring his *philoi*.

33 On veiling, see Llewellyn-Jones (2003) esp. 299 on the *Ajax*; also Lee (2015): 154–60. Cairns (2002) esp. 75 notes the many emotional reasons for veiling in Greek culture (shame, grief and anger, among others), and argues for its use by men in emotional extremes as part of placing themselves 'in a feminized predicament' (76–7). Ajax is covered by a woman using her own cloak (thus an explicitly female garment), as he cannot accomplish the task for himself. Cairns (2002): 81–2 notes that veiling can be a response to a challenge or threat to 'one's social self [or] public identity', an idea which is especially fitting to the covering of Ajax once his identity has come under threat by his failure to sustain it through praise. Finglass (2009) provides the most compelling argument for rejecting any possibility bar that Tecmessa is covering Ajax in her own cloak.

34 O'Higgins (1989): 48. See also Rosenbloom (2001): 122, who claims that Ajax 'naively' assumes that heroic deeds will speak for themselves, and is thus destroyed when he finds they do not. Rosenbloom is correct to note the importance of speech in confirming the validity of heroic deeds in the *Ajax*, but his claim about Ajax's own failure to recognize this element is unfair – Ajax fully grasps that his deeds will not speak for themselves, and his complaint in this play (later taken up in a slightly different way by Teucer in his defence) centres around the fact that others do not speak of them, or praise them, in the way that Ajax believes they should.

35 9.115–56, 9.300–6, 19.74–144.

36 Heath and OKell (2007): 365–6. Finglass (2011): 38–9 suggests instead that this detail may have appeared in the epic tradition, and Sophocles is 'reaching back to an epic precedent ignored by his tragic predecessor'. If so, this would still involve some element of surprise and additional negativity to the portrayal of Ajax for Sophocles' audience, even if the effect were not *as* surprising as Heath and OKell suggest.

37 The familiar formula appears again here, too: Ajax is κράτιστον Ἀχιλέος ἄτερ μάχᾳ 'best apart from Achilles in battle' (27).

38 Köhnken (1971): 102 argues that that Pindar's claim here is that Ajax failed to receive his due recognition for being the 'stärkster' warrior (strongest).

39 On the second reading as more likely, see McNeal (1978): 151–2, although Willcock (1995): 79 disagrees.

40 Fearn (2007): 121–43.

41 Pindar describes Ajax as 'strongest after Achilles' (27–8), again demonstrating the strength of the poetic tradition against which Ajax is fighting in the *Ajax*.

42 Nagy (2017); Nagy (2021).

43 On the ongoing interest from archaic and classical poets and artists in reconfiguring the *kleos* of individual heroes, from Homer onwards, see also now Stelow (2020) on Menelaus, although she does not consider tragedy's role in such a reconfiguration.

44 cf. *Ant.* 50. There are also two instances in fragmentary Sophoclean plays at frs. 658.3, and 188.1 *TrGF.*

45 See further Finglass (2011): 182.

46 Hesk (2003): 28 and 29 on the further Homeric elements in the vulture simile; see also 164–71.

47 Cairns (2006): 103–8.

48 Starobinski (1974): 23.

49 As we shall see in Chapter 5 on the *Trachiniae*, the transition into becoming 'unspeakable' recurs as a problem when the praise discourse for heroes dissolves.

50 Nooter (2012a): 31–55.

51 See Chapter 1: 25–7, for the similar possibility of 'boasting' over Philoctetes' bow experienced by Neoptolemus, based on a stronger foundation.

52 Rodighiero (2012): 27 also reasonably suggests that the chorus' words here could have drawn attention to a lively choreography.

53 Whether this reference should be taken as extradramatic has divided commentators: Finglass (2011): 347 sees it solely as a reference to the usual practice of celebration and worship of the gods, whereas Henrichs (1994): 70 includes it among examples of a playwright 'empowering' the choral performers to acknowledge their ritual role in the performance and draw attention to their dual identities as characters and performers (75).

54 Nooter (2012a): 45–6 shows that the chorus fail to respond to Ajax's own poetic tone, since they are excited and delighted by his speech, which is threnodic and not usually expected to inspire such a response.

55 See Chapters 3 and 5. Rodighiero (2012): 49–50 points to the connections with Pindaric poetry in the chorus' song here, which may almost have led the audience to an expectation of the song moving into praise for Ajax, an expectation undermined by the content of the remainder of their ode.

56 Goldhill (2013): 106–7 notes too here that the chorus' lack of authority is grounded in their personal response to Ajax's situation.

57 O'Higgins (1989): 48–9 is right therefore that Sophocles' *Ajax* dramatizes a gap in the *kleos* of Ajax, by 'disinheriting' the Homeric tradition but providing no new alternative poetic *kleos*-establishment, although she does not recognize the absence of tragic choral praise as a particular feature of this failure to provide an alternative.

58 Similarly O'Higgins (1989): 55 n30. Pallantza (2005): 230 sees the chorus' attitude in their odes as 'antiheroic', contrasting with Ajax's epic and heroic ideals.

59 As the chorus of Euripides' *Heracles* achieve more successfully – see Chapter 3.

60 Seaford (2019): 74.

61 *Il.* 11–16 for the defence of the Greek ships, and 7.38–312.

62 Barker (2004): 11 notes the echoes of Achilles' complaint at *Il.* 9.334–45 in Teucer's comment at 1110–11 that Ajax did not come to Troy 'for Menelaus' wife'.

63 Michelakis (2002): 148–50 demonstrates the connections between the two plays effectively, arguing that in both the question of the 'social memory' of a hero is being rehabilitated by this kind of speech.

64 Gregory (2018a): 139–41 provides a balanced discussion of the changes, which she describes as differences in 'narrative emphasis and detail'.

65 Rosivach (1976): 58 argues that Teucer's purpose in this recounting is to strike at Agamemnon's pride rather than praise Ajax, explaining the lack of focus on full praise for Ajax's deeds. Holt (1981): 285–7 comments on the 'lack of nobility' in both debates. Similarly Goldhill (1986): 160 contrasts unfavourably the 'greatness' of Ajax with the 'aggressive oversimplifications' of Teucer, Menelaus and Agamemnon.

66 Hesk (2003): 117.

67 It is only when Odysseus intervenes that Agamemnon can be persuaded, as even the rather biased chorus acknowledge (1316–17).

68 O'Higgins (1989): 53 n13 notes that '"Best . . . after" is a promise that is then taken back' in the *Iliad*, making it more disappointing than a simple second place. The same effect of a retracted promise is found in Odysseus' formulation here – by delaying the exception Sophocles not only recalls the traditional formulation, but also implies that Odysseus will finally vindicate Ajax's attempt to claim this identity for himself before that possibility is firmly removed.

69 I do not agree with Murnaghan (1989): 182 that this is a concession of victory from Odysseus – Odysseus concedes nothing about himself in including this comment here – and his inclusion of Achilles in the formula thwarts Ajax's desires rather than fulfilling them, as she claims. Similarly Garvie (1998) ad loc. claims that Odysseus 'validates Ajax's perception of himself' – this does not take sufficient account of the difference between what Ajax claims and what Odysseus will allow.

70 So Pindar in fr. 181 SM – see further Kurke (1991): 101.

3 Euripides' Heracles, 'Glorious' How?

1 Barlow (1981) brings out the many similarities between Euripides' Heracles and Sophocles' Ajax in her valuable analysis.

2 E.g. Silk (1985): 12–16, Papadimitropoulos (2007): 132–5 and Mikellidou (2015), who argues that this transition is associated with Heracles' *katabasis*.
3 Gregory (1977): 260–2.
4 Dunn (1997): 98.
5 Galinsky (1972): 10–15.
6 Galinsky (1972): 23–39.
7 Foley (1985): 175–200 and Swift (2010): 121–51, esp. 122, 155–6 for the importance of reading Heracles' presentation in tragedy as a development of his portrayal in other genres, particularly in relation to epinician.
8 In contrast to Eur. *Or.* 241, 470 and 477, for example, where Menelaus and Tyndareus upon their entry on stage are identified primarily by their family ties with the speaker. Similarly Eur. *Supp.* 100, Soph. *OT* 639.
9 Similar examples of individuals fearing or anticipating their enemies' laughter appear at Soph. *El.* 1153, *Phil.* 258 and 1021–4, *Aj.* 454 and 1042–3, Eur. *Med.* 383, 404, 797, 1049, 1355, 1362 (Medea is particularly concerned about this risk – see Chapter 6). See further Dillon (1991): 346–8.
10 Contra Burnett (1971): 159–63. Yoshitake (1994): 137–40 argues convincingly that the *Heracles* supports the importance of preserving reputation through suicide by having Heracles take up and validate Megara's and Amphitryon's earlier arguments. Walsh (1979): 305 argues that Megara fails her family by prioritizing 'public' honour over private ties here, but no character in the play levels this charge against her, not even Amphitryon in their dispute about whether she is right to choose death.
11 Foley (1985): 181–2 draws out interesting associations in the *Heracles* between Lycus and blame poetry.
12 Cairns (1993): 15–18, on the connection between shame and self; see also 18–26.
13 Mikalson (1991): 72–4 and specifically on Lycus 258 n17.
14 Chapter 2.
15 Swift (2010): 132–3. καλλίνικος occurs as a cult title for Heracles – see Sourvinou-Inwood (2003): 363; Stafford (2012): 90, 176. Heracles' use of the term also picks up on its appearances elsewhere in the play when it is used as an identifying feature which focuses on his glorious deeds – as at 49, 180, 570 (applied to his club). It is important as a marker of epinician style, as at 681 and 789. See Carey (2012): 29–30.
16 As elsewhere at 50, 265 and 568–70, where Heracles' victory over the Minyans is noted as a great service from Heracles to the people of Thebes.
17 See further Lardinois (1995): 75–6 on the use of πᾶν in this kind of *gnome* to emphasize its authority, and 106–7, 173, 212, 254, 263 on the use of *gnomai* in praise and blame poetry. On the use of *gnomai* to identify praiseworthy topics in Pindar and Bacchylides, see Bundy (1962): 7–8, 28–9, 37–8, 52–61, 81, 88–9; also Kirkwood (1982): 13–14.

18 On authoritative choral wisdom expressed through gnomic statements, see Swift (2010): 38–9 and Calame (2013a): 39–40.

19 Konstan (2007): 192 considers this issue within the wider context of ethical discussions of violence in Greek society.

20 Padilla (1994): 292. See also Gibert (1997): 255 and n40 on the ambiguity. On the parallelism between Lycus' intentions and Heracles' act, see Kraus (1999): 140–3 and Papadopoulou (2001): 116.

21 Delgado (2015): 97–8 has demonstrated effectively how Megara's hopes for her children draw on folktale traditions of royal inheritances, so these are less troubling than the children playing with the weapons.

22 See Conacher (1967): 82, who describes this as 'humanizing' the myth. Padilla (1994): 294 argues that the innovation allows for Heracles' labours to be a duty to Amphitryon, so that both Heracles' fathers in the *Heracles* have sent him to undergo dangerous trials rather than caring for him.

23 Griffiths (2006): 21 notes that this innovation 'allows Euripides to place Heracles firmly within a family context', but does not fully recognize that the result of this change for Heracles is not only negative in terms of the results of the madness, but also in relation to the blame to which this leaves him exposed within that family context.

24 On the role of choruses as public singers in Greek society, see Goldhill (1996): 252–5 and Swift (2010): 1–3. Cropp (1986): 193 also acknowledges the chorus of the *Heracles*' role in representing the wider community.

25 Contrast Soph. *OT* where a chorus with the same group identity as the chorus of the *Heracles* (Theban elders) are identified by Creon simply as ἄνδρες πολῖται (514), or *Ant.* where they are simply σύγκλητον γερόντων (159).

26 The chorus of Aeschylus' *Agamemnon* similarly explicitly claim 'authority' based on age and prowess in song (104–6).

27 Segal (1993): 21.

28 On the choral self-referentiality here, see Henrichs (1994), esp. on this chorus 70.

29 On the significance of the choral garlands here for emphasising the self-referential performative aspects of this ode, see Henrichs (1996): 54–5.

30 Nagy (2013): 254–5 sees the reference to the Maidens as an 'ongoing mimesis' of an idealized performance in the choral performance here. See also Henrichs (1996): 54–60 on the Delian Maidens as role models for the Theban chorus as part of a poetic construction of their role as ideal poetic performers. On the reference to the swan, see Bond (1981): 239–40 who also points to the associations between the swan and the cult of Apollo at Delos.

31 There may be a textual problem here, but Hermann's καλλίχοροι is fairly universally accepted, and Diggle's justification of its function ((1981): 53) seems to clear up any lingering doubt.

32 Detienne (1996), esp. 47–9, points to Theocritus' comment about the role of Simonides in conferring memory (*Testimonia* 13 – Theocr. 16. 42–7) upon his patrons through song, as well as the songs of Pindar. An explicit invocation of Mnemosyne (described as λιπαράμπυκος) in connection with the poetic celebration of glorious deeds (explicitly through songs connected to fame: κλυταῖς ἀοιδαῖς) appears in Pind. *Nem.* 7.15–16, and the connection is also indicated at *Ol.* 8.74, and *Isthm.* 6.75 (where Dirce and Mnemosyne both appear as the capping elements of Pindar's celebration of the victor, presenting some striking similarities with the second and third choral celebrations of the *Heracles*). Elsewhere praise song itself conveys a 'memorial' at *Pyth.* 5.49 and *Isthm.* 8.62.

33 Rehm (1996): 53.

34 Swift (2010): 131–3.

35 The streets of the city are invited to ἀναχορεύσατ' at 783.

36 Bond (1981): 265 points to the 'atmosphere of ritual' in this song, which adds an authoritative, public element to the voice of the chorus.

37 Swift (2010): 148.

38 Rutherford (2012): 76.

39 There may have been other tragic choruses which performed a very similar role; although Aeschylus' *Children of Heracles* is no longer extant, it is clear from the surviving fragments that at least one set of choral lyrics celebrated Heracles' heroic deeds (fr. 74 *TrGF*). See further Wright (2018): 30–1, and for the chorus and Heracles in the *Trachiniae*, Chapter 5.

40 Rehm (1996): 53. On the epinician aspect of this ode as a whole, see Swift (2010): 124–9 and Carey (2012): 28–9; on the specifically Pindaric features, see Barlow (1996): 139.

41 Steiner (1986): 35–6; Carey (2012): 28.

42 On the Euripidean chorus' role in providing the wider mythological background for the events of a tragedy, see Murnaghan (2016): 419–21, and Kranz (1933): 253–7, who connects these 'balladic' choral odes with the mythical narrative techniques of Stesichorus and Bacchylides.

43 Young (1971); Rutherford (2011): 110. On myths of Heracles himself providing useful exempla in Pindar, see Rutherford (2011): 121–2.

44 Parry (1965), who also points to how the excess of praise for Heracles leads to the danger of his rising 'too high' which an epinician poet would *usually* successfully guard against, and creating a foil against which his 'fall' takes place (364, 374).

45 Bond (1981): 154 also notes that the chorus sing a 'panhellenic' version of Heracles' labours. A secondary effect is to effectively support Amphitryon's earlier insistence on the wide-ranging quality of Heracles' heroic reputation.

46 On the allusions to Lycus as another 'beast', see Rehm (1996): 53 and Kraus (1999): 142.

47 Most extensively Griffiths (2002), also Burnett (1971): 177–80.

48 Lee (1982): 46–7 for the importance of Iris' and Lyssa's equal status in giving both goddesses' opinions weight within the play.

49 Holmes (2008): 263 points out that Heracles almost does not recognize himself in the extreme 'self-alienation', which causes him not to appreciate the results of his actions.

50 On labour being associated with the heroic quality of ἀρετῆ in the same terms (ἀρετὰ δ' ἐπίμοχθος) but resulting in glory, *eukleia*, see Bacchyl. 1.180–4.

51 In contrast, Aethra of the *Suppliant Women* identifies Adrastus to Theseus via name and title immediately (105). Even though this recognition cannot rely on a prior relationship or knowledge of the individual's appearance, as Theseus' recognition of Heracles could, still it is not accompanied by the kind of lengthy listing of heroic deeds with which Amphitryon describes Heracles to Theseus – Adrastus' name is apparently sufficient to progress the conversation.

52 E.g. Gregory (1977): 271–5; Yoshitake (1994): 153; Papadopoulou (1999): 305.

53 Kraus (1999): 150 makes the interesting argument that Theseus offers Heracles various 'cult selves' to take up as his identity in the titles at 1250–1, as well as what I am describing as his 'heroic' self.

54 Walsh (1979): 306–8 recognizes the public nature of the move to Athens, as distinct from the private realm Heracles failed to maintain through care for his family (306).

55 Theseus' earlier indication of trust in the tales of singers at 1315 (despite Heracles' dismissal at 1346), also presents Theseus and Athens as providing a poetic landscape rather than one removed from public praise.

56 Bond (1981): 408 ad 1386–8 notes some textual issues here, and dismisses these lines as an 'antiquarian's footnote'; Barlow (1996): 183 agrees that they 'come oddly here', although she allows the lines to stand. Kovacs (1998), and Diggle (1981) do not object to the lines, although both accept Wakefield's (1794) conjecture of 'ἀγρίου' to improve the sense of 1386.

57 Foley (1985): 155–200. Rehm (1996): 54–5 sees these developments as part of the full horrifying extent of Hera's overthrow of Heracles (and the overthrow of 'natural order' and challenge to narrative patterns enacted across the play), in that she has even overthrown the poetic celebrations for his triumph and turned these to celebrations of his destruction (1303–7). See also Henrichs (1996): 61–2 who points out the perverted nature of this description in what is, itself, a dance performed at a festival for Dionysus, and links this 'tragic perversion' to the *Bacchae*.

4 Euripides' *Suppliant Women* and the Female Subversion of Praise

1 On Theseus as Athens' 'own' hero, see Walker (1995): 13–15 and Mills (1997): 2–6. On Theseus as founder of Athens' democracy, see Davie (1982), Calame (1990):

259–60, Walker (1995): 35–64 and Mills (1997): 97–104. Loraux (1986): 66–7 adds some useful caveats on the idea of Theseus as 'democratic' hero.

2 The use of praise as a method of persuasion is similar to its deployment against Neoptolemus in the *Philoctetes* – see Chapter 1.

3 In contrast, Tecmessa speaks her last line at 973 of the *Ajax*, so that the remaining 450 lines are spoken entirely by men, and Lyssa and Iris finish their conversation at 874 of the *Heracles*, after which follow another 550 lines spoken only by male characters.

4 See most recently Mendelsohn (2002) for a reading of the play entirely along gendered lines.

5 E.g. Goff (1995) on Aethra, or Foley (2001); Loraux (2006); Holst-Warhaft (2002) on the interaction between lament and civic discourse (for more detail see below).

6 See 108–11 below.

7 Kovacs (1998) reads the novel Euripidean term εὐτεκνίᾳ at 66 as being a positive description of Theseus (the 'noble son' Aethra bore), but the more straightforward reading is to take it as referring positively to the fact that Aethra, whose son is still alive, is considered blessed by the chorus, who have lost their sons. Collard similarly (1975) emphasizes the contrast it sets up with δυστυχίαν (cf. also his note on 955). This contrast between childlessness and the 'gift' of children is supported by its use at *Ion*. 470. The contrast between this family-focused way of identifying Theseus, as opposed to the identifications which focus on praiseworthy deeds found in the *Heracles* (chapter three) is striking. For more on the contrast these neutral descriptions present with the situation in Euripides' *Heracles*, Sophocles' *Ajax* and Sophocles' *Trachiniae* while their heroes are off-stage, see Chapters 2, 3 and 5.

8 Morwood (2007); Collard (1975) ad loc. On the frequent ancient comparisons between Heracles and Theseus, see Barlow (1981): 3 and Mills (1997): 108, 138. Plutarch (*Vit. Thes.* 6–12) reflects this connection in his claim that Theseus deliberately 'imitated' Heracles' great deeds. See further Chapter 3 on this praise vocabulary for Heracles in tragedy.

9 E.g. *Ol.* 9.2, *Pyth.* 1.32, 5.106, 11.46, *Nem.* 3.19, 4.16, *Isth.* 1.12, 5.54. Elsewhere in Euripides the term appears in epinician passages, e.g. Eur. *El.* 761–899 (Swift (2010): 156–70), *Alexander* fr. 62d.53 (Kampakoglou (2018)), and see Chapter 3.

10 Aethra refers to the boar at 316–17, Theseus talks of his deeds generally at 339–40, and at 573, and the messenger refers to the club stolen from the robber Periphetes as in Theseus' possession at 714.

11 Mendelsohn (2002).

12 In the case of Aethra, her presentation as legitimate wife of Aegeus is the unexpected element in the *Suppliant Women*. More usually (Apollod. III. 15.7, Hyg. *Fab.* 37, Plut. *Vit. Thes.* 3.3–4, Eur. *Med.* 665–81 (implied)), Theseus is conceived in an extra-marital relationship as Aegeus travels to Athens via Troezen, but Euripides

has Aethra highlight the legitimacy of the relationship in direct contrast to this tradition (5–7), as a result drawing attention to her presence and speech in the opening lines of this play. Mendelsohn (2002): 143–4 discusses this newly legitimized marriage for Aethra as presenting a contrast to the problematic Argive and Theban marriages explored throughout the play. Mills (1997): 105 sees it as designed to be flattering to Theseus. Evadne seems to have been a Euripidean invention, interpreted in various ways by critics, for example for the sake of emphasising the individual, pathetic consequences of mourning according to Romilly (1961): 38–9; or as a lesson in the costs of war for Rehm (1994): 120–1.

13 E.g. *Nem.* 7.77–9, *Pyth.* 8.57. See further on this imagery in tragedy in Chapters 1 and 3.

14 Particularly imperial action – see further Mills (2020): 21–2. On the contemporary political resonances of πόνος in this speech, see Michelini (1994): 230–2 and Loraux (2014): 44–6. Hesk (2011): 130–3 discusses Aethra's speech in relation to an Athenian concern with εὐβουλία, and Sissa (2020): 219–20 notes how she draws on the language of Greek political theory.

15 Loraux (2014): 45 notes the connection between πόνος and glory through words (particularly the songs of Pindar) – and see 53–7 on the connection with Heracles. See also Storey (2008): 42–3.

16 McClure (1999a): 263 describes Aethra's public authority as 'maternal' here, and considers it rooted in the ritual context within which she appears. Goff (1995): 71–4 gives a useful analysis of the roots (maternal, political and ritual) of Aethra's authoritative speech, as well as her concern with articulating a wider Athenian identity in the process of persuading Theseus (76–8).

17 E.g. Ajax's father Telamon in Soph. *Aj.* 764–6, Amphitryon in Eur. *HF* 170–205. Even absent fathers can be used as a spur, as is the case for Orestes in Aesch. *Cho.* 503–7, or in Soph. *Phil.* where the promise of living up to Achilles' reputation is held before Neoptolemus. For more on the influence of their fathers as a spur to win praise in the cases of Neoptolemus and Ajax, see 21–5, 46–50. In Euripides' *Hippolytus*, Phaedra wishes for *civic* success in Athens for her sons (420–3), and that they should have good reputations (717), but she does not intend for them to take any direct action to improve their reputations; rather, *she* will act to ensure this.

18 In this regard, while I agree with Sissa (2020): 222–3 on the importance of recognizing the intellectual, political and panhellenic language developed by Aethra, I do not agree that this makes her speech 'trans-gendered'. Aethra's speech is gendered feminine in the *Suppliant Women*. However, this feminine marking comes about through its contribution to a discourse which is not usually gendered feminine: the encouragement towards seeking praise and concern with reputation that the female characters in this play repeatedly demonstrate.

19 Rehm (1994): 112 describes Evadne's appearance and suicide as the most 'theatrically daring moment in the history of the stage', and argues (111) that if the scene had been lost, no lacuna would have been noted. Collard (1975), esp. 353, rightly notes, however, how her arrival has been prepared in the preceding scenes, suggesting that Rehm's assessment may slightly exaggerate the surprise of Evadne's appearance, if not its dramatic impact.

20 See Mendelsohn (2002): 199–200 on the strength of the unusual detail that Evadne has been locked away and guarded by her father, rather than simply expected to stay inside. Chong-Gossard (2008): 217–19 points out that the detail is somewhat unclear, however.

21 It is possible that Aethra, Evadne and Athena were all played by the same actor (see Storey (2008): 106–7), strengthening the connections between their various speeches. However, Collard (1975): 20–1 proposes to give Evadne to the same actor as Theseus, and since either distribution is plausible, it is difficult to read too much significance into the sharing of parts.

22 Capaneus' boastfulness is a key part of the tradition. In Aesch. *Sept*: ὁ κόμπος δ᾽ οὐ κατ᾽ ἄνθρωπον φρονεῖ - 'his boasting is not in accordance with being a mortal man' (425), and his speech is described by the messenger (427–31), before the speech of his shield is quoted (434). See also Eur. *Phoen*. 1174–5 where it is claimed ἐκόμπασεν, and Soph. *OC* 1318–19 where he εὔχεται.

23 Mendelsohn (2002): 207.

24 Dee (2015): 266.

25 Torrance (2013): 168 makes the interesting suggestion that there is a metapoetic meaning implied here too, so that Evadne is being instructed not to tell a new μῦθον to the *audience*, at a moment of innovation in Euripides' treatment of the Seven and their fate. If so, this would indicate a further level of poetic self-consciousness in the portrayal of Evadne in this scene.

26 Chong-Gossard (2008): 224–5.

27 See 9, 76–7.

28 Mendelsohn (2002): 203–4; Loraux (1987): 29 and n58 associates much of Evadne's language here with 'virility'. On ἀρετῇ as a praiseworthy quality of heroic excellence, see Chapter 1: n36.

29 Morwood (2007) ad 984–5.

30 Collard (1975): 360–1 points to the common trope of celebratory songs (ὑμέναιοι) which became laments (γόοι) found throughout tragedy. See also Alexiou (2002): 57–8. There are substantial problems with the text in Evadne's monody (see Collard (1975): 360–1). The adjective applied to either γάμων or ἀοιδαῖς must be supplied (fortunately both nouns remain); I print here Kovacs' supplement.

31 Most commonly light imagery, especially to begin a song, features in the *paian*. See Eur. *Ion*. 82–7 for a tragic example, and see Swift (2010): 68, and 73 on light imagery

referring to a paianic context in the *Alcestis*. On the imagery of light or 'radiance' brought by commemorative poetry in Pindar, see Segal (1998): 242–5, and for the wider poetic connections between light and fame see Hutchinson (2012): 279–80. Garrison (1995): 124 also points out the connection with Capaneus which the light-focused imagery in Evadne's speech develops.

32 There are further textual issues here. I print Kovacs' (1998) text, but see Collard (1975): 362–4 on the problems.

33 Rutherford (2001): 110.

34 See Mastronarde (2002): 82–4, and 83 on the use of the Doric ᾱ for η.

35 This term is a hapax. Euripides elsewhere uses compound adjectives from 'bronze' (χαλκο- or χαλκεο-) to describe epic warriors, for example, Hector is χαλκεομήστορος at *Tro.* 271, and the Danaans are χαλκεόπλων at *Hel.* 693. Later in the *Suppliant Women*, the sons of the Seven will be described as χαλκοπληθῆ (1220). There is also a persistent tragic connection between the wars against Thebes and bronze weapons or armour; at Eur. *Hypsipyle* fr. 752f.30–1 the original expedition against Thebes is described as χαλέο[ι]σιν ὅπλο[ις, and the shields of those fighting at Thebes are χαλκοδέτων in Aesch. *Sept.* 161. Bronze-wearing warriors formed from similar compound adjectives are found in Bacchylides (*Ep.* 13.109 (describing Hector) and *Ep.* 11.123 for the Atreidae (who are χαλκοθωράκων), Pindar (*Pyth.* 5.82 – the Trojans are χαλκοχάρμαι and fr. 52f.108 SM where Neoptolemus' soldiers are χαλκοκορυ[στ]ὰν), Hesiod (fr. 165.14 MW) and the Homeric epics (e.g. *Il.* 4.448, 7.41, 8.62, 10.287, 11.694, *Od.* 1.286, 4.496). The fight which Theseus himself is said to appreciate is χαλκεοκτύπου μάχας in Bacchyl. *Dithyrambs* 18.59, and Theseus is similarly χαλκοθώρα[κα] in *Dithyrambs* 17.14–15. Memnon too attracts this kind of description in poetry – he is Μέμνονα χαλκοάραν in Pind. *Isthm.* 5.41, and Μέμνονα χαλκοκορυστήν in Hes. *Theog.* 984. Bronze compounds also make up common epithets of Hector, as at *Il.* 5.699, 6.398, 13.720, 15.458, 16.358, etc.). Conversely, compound adjectives from χαλκο- or χαλκεο- are extremely rare in classical Attic prose (I count 5 instances, all forms of χαλκότυπος), suggesting they are markedly poetic forms.

36 Although it is not uncommon to find Athena at the end of a Euripidean play (see similarly *IT*, *Ion*), particularly a 'political' play (Kennedy (2009): 71), various aspects of this appearance have been noted as unusual. Rehm (2002): 31 treats her appearance as entirely unexpected, pointing to the apparent spatial transformation caused by the movement from a space focused on Demeter to a space controlled by Athena. Anderson (2015): 312–13 highlights how the audience is led to expect the traditional burial of the Seven at Eleusis, rather than the oath, but then hear nothing of this from Athena. Conacher (1956): 26 argues that Athena's comments add to the 'irony' of Theseus' comments about just gods in the *Suppliant Women*.

37 This kind of promise has itself a strong epic precedent, in the remark of Helen at *Il.* 6.357–8.

38 Most notably in the *Epigonoi* itself, the epic poem which apparently narrated and celebrated their exploits and was known to Herodotus (4.32.1). There also seems to have been Sophoclean and Aeschylean *Epigonoi* tragedies. See similarly Pind. *Pyth.* 8.42.

39 Kavoulaki (2008): 305 connects Athena's invocation of the sons' epic potential here to the burial of the Seven, but the full web of connections Athena develops with epic, poetic language has not fully been explored.

40 Collard (1975): 419.

41 The focus on the seven gates attacked by Seven heroes makes up a substantial part of Aeschylus' *Sept.* (375–652), and the description of Thebes by its towers recurs in *Sept.* 30, 251, 469. Elsewhere in tragedy, Euripides refers only to the πύργωματα of Troy or Thebes (*Cyc.* 115, *Tro.* 46, 1174, *Hel.* 51 *Phoen.* 287).

42 πόλεος is an epic form – see Collard (1975): 421. On the Homeric lion simile as a 'model' for tragic metaphors featuring lions, see Wolff (1979), esp. 144–8 and Konstantinou (2012): 128–9. Griffiths (2020): 164–8 notes the potential for violence, and thus dangerous quality, indicated by the description of children as lion cubs in tragedy. See also Mendelsohn (2002): 220–1 for the suggestion that the recalling of lion imagery, first seen at *Supp.* 140, brings back a dark note of bestiality.

43 See Chapter 1: 36–8 on Heracles' promise in the *Philoctetes.*

44 Mendelsohn (2002): 221 notes other similarities between the appearances of Evadne and Athena.

45 Swift (2010); Rutherford (2012): 217–21; Andújar et al. (2019): 1–6.

46 Michelini (1991): 29 and n86.

47 See Collard (1975): 348–53 who notes epic colour in the description of the sons, the reference to Artemis, and the unique form πτύχα (979) derived from the epic πτύξ.

48 Henrichs (1994).

49 Collard (1975), esp. 115–25, 179–80, points to repeated use of epic language in the choral passages; see similarly Morwood (2007) on lines 16–19, 47, 60–2, 69–70, 80, 263–85, 365, 525, 599, 603–4, 647 and 1146.

50 The other is the θρῆνος. The two types of poetic lament have slightly different performance techniques and purposes in Homeric epic (see Murnaghan (1999): 206–8), but by tragedy the terms are used interchangeably (Swift (2010): 301–4).

51 Often featuring either music which is not musical, or music which has gained negative qualities from tragedy which do not suit choral or musical performance, as at Aesch. *Supp.* 681, *Ag.* 1142 or *Eum.* 307–96 for the furies' 'hateful' (308) binding music, Soph. *OC* 1220–3, Eur. *Tro.* 121, *Phoen.* 784–97. See further Rutherford (2012): 141–3.

52 There may also be a further, allusive reference to the chorus *qua* chorus when they describe themselves as currently at Καλλίχορον θεᾶς ὕδωρ (619), since this well was apparently associated with the first female choral performances at Eleusis (Paus.

1.38.6). For more on the adjective καλλίχορος as connected to choral self-referentiality in Euripides, see Cook (2021): 83, with examples at *Hcld.* 359, *Herc.* 690, fr. 453.7 *TrGF*, *Hel.* 1454, *Phoen.* 786.

53 Loraux (2002): 58–60.

54 Stesichorus fr. 271 Finglass, see further Davies and Finglass (2015): 262–3. Sophocles Nauck fr. 764 and *OC* 1221–2. Another Euripidean example appears at *IT* 182–5. See further Swift (2010): 71–2; Rutherford (1994): 121–4 on the problematic juxtapositions of songs to Apollo and Hades in relation to the paean, in tragic lyric.

55 Kavoulaki (2011): 367–8 notes the autonomy of the chorus from Adrastus as a significant difference between this female chorus of suppliants and the chorus of Aeschylus' *Suppliant Women*, with whom they otherwise share many similarities.

56 Easterling (1991). See also Murnaghan (1999), esp. 205–7.

57 Scully (1996): 69 discusses the contrast in terms of two competing types of ritual, and further argues for a contrast of concerns about the οἶκος vs. concerns about the πόλις split between the female and male voices in the *Suppliant Women*.

58 Foley (2001): 39–40 argues that Theseus, along with the messenger who has complained about Adrastus' laments, attempts to suppress the public female lamentation as part of taking control over the funeral rites. See also Loraux (1986): 47–9. Kornarou (2008): 35–6 describes the chorus' ongoing lament as 'resistance to being incorporated into the civic system'.

59 Murnaghan (1999): 217; Dué (2006): 42–3.

60 Dué (2006): 40.

61 In other extant plays featuring the expedition of the Seven, the choruses are either associated with the city of Thebes (Aesch. *Sept.*) or uninvolved in the action, as visitors (Eur. *Phoen.*). We do not know who formed the choruses in Aeschylus' *Eleusinioi* or *Epigonoi*. In other suppliant plays, the chorus often has some association with the city being asked for aid, so that their stake in the action is slightly more remote – e.g. Soph. *OC*, Eur. *Heracl.* – although Aeschylus' *Suppliant Women* features the chorus as the suppliants themselves.

62 While both the *Ajax* and the *Heracles* feature the wives (or similar, in the case of Tecmessa) of male heroes with a concern for their husbands' *kleos* and reputation (Chapters 2 and 3), both heroes are also surrounded by male relatives and, significantly, by male choruses, presenting a substantially different situation to that found in the *Suppliant Women*. The *Philoctetes* has no female characters at all.

63 Toher (2001): 340–2; Anderson (2015).

64 Plut. *Vit. Thes.* 29.4–5.

65 McDermott (1991): 126–7 points out that the innovation of Theseus' needing to fight is highlighted by the description Theseus gives of himself as καινὸς ἐν καινῷ δορί (597). Lloyd (1992): 79 suggests that the *agon* demonstrates an initial, unsuccessful attempt to persuade the Thebans through speech rather than battle.

Michelini (1994): 247 argues that the play therefore presents the 'impossibility' of reaching closure through *logos* rather than violence.

66 Mastronarde (1986): 203–5 argues that the contrast between Theseus' views here and their unsatisfactory results later in the play suggests a characterization of Theseus as an optimist throughout the *Suppliant Women*.

67 Plat. *Phaedr.* 269a, taken by West (2003) to be a reference to the epic *Thebaid* (fr. 4*) although the attribution is uncertain. See also Torres-Guerra (2015): 239–40.

68 E.g. *Ol.* 11.4, *Pyth.* 3.64, *Nem.* 3.4, *Pae.* frs. 52c and e. See also Bacchylides' description of himself as 'honey-tongued' (μελίγλωσσος) 3.96. In the *Odyssey* (12.187) it is applied to the most dangerous kind of *kleos*-granting seductive song, the song of the sirens (see Segal (1994): 100–6; Doherty (1995)), and it appears as a descriptor of beautiful song in the *Homeric Hymns to Apollo* (519) and *Pan* (18), where it refers to the song of the nightingale.

69 *Ol.* 6.11–19. The scholiast on *Ol.* 6.15–17 claims that this quotation was taken from the *Thebaid*, see fr. 6 West.

70 Michelini (1991): 18 makes the intriguing suggestion that Adrastus' comment about poetry and the persuasive speaker at 180–3 (which follows a lacuna of some kind) may have been a way of emphasizing this contrast with the poetic tradition, and between his 'poetic' self's usual persuasiveness and his failure to persuade Theseus.

71 Scodel (1999): 139–40 describes Adrastus' rhetoric as an 'unsuccessful performance' in comparison to those of Aethra and Theseus. Similarly Michelini (1991): 16–17 points out that the 'dramatic arrangement undercuts the suppliant's potential for persuasive eloquence'.

72 Mastronarde (1979): 64 describes this as 'one of the most remarkable interruptions of all tragedy', and points to its being a strange break in Adrastus' otherwise lengthy silence (263–733), especially given that Adrastus does not successfully break into the conversation at all.

73 There is some textual corruption here, but once the manuscript's εἰσορῶ is (rightly) rejected, Collard's (1975) ἱστορῶ, or Kovacs' (1998) ἀνιστορῶ (printed here) are equally acceptable, and the remainder of the introduction from Theseus does not seem problematic.

74 Kovacs (1996): 75–6 proposes deleting these lines (232–7) along with 238–45, partly on the basis that 'the whole passage should perhaps stand or fall together', and with the objection that the discussion of the role of young men in democracies is problematic. I am not convinced that the material, given its themes of youth and management of the state, is sufficiently irrelevant to be removed primarily on these grounds (for the connection of this passage to discussion of both themes in the *Suppliant Women*, see Thury (1988)), and am inclined to agree with Collard (1975) and Morwood (2007), who retain the passage.

75 Mendelsohn (2002): 189–90 suggests that the 'echo' of Adrastus' and Theseus' earlier disagreement undercuts Theseus' invitation here. Similarly Burian (1985): 147 claims that, while polite, Theseus' terms have the effect of keeping his earlier condemnation before the audience. Mills (1997): 124–5 sees only an attempt by Theseus to 'rehabilitate' Adrastus by this invitation, in a rather optimistic reading.

76 Zuntz (1955): 23 and Collard (1972): 39–52 are among the few scholars to read the speech 'straight'. Fitton (1961): 437–40 argues that the speech is 'absurd and intended to be so'. Burian (1985): 147–8 attempts to read Adrastus' speech as a genuine, but failed, attempt at praise.

77 Loraux (1986): 82–4.

78 Michelini (1994): 242–5 argues that despite its presentation as a public funeral speech, and similarities in content with an *epitaphios,* the speech cannot be considered a typical Athenian *epitaphios* as it discusses individuals rather than a collective, and see similarly Scodel (1999): 132. Cf. however Hesk (2013), esp. 55–6, who adds some very reasonable caveats to the reading of this individual praise as too unlike the 'democratic' Athenian approach. Sammons (2021): 319–20 sees the speech as a failed attempt to blend the *epitaphios logos* with an epic catalogue of heroes, an intriguing suggestion.

79 On Euripides' or Adrastus' apparent divergence from mythical tradition here, Smith (1966): 162–3 describes the contradictory speech as 'satirical', Fitton (1961): 437–8 as ironic, and the portrayals are judged rather more moderately by Mendelsohn (2002): 191 as 'difficult to take at face value'. Grethlein (2003): 173–4 sees the speech as demonstrating the tension between 'ideal' portrayal of the *epitaphios* and 'realistic' images which are handed down through tragedy. However, Torrance (2013): 167–70 argues that Adrastus' eulogies do *not* explicitly contradict tradition, and thus represent a 'new' account which is nonetheless not so drastically opposed to earlier accounts as other scholars have argued.

80 Views on Theseus' comments about Amphiaraus and Polyneices often align with scholars' views of the funeral speech as a whole. Morwood (2007): 215 and Storey (2008): 71–2 read Theseus' view as a 'corrective' of that of the Theban herald. Conversely Smith (1966): 170 describes Theseus' concluding remarks (which he attributes, probably wrongly, to Adrastus) as 'fatuous', which adds to his overall critical reading of the funeral speech. In a more moderate view, Gamble (1970): 403–4 sees the presentation of the two viewpoints here as Euripides' demonstration of the contradictions and uncertainty of 'human life'.

81 Foley (2001): 42–3 includes Evadne as a further example of Theseus' failure to entirely control 'female hysteria' in the play, suggesting that both aspects of Theseus' instruction on how to commemorate and praise the dead fail to be fully embedded in Adrastus' or the Argives' response.

82 Toher (2001): 337–8 argues that Adrastus' participation in the funeral oration shows his restoration of status to the 'king of the Argives', but given that his handling of the mothers' grief and of the oath between himself and Theseus needs additional correction (by Theseus and then Athena), his status of independent leader in this situation does not seem secure even after the funeral oration is given. Mills (2020): 90 describes Adrastus as 'rehabilitated', but argues that this rehabilitation is not total, and that Argos' 'wretched' path prevents its being so. Collard (1975): 209 suggests that Adrastus learns from suffering, particularly from Theseus' instruction in the conversation with the Herald. Zeitlin (1990): 146 argues that it is Adrastus' ability to 'admit the error of his ways' which enables him to speak for the dead and demonstrates his movement from the Argive to the Athenian way of thinking, which he has learnt from Theseus. Conversely Morwood (2012) argues that it is Theseus who learns to move beyond Athenocentricism through his interactions with his mother, Adrastus and the chorus.

83 E.g. Eur. *Heracl.* 315, Aesch. *Ag.* 258 and 783, where the verb appears alongside an epinician image of praise speech as a projectile to be fired neither too far nor not far enough (e.g. Pind. *Nem.* 6.26–8, or *Ol.* 2.83, 89–90).

84 The end of Aeschylus' *Suppliant Women,* the only other extant play with a suppliant chorus, features a choral ode celebrating Argos, its people, and its local gods (1018–33). Other suppliant plays feature similar celebrations of the city e.g. Eur. *Heracl.* 748–83, 892–918, Soph. *OC* 668–719.

85 Rehm (1988): 284–8 (contra Collard (1975)) envisages a staging for the chorus of boys and main chorus of women at the start of the *Suppliant Women* which provides a gendered contrast between the male (boys') chorus and Adrastus, and the female (mothers') chorus with Aethra, before the movement of the choruses enables Theseus and Aethra to be joined in the playing space in the same way that they become connected in pity.

86 Given their roles in the play Griffiths (2020): 77–8 argues that the chorus of boys in the *Suppliant Women* should be seen as 'dramatic adults' rather than 'dramatic children', i.e. adolescents, although she notes that the staging does not preclude a child chorus. They are particularly well suited to being among those educated by Adrastus' speech, which Theseus wishes addressed to the young (νέοισιν 843), and which Adrastus claims specifically as being educative and as aimed at the raising of children (913–17). See Loraux (2006); 83–4 for more on the didactic aspects of this funeral speech and of the *epitaphios* more widely. There is an oddity in Theseus' description of the speech's audience, since he describes the audience for the speech as ἀστῶν, which should not apply to the Argive sons of the Seven. Collard (1975): 320 is likely right to see this description as adding an effective ambivalence as to whether the sons or the theatre's audience are being addressed – see also Rehm (2002): 33–4 who points to the Athenian young as the key audience for the speech, and Storey (2008): 64.

87 Halleran (1985): 21 connects the chorus of boys to Adrastus as 'secondary characters', noting that their entrances to and exits from the stage are always alongside him, which makes their failure to follow his kind of speech especially remarkable.

88 On direct address of the dead as a key feature of lament, see Alexiou (2002): 131–50. On this as typically tragic, see Collard (1975): 401–2, who also notes (398) the extensive echoes of Aeschylus *Agamemnon* in 1123–6.

89 On how Greek female lament is integral to spurring on revenge, see Alexiou (2002): 21–2 and Holst-Warhaft (2002), esp. 2–5, 97–8. On the representation of this relationship in tragedy, see Foley (2001): 23–4, 151–4.

90 Mendelsohn (2002): 218, but Morwood (2007): 233 is surely right to view this reading as mistaken – the mothers' eagerness to complete the boys' promise to be an avenger does not suggest that their own contrasting wishes have been 'overwhelmed'.

91 There is some confusion as to the division of these lines between speakers both here and at line 1151, but Collard (1975); 392–4 is convincing, and has been followed here. Morwood (2007): 132 prints the alternative possible text but (232) also recognizes the strong case for having the chorus take up the boys' comment, as well as assigning the comment at 1151 to the chorus rather than the sons.

92 Michelini (1994): 245; Mendelsohn (2002): 196. Morwood (2007): 217 describes Adrastus' rejection of πόνος here as 'gracelessly ungrateful', which is strong but not unwarranted.

93 Burian (1985): 149 similarly describes the sons' intentions as demonstrating 'the failure of reasoned discourse to change the pattern', but does not recognize that this is due to a competing *type* of discourse persuading the sons, instead attributing to their failure to be taught to the influence of 'ancient passions'. Toher's (2001): 338–9 reading of this moment as a 'regeneration' shared between the Argive boys and Adrastus is accordingly rather too optimistic.

94 Loraux (2014): 47.

95 Rutherford (2012): 140 also connects this image to Homeric metaphors of violence, but notes the 'perversity' of a harvest such as this.

96 Chong-Gossard (2008): 216–26.

5 Unpraised and Unpraiseworthy: Deianira and the Destruction of Heracles in Sophocles' *Trachiniae*

1 The dates of both the *Heracles* and the *Trachiniae* are uncertain, the *Trachiniae* particularly so, but it is most likely that the latter is the earlier of the two plays. See Easterling (1982): 19–21.

2 See Easterling (1982): 72 on the rhetorical precedence for this type of personal rebuttal of a maxim, although it is not very common elsewhere in tragedy. Heiden

(1989): 1–2 has argued that the unusual nature of this prologue, in which a character seems to speak to the audience with no other characters present, threatens to break the dramatic illusion and highlights the theatricality of Deianira's character. In my view this unusual opening statement and the attention drawn through it to Deianira as a *character* further gives it a programmatic sense, demonstrating for the audience the concern with speech and its effectiveness which will be an essential facet of her character in this play.

3 Allen-Hornblower (2016): 98–9 connects Deianira's initial statement and following descriptions of her life with a character which prioritizes cautious observation as a means to gathering information.

4 Heiden (1989): 33–4 correctly describes this comment as part of Hyllus' tendency to 'exaggerate the extent of his knowledge', which he demonstrates throughout the play, but does not recognize in Deianira's questions a desire to replace this exaggeration with a more accurate report, instead claiming that Deianira repeatedly interprets Hyllus' report in terms of her own expectations of negative news. Deianira's questions, however, are neutral in content: rather than indicating any unusual degree of fear, she asks for precise information about Heracles' location and status, as well as casting doubt on the veracity of the report Hyllus brings. Further, in her discussion of the prophecies, rather than demonstrating any 'expectation of disaster' (Heiden 1989: 34), Deianira technically gives more weight and detail to the positive potential meaning of the prophecy (80–1), than to the negative (79), which she passes over more quickly. Heiden's reading is part of a trend of scholars who read a persistent and unnatural level of fear or anxiety as the central trait of Deianira's character. See also Morwood (2008): 29–31, Mossman (2012): 495, Rabinowitz (2014): 192 and Mattison (2015): 14–15.

5 Lawrence (1978): 290.

6 Steiner (1994): 85–6.

7 Mueller (2015): 161–2 connects these comments also to the oracular nature of the *deltos*, and to the performative aspect of action which is itself part of a performance.

8 Barrett (2002): 96–101 on how named characters can perform the role of an unnamed messenger, as Hyllus does here.

9 Segal (2000) discusses the confusion which arises from the multiple versions of the oracles.

10 Kraus (1991): 81. Bowman (1999) argues that Nessus' speech does function as prophetic speech within the play, but that Deianira's reliance on it, despite its lack of authority and in preference to the prophecies given her by her husband, constitutes a form of adultery, with destructive results.

11 Heiden (1984): 67–9.

12 On Nessus and Heracles' understanding of the centaur's role, see Fowler (1999): 165–7, who connects this realization strongly to the myth of Heracles' apotheosis.

13 Contra Gardiner (1987): 124–5.

14 Hyllus' description of the offstage event also indicates that Lichas has conveyed Deianira's message and gift without adding any further information, as Hyllus claims that Heracles has received the instructions from Deianira (759), and that Lichas repeats the false description of Deianira's gift on Heracles' demand (775–6) without Lichas' being reported as saying anything additional.

15 Gardiner (1987): 121 notes the autonomous position of the chorus, but this still does not prevent their obeying Deianira's commands whenever she gives them.

16 Janka (2004): 147 rightly sees this as a choral intervention to attempt to protect Deianira, but their tactic of recommending silence has been indicated by her preceding request, it is not a suggestion which they make independently.

17 The chorus of the *Iphigenia at Tauris* also lie for Iphigenia to conceal her escape (1056–77, 1293–1301), although to be granted this, Iphigenia supplicates the chorus of the *IT* (1069–70), while Deianira needs only to give a command to her own chorus. See Foley (2003): 16 on choral deception. Chong-Gossard (2008): 155–74 discusses choral silences at the request of women, aimed at 'covering up' wrongdoing, in terms of 'female solidarity' in Euripides, demonstrating how the female characters often appeal to shared female experiences to establish this solidarity (156). See similarly Montiglio (2000): 252–6. Deianira's silence differs significantly from these (generally Euripidean) silences, in that she takes pains to distinguish herself from the chorus in their early meeting (see further below).

18 *Ant.* 1251, *OT* 1073. Burton (1980): 43 notes the contrast as 'curious' but does not recognize that it follows Deianira's command for silence.

19 Dewald and Kitzinger (2015): 97–8 argue that Sophocles here represents a failure of language, as Deianira's silence implies that she is not *able* to speak about what has happened. However, Deianira's deliberate choice of silence at this moment fits within the wider pattern of her careful, controlled speech, rather than demonstrating incapacity.

20 See Chapter 3.

21 Segal (1977): 62; Foley (2001): 95; Rabinowitz (2014): 194–5.

22 Mossman (2012): 496; Mattison (2015), esp. 12–13, 24.

23 Mattison (2015): 14–15 argues that Deianira attempts to 'infect' the chorus with her own fear; I do not see any evidence for this in her language. Instead she makes her fearfulness in this situation part of the contrast she draws between the 'group' truth they claim to represent, and Deianira's own, lived truths which she argues for throughout the play. See Swift (2010): 253 on the imagery in Deianira's description, which is typical of descriptions of *parthenoi* in wedding songs.

24 Rehm (1994): 72–3, and see further below. Similarly, at 523–5 the chorus' later retelling of Deianira's experience presents it as part of a wedding, when they describe Deianira as 'awaiting her bridegroom' (525). See, for more on Deianira's

contrast between herself and the chorus and its roots in wedding imagery, Seaford (1986): 50–5. Ormand (1999): 38–9 notes that Deianira's association between marriage and fear is treated by her as typical: exceptional in degree, but not the fact of fear itself.

25 Seaford (1986), esp. 55–9, and Ormand (1999): 42 have both argued that in fact Deianira's transition to (happily) married woman is incomplete, and this is part of the reason for the destruction which the play represents. I would not contradict these valuable arguments, but rather state that Deianira at least *claims* this status for herself in her interactions with the chorus and Iole, even if an external audience may interpret her position differently.

26 Davies (1991): 154–5. Segal (1995): 73, 76–9 and 88–9 notes further how Iole's 'marriage', as conducted by Heracles, violates the norms for a civilized marriage, including the death of her father and destruction of her city. Kratzer (2013): 44 discusses Deianira's language here in terms of jealousy.

27 There is a significant difference between tragic women who draw attention to their 'public' speech as problematic (for example Clytemnestra in Aesch. *Ag.* 855–7, Electra and Chrysothemis in Soph. *El.* 310–15, 328–30, Heracles' daughter in Eur. *Heracl.* 474–5, or Medea, Eur. *Med.* 214–15) and those who do not, as Deianira does not.

28 Rabinowitz (2014): 195. Wohl (1998): 39 argues convincingly that Iole's silence also allows Deianira to project her own construction of Iole's identity on to Iole.

29 Wohl (1998): 44–5 has argued that the gendered spaces of inside and outside the house are clearly demarcated, with no overlap, in that Deianira's meaningful actions take place inside, and Heracles returns to it only once he has been feminized by the robe. It is important to note, however, that Heracles does not *enter* the house at the end of the play; instead he is removed immediately to the site of his pyre (Hyllus even summons the chorus to leave the house behind entirely at 1275).

30 Allen-Hornblower (2016): 155–8 and n412.

31 Kurke (1991): 6 on the role epinician plays in returning and reintegrating an athletic victor to his home.

32 E.g. Pind. *Ol.* 2.5, 10.59, 13.14, *Pyth.* 1.59, 8.26, *Nem.* 1.9, 3.67, *Isth.* 1.22 etc.

33 Easterling (1982): 136–7; Stinton (1986): 126; Heiden (1989): 77–8; Kratzer (2013): 28–30.

34 See further Chapter 3 on Euripides' *Heracles*.

35 Weiberg (2018): 25–6 has persuasively connected Deianira's inability to talk of the assault to her experiences of trauma.

36 A significant contrast with the attitude of Megara in Euripides' *Heracles* – see 119–20 for Megara's desire to uphold Heracles' praiseworthy reputation.

37 The use of this phrase to imply potential for doubt seems especially common in Sophocles' tragedies. Ajax makes use of a similar turn of phrase in his 'deception speech': ἡμεῖς δὲ πῶς οὐ γνωσόμεσθα σωφρονεῖν / ἔγωγ'· (*Aj.* 677–8): here the generalized claim to begin with, combined with the fact that Ajax's words (whether deliberate deception or not) do not match his actions as the play progresses, make a straightforward reading difficult. Antigone uses the same phrase at *Ant.* 464 to claim that death must bring someone like her κέρδος, yet shows in her following laments (806–943) that her death is not a κέρδος to her. Similarly, Deianira's speech as the play progresses will show (as with Ajax) that there is some mismatch between the feelings she claims here and the reality. There is also another use of this phrase by Deianira with an even stronger sense of doubt implied at 444, when she says οὗτος γὰρ ἄρχει καὶ θεῶν ὅπως θέλει, / κἀμοῦ γε· **πῶς δ' οὐ** χἀτέρας οἵας γ' ἐμοῦ; (443–4). Deianira apparently argues for the reasonableness of Eros 'ruling another woman'; but given that she promptly acts to try and forcibly change her husband's feelings by making him love her alone, her actions do not seem to support her claims. It appears again at 718, where Deianira is 'sure' that the poison will be about to kill Heracles, and yet she waits to hear whether she is right before acting (somewhat unusually, for a tragic character), again suggesting that her words and her attitude do not entirely match.

38 Kirkwood (1941): 206 also describes her response as 'dubious', and Heiden (1989): 64–5 similarly notes the 'ambivalence' in her response.

39 Contrast the (deceptive) praise Clytemnestra displays as part of her welcome to Agamemnon, esp. Aesch. *Ag* 896–913. In Eur. *El.* Electra complains at 157–66 that Clytemnestra's welcome to Agamemnon did not (at least according to her version) involve the appropriate garlands and context of praise for a wife welcoming home a victorious husband, suggesting that this would be an expected welcome from wife to returning husband.

40 E.g. *Ol.* 5.23–5, 7.24–6, 12.6–12a, *Pyth.* 3.80–106.

41 In comparison, Pindar's inclusion of this sentiment is generally phrased either as an instruction against reaching too far (e.g. 'seeking to become a god' in *Ol.* 5.23–5), or that generally, mortals should expect to face troubles along with doing well. They do not include such explicitly negative emotions as fear, as Deianira does, nor is the risk to the achiever usually expressed in such direct, threatening terms. Easterling (1982): 2–3 connects this phrase to the mutability of human fortune as a central theme in the play, Allen-Hornblower (2016): 107–10 discusses it in connection with the generalizing tendency towards pity which helps associate Deianira's perspective with that of the play's spectators.

42 The *OCT* (1990) emendation, followed by Davies (1991), gives this attractive antithesis, but if γενέσθαι is preferred, the strength of Deianira's blame for Lichas'

behaviour remains clear and her apparently unwarranted criticism of Heracles' presumed involvement is preserved.

43 Unlike Clytemnestra, for example, who targets both her husband *and* Cassandra, and explicitly blames Cassandra for her (involuntary) involvement with Agamemnon: Aesch. *Ag.* 1440–7.

44 Jebb (1908) ad 27 points to the clear scepticism of εἰ δὴ.

45 Cf. 134–8.

46 Plato in *Laws* 700c–701b complains about the mixing of genres as moving away from what was 'lawful and just', and connects this explicitly to the 'lawlessness' in theatre audiences caused by tragedy, suggesting that at least in some Athenian circles the mixing of genres of the kind seen throughout the choral songs in this tragedy could be felt to be peculiar or problematic, even if this view is clearly strongly expressed as part of Plato's development of a particular political viewpoint. On the 'unsettling' mixing of genres in this song, see also Weiss (2020): 173.

47 On the *hymenaic* elements of 205–7, see Swift (2011): 410.

48 Seaford (1987): 111.

49 Swift (2010): 253 also recognizes that in picking up wedding imagery here, the chorus are continuing a pattern set by Deianira in her earlier address to them.

50 Swift (2010): 65; Swift (2011): 410.

51 Rutherford (1994): 120. See also Calame (2005b): 225 on the 'ambivalence' caused by this generic mixing. There is some potential overlap between the *paian* and the *dithyramb,* but the forms are distinctive enough to deserve separation (see further Harvey (1955): 172–4), and the introduction of Dionysiac elements in particular make this an uneasy combination of genres at this point in the chorus' song. See Loraux (2002): 71–2 on the capacity of the tragic choral voice to make 'dangerously close' connections between the Muses, Dionysus and Apollo.

52 Allen-Hornblower (2016): 117–19; Weiberg (2019): 180.

53 The text is uncertain here, but Easterling (1982): 138 provides a good rationale for θάτηρ (following Zieliński) to replace the corrupt μάτηρ.

54 Rodighiero (2012): 66–7. See also 78–9 on the epic features used to describe Heracles.

55 Compare Eur. *HF,* where Heracles is repeatedly praised in epinician terms (Chapter 3). The use of epinician features in *Trach.* 497–530 is discussed at length in Swift (2011), who sees a clash evoked between the roles and presentations of Heracles in tragedy and epinician.

56 On the confusion of participants in the contest and their roles, see Rodighiero (2012): 63, 75.

57 Wohl (1998): 19–20; on the erotic connotations of the language, see also Janka (2004): 140–2.

58 Specifically Bacchylidean: see Rodighiero (2012): 63, also on the mixing of genres which this song represents, 63–5.

59 Rodighiero (2012): 95.

60 Seaford (1987): 111; Ormand (1999): 41.

61 Rodighiero (2012): 98–100 sees sufficient negative references in the choral language here to read this part of the ode as an 'anti-epithalamion'.

62 See Kowalzig (2004) on Plato's objections to tragic choral performance blurring usually gendered choral performance, and Lardinois (2011): 170–1 on choral praise as gender-segregated, so that the female chorus of the *Trachiniae* attempting praise for a male subject is perhaps particularly problematic.

63 Lardinois (2011): 163–5.

64 Swift (2011): 410.

65 On the geographical references to competitors' home cities as typically epinician, see further Swift (2011): 396.

66 Janka (2004): 97.

67 Nooter (2012a): 66.

68 Loraux (2002): 61–2.

69 Loraux (2002): 62.

70 See similarly Janka (2004): 98–9. Janka sees the ode at 634–62 as a turning point which structurally links together the positive and negative first and second halves of the play, thus the intermingling of elements within it.

71 Bagordo (2003): 149–52. Both fragments are attributed to Simonides by Page and Bagordo himself, but anonymous in the *PMG* listing.

72 Janka (2004): 103–6 also points to how the chorus' use of the first-person plural in 647 and 649 suggests the chorus' identification with Deianira.

73 The term ἄσπετον is rare in tragedy (three instances), appearing more frequently in epic (thirty-seven instances). It is likely that its infrequency would have made its use here especially notable. Similarly, the clustering of descriptions of the burning caused by the potion as 'unspeakable', here, referring to the tuft of wool at 693–4, and the robe as described by Heracles at 1057 makes the description especially marked. Nooter (2012a): 73–4 notes Heracles' change in status from 'the world's most talked-about hero' to this unspeakable sight.

74 Allen-Hornblower (2016): 143–4 on the chorus' return to an earlier theme here, although she connects this revelation with the chorus' purpose of exculpating Deianira.

75 See 93–5.

76 On the extremely physical aspect of the robe, see Pozzi (1994): 585 and Kratzer (2013): 46–7.

77 The *Trachiniae* never explicitly refers to the apotheosis of Heracles after the play has ended. Recognition of Heracles' future cult role would enable the introduction of a

different dimension of praise into how characters or the chorus speak about him. Swift (2011): 406–9 argues that the inclusion of epinician elements in the choral ode at 497–530 itself reminds the audience of the apotheosis (usually celebrated in epinician), which is not implausible, although she rightly points to the contrast this would present between the Heracles of the *Trachiniae* and his usual future fate. Even if this association is assumed, there remains no *direct* praise for the divine Heracles in the play.

78 Wender (1974): 14; Machin (1981): 274. Although Deianira kills Heracles without a (typically masculine) sword, she does bring about her own death using one. See also Loraux (1987): 9–11 on possible gendered readings of tragic deaths, and Winnington-Ingram (1980): 81 n28, who connects this mode of death with the sexual relationship between herself and Heracles.

6 Medea and the Mastery of Blame

1 On connections between Deianira and Medea, see Mossman (2011): 20–3.

2 Mossman (2011) has also argued that Jason is feminized in the *Medea*, but attaches this quality to his behaviour and situation, whereas I shall argue here that the terms of Medea's blame for his behaviour have this gendering effect.

3 See Swift (2013): 140–1 on some of the complications caused by the chorus' apparent song to disavow their own ability to sing here; she seems them as representing a conflict between their gendered identity as women, which Medea encourages them to identify with most strongly, and their identity as a chorus.

4 Mastronarde (2002): 240–7; Mossman (2011): 257–9; Thomas (2018): 113.

5 See Introduction: 2.

6 Rehm (1994): 99; on the unusual combination of dialect and metre, see Swift (2013): 141. The use of Ionian may also be a further reference to epic features, but it is potentially operating on both levels, given the significance of blame for Medea's speech generally.

7 Swift (2010): 120–1 on the problematic features of praise/blame poetry as represented within the ode itself, particularly the chorus' mingling of future blame into this new song, which matches Medea's own practice throughout the play.

8 Mossman (2011): 259.

9 Mastronarde (2010): 118.

10 Knox (1977): 224.

11 Rabinowitz (1993): 153.

12 Boedeker (1997): 108–9.

13 Rehm (1989), esp. 106–11.

14 Foley (1989; rev. 2001) suggested influentially that the debate Medea holds with herself at 1019–80 represents a struggle between Medea's two gendered selves, each

of which embodies one part of these virtues. For the recognition of male or heroic qualities in the presentation of Medea, see e.g. Maddalena (1963), followed by Knox (1977) Seidensticker (1990), Bongie (1977) and Burnett (1973).

15 See Introduction: 15–16 on these generalized blame traditions.

16 On Medea's similar use of the *agon* as a form of 'performance of self', see Scodel (1999): 137.

17 Rabinowitz (2004): 52 notes that her choice of vocabulary also has a masculine effect. However, while her description may be masculinized, her need to excuse her exit from the house into the public arena is a type of speech limited to female characters in tragedy (see Chapter 5: n27).

18 On the Corinthian friendliness to Medea in this version, see Easterling (1977): 180. The Nurse comments that she is loved by the Corinthians (15), possibly alluding to the myth which is noted by the scholiast to Pind. *Ol.* 13.74 that Medea had saved the Corinthians from famine.

19 Rabinowitz (1993): 129–30 argues that Medea's supplications position her as victimized and thus sympathetic; McClure (1999b): 373 calls it a 'typically feminine' aspect of her persuasion; see further Boedeker (1991): 98–9 and Foley (2001): 258–9; Allan (2007): 121 suggests Creon's acceptance of Medea's supplication demonstrates his piety rather than simply her persuasiveness.

20 Luschnig (2007): 2–3.

21 Per Mastronarde (2002), Kovacs (1996) and Diggle (1984), although there is some corruption here, and Kovacs (2001) does not print γόον.

22 The Nurse's connection of banquets to consolation for grief may suggest the kind of poetic consolation which rejects lament found in Archilochus frs. 11 and 13 West, but rejects the claims made by poets such as Hesiod (*Theog.* 98–103) or Pindar (*Isthm.* 8.1–11) that poetry *can* console those suffering grief. The Nurse thus enters tragedy, through her words, into a longstanding poetic debate. Segal (1993): 20–1 connects this to the 'paradox of tragic song' in that tragedy is itself a song which does not heal through pleasure, and dwells on suffering. Similarly, Pucci (1980): 24–32 sees a characterization of Euripides' own tragic writing in the Nurse's description of song's potential. For a slightly different view on the Nurse's comment as rejecting older forms of poetry, see Crane (1990). Gentili (1988): 41 suggests that this comment reflects poetry's failure to 'probe' human suffering, in comparison to the new dialectical style of philosophy. Thomas (2018): 110–12 reads this passage as part of Euripides' comment on musical innovation, indicating the playwright's own engagement with 'new' musical styles.

23 Kousoulini (2019): 29 on the 'emotional involvement' thus revealed by the Nurse.

24 Mastronarde (2002): 192.

25 McClure (1999b): 380–1, and see Chapter 1: 29 on Philoctetes' similar facility with the combined genres of blame and lament.

26 Pucci (1980): 116–31; Thomas (2018): 116–18.

27 Pucci (1980): 122–3.

28 Rehm (1994): 106. There are also references to Pindaric praise poetry in the style; see Mastronarde (2002): 305.

29 See similarly Swift (2013): 144. Mastronarde (2002): 347 suggests that the chorus may be responding to the Nurse's initial statement and confirming that their song is 'incommensurate with the horrors facing them'.

30 Luschnig (2007): 151–4 for some discussion of the potential political ramifications for the Athenian audience hearing this ode.

31 Knox (1977): 196.

32 Boedeker (1997): 129–30.

33 Describing Ajax (Soph. *Aj.* 41, 744), Zeus (Aesch. *PV.* 29, 376), Hephaestus (Eur. *Phaethon* fr. 781, 258), Neoptolemus (Soph. *Phil.* 328) and Heracles (Soph. *Trach.* 269). The term is also used once of Electra's anger (Soph. *El.* 176), and for Hera and the Erinyes (Eur. *HF* 840 and *IT* 1439). On Medea associated by her wrath with Achilles, see Mastronarde (2002): 345–6.

34 Mastronarde (2010): 264.

35 Foley (2001): 260–2 and n61. On Clytemnestra, see Katz (1994): 84 and McClure (1999a): 72–5. On the 'masculinized women' of tragedy, see Gould (1980): 56–7 and Foley (1981): 151–2. Mossman (2011): 31–9 provides some useful caveats.

36 Gould (1980): 55–6; Carson (1990): 159; Allan (2002): 61; on narratives of women's destructive sexuality, see Goldhill (1995): 145.

37 Sanders (2013): 45.

38 On the traditional generalization of blame for an individual woman becoming blame for the entire class, see Loraux (1994): 72–100 and McClure (1999b): 377; on these as especially common in Euripides, see Pomeroy (1975): 106–8.

39 Mastronarde (2010): 136–7 sees the chorus' responses to Medea as evidence of her 'manipulative power'.

40 Jason's description of Creon's daughter as a νύμφη not only implies that he thinks of her as young and nubile, sexier than Medea (Sanders (2013): 46), but also sets up a parallel to Medea's younger self, since Jason later uses very similar terms to talk of their early relationship at the time when their children were born (1336). Jason effectively implies that he has replaced Medea with a younger model. Medea potentially echoes this insult in the description of the bride as νεοζύγου (new-wed 804), which is a hapax, emphasizing the bride's newness.

41 In Euripides λέκτρα refers more often to the bed than its occupant, but it frequently appears where situations of sexual irregularity and almost exclusively infidelity (including where divine relationships interrupt mortal marriages) are being discussed, as at *HF* 345; *El.* 1037; *Hipp.* 14 (even if the impropriety is in Hippolytus' eyes only), 463, 860, 944; *Andr.* 35; *Hec.* 635; *Tro.* 404, *Ion.* 819; *Hel.* 637, 666, 794;

Phoen. 49, 59; *Or.* 1009; and *IA* 1275. The only cases in Euripides where λέκτρα does not occur in this context are at *Supp.* 56 in relation to Aethra's marriage to Aegeus (although given the more usual mythical background for this relationship, the portrayal of it here as a 'regular' marriage is itself odd), *Tro.* 745, where Andromache calls her marriage bed δυστυχῆ, and 981 where Hecuba claims that Athena dislikes the λέκτρα; *Hel.* 1400 where Helen claims to be honouring her first 'marriage-bed' in the faked funeral; and *Phoen.* 14 where it is the childless bed of Laius and Jocasta.

42 Mossman (2011): 277 sees this verbal mirroring as undermining Jason's attempts to deny the accusation.

43 McClure (1999b): 387, who also points out that Medea's later (1364) accusation that Jason's desire is a νόσος makes use of a term most often used in Euripides for specifically female desire.

44 Buchan (2008): 7–8. The chorus' reference to ἔρωτες . . . ἀνδράσιν may also indicate Jason rather than Medea as their focus; see Mossman (2011): 279.

45 Page (1938) ad 155 describes the chorus' verb as 'not very tactful' given its emphasis.

46 Sanders (2013): 46–7; Calame (2013b): 149.

47 The verb is not common but is found elsewhere in explicitly sexual contexts in Euripides – as at *Ion* 17, 1484; *Phaethon* 45 See also Hom. *Od.* 5.65, 5.119. In both Euripides and Sophocles it can mean the more neutral 'lie down' in the context of illness, as at Soph. *Trach.* 106, 1041, 1242; *OT* 961; Eur. *Or.* 152.

48 Mossman (2011): 222 also reads erotic implications in this phrasing.

49 McClure (1999a): 26–7; Foley (2001): 112; Murnaghan (2009): 238.

50 Allan (2007) argues that the 'oath' Medea claims to have performed with Jason is not meant to be seen as legitimate by the audience. However, while an audience might have judged this to be the case, Jason himself never even implies that the 'oath' she holds him to is invalid, which would presumably have been a valuable point in his defence.

51 On this as traditional blame, see Zeitlin (1996): 343–4; see also McClure (1999a): 40–7 in relation to women's role in lament. Archilochus in fr. 13 West rejects lament as γυναικεῖον ('womanish' fr. 13.10), in the same fragment which contains ideas similar to those raised by the Nurse in her rejection of lament (190–204), and suggests in the same fragment (lines 1–2) that lamenting to the wrong extent might be a source of blame: κήδεα μὲν στονόεντα Περίκλεες οὔτε τις ἀστῶν / **μεμφόμενος** θαλίῃς τέρψεται οὐδὲ πόλις.

52 Although in her early, off-stage lamenting, Medea more resembles the male Ajax of Sophocles than a female sufferer such as Hecuba, whose misery is played out entirely on-stage (Knox (1977): 76; Foley (2001): 260 and with a further comparison to Hecuba 260 n61).

53 Barlow (1989): 163–4; Boedeker (1991): 99; Foley (2001): 258–61.

54 Foley (2001): 261–2 argues that Medea is converting herself to a more masculine, heroic figure, and dropping a 'feminine mask'. See also Levett (2010): 62.

55 Knox (1977): 206–11 saw the end of the play as moving Medea beyond humanity, into the position of a *theos*, removed from the action, thus her emotional detachment, which Jason does not share. See also Pucci (1980): 158–61 for a variety of earlier views; Mastronarde (2010): 186 deals with the dramatic conventions involved in her appearance as a *deus ex machina*, cf. Rutherford (2012): 95–7.

56 Rabinowitz (1993): 135–6 traces a 'backdrop' of sea-based imagery as part of Euripides' emphasis on the Argonautic myth. Mastronarde (2002): 258–60 suggests there may be a rather unflattering allusion to trading by sea in Jason's language.

57 Bongie (1977): 43; Mastronarde (2002): 260.

58 Mossman (2011): 269–73.

59 Blundell (1989). Medea's actions simultaneously attempt to reinforce this code by contravening it, since she will destroy her own *philoi* to harm her enemies. See also Belfiore (2000): 131–2; Rehm (2002): 261–2; Williamson (1990): 24–5 notes her long history of harming *philoi* and not correctly identifying enemies during her association with Jason.

60 Boedeker (1991); Rabinowitz (1993): 142–5; Foley (2001): 258–60; Mastronarde (2002): 8.

61 Her narration of sections of their previous adventures, and of Jason's death to come, also effectively show her taking a role in the construction of his entire mythical identity. Segal (1996): 37–8 is persuasive on how she 'recasts' his life story, shaping it from a 'woman-centred view' which centres his entire story on his relationship and marriage to her, and significantly diminishing the Argonautic aspects (and the Argo itself at 1386–8). While Segal's interpretation is extremely effective, I would also argue that it is not simply a matter of Medea's role as speaker or narrator which makes her able to affect this change, but her awareness of and facility with the genres of praise and blame speech.

62 On Medea's self-construction and presentation, see Pucci (1980): 62–82 and Luschnig (2007): 188–98.

63 While Medea is always involved in helping Jason with the bulls and providing assistance or advice, a major role in dealing with the dragon seems to have been a later addition to the tradition, and may well be a new or exaggerated feature of her account here. See McCallum-Barry (2014): 25–9.

64 Mossman (2011): 266–7.

65 See Chapter 4 on Evadne's seeking after the same term.

66 Luschnig (2007): 196 associates this language with Medea's desire to 'change the stories' of herself and Jason. This claim to victory is particularly incongruous when it is associated with the act by which she intends to attain that status – the murder

of her children – but provides an interesting comparison with Euripides' Heracles, who also self-identifies as καλλίνικος as the result of his (unknowing) slaughter of his children (Eur. *HF* 961): see Chapter 3.

67 See Mossman (2011): 219 on the epinician implications of this song and implied contest.

68 Mossman (2011): 253–4.

69 Bongie (1977): 44.

70 This anticipation of mockery is similar to that mentioned by the chorus and characters of the *Ajax* – see Chapter 2. However, the case presented in the *Ajax* is less unusual, as the feared mockery was of a male character, and as Rehm (1989): 109 points out, the last thing Medea could be considered after killing Creon and his daughter is 'laughable', unlike Ajax, whose violence is laughable because it is so wildly ineffective after the intervention of Athena.

71 Blundell (1989) on harming enemies and helping friends, but see Foley (1989): 66 and Williamson (1990): 26. On the concept of the 'Sophoclean Hero', see Knox (1964).

72 Although Rehm (1989): 109–11 sees this as Medea lapsing into an unsuitable masculine λόγος, as a result of her failure to establish a better female version.

73 On praise or blame as motivating factors, see especially Chapters 1 and 4.

74 Medea's ability to consider the effects of multiple identities and argue for the prioritization of one over another for the best effect for her desires, can also be seen in her requests that the chorus prioritize their shared identity as women over differences in ethnic identity, shown deftly by Swift (2013): 134–8.

75 As Segal (1996): 39 points out, Medea continues to identify herself as 'mother' (1397), while Jason is unable to similarly self-define as 'father'. See further on Medea's past and present violence primarily resulting in the destruction of identities rooted in familial ties (e.g. 'daughter', 'sister'), Sanders (2013): 47–8.

76 Blondell (1999): 166; Segal (1996): 21–2.

77 Williamson (1990): 19 also rightly points out that much of Medea's arrangement with Aegeus is in itself similar to the contracting of a new marriage, like Jason's to Creon's daughter, in terms of the benefits she and he gain from it, and in the way she describes it to Jason at 1385.

78 Luschnig (2007): 72–3. See also Segal (1996): 27–31.

79 Mossman (2011): 367.

Conclusion

1 For example, in fr. 97 from the *Alcmene*, someone speaks against being praised while suffering misfortune, Amphion in the *Antiope* criticizes the praising of

dangerous behaviour in fr. 194, and in fr. 347 the question of praising properly is connected in the *Dictys* (perhaps) to patriotism, since the person who praises a foreign land above his own is to be judged as 'not thinking well'. There are also examples of choral performance as part of establishing *kleos* in fragmentary tragedy, for example the *Erechtheus*, in which the chorus describe themselves as 'singing garlanded' (fr. 369.3), and say they will be unfolding the voice of works in which the wise are 'celebrated', κλέονται (369.7).

Bibliography

Ahrensdorf, P. J. (2009) *Greek Tragedy and Political Philosophy: Rationalism and Religion in Sophocles' Theban Plays* (Cambridge; New York: Cambridge University Press).

Alexiou, M. (2002) *The Ritual Lament in Greek Tradition* (Oxford: Rowman & Littlefield).

Allan, A. L. (2007) 'Masters of manipulation: Euripides' (and Medea's) use of oaths in *Medea*', in A. H. Sommerstein and J. Fletcher (eds), *Horkos: The Oath in Greek Society* (Bristol: Bristol Phoenix Press) 113–24.

Allan, A. L. (2011) '"Am I Not the One...?"(Sophokles' *Phil.* 114): Neoptolemos and the Allure of Kleos', *CJ* 107: 1–26.

Allan, W. (2000) *The* Andromache *and Euripidean Tragedy* (Oxford: Clarendon Press).

Allan, W. (2002) *Euripides'* Medea (London: Duckworth).

Allan, W. (2005) 'Arms and the man: Euphorbus, Hector, and the death of Patroclus', *CQ* 55: 1–16.

Allan, W., and A. Kelly (2013) 'Listening to many voices: Athenian tragedy as popular art', in A. Marmodoro and J. Hill (eds), *The Author's Voice in Classical and Late Antiquity* (Oxford: Oxford University Press) 77–123.

Allen-Hornblower, E. (2013) 'Sounds and Suffering in Sophocles' *Philoctetes* and Gide's *Philoctète*', *Studi italiani di filologia classica* 11: 5–41.

Allen-Hornblower, E. (2016) *From Agent to Spectator, Witnessing the Aftermath in Ancient Greek Epic and Tragedy* (Berlin; Boston: De Gruyter).

Anderson, A. S. (2015) 'The Seven Against Thebes at Eleusis', *ICS* 40: 297–319.

Andújar, R., T. R. P. Coward, and T. A. Hadjimichael, eds (2019) *Paths of Song: The Lyric Dimension of Greek Tragedy* (Berlin; Boston: De Gruyter).

Austin, N. (2011) *Sophocles' Philoctetes and the Great Soul Robbery* (Madison, US: University of Wisconsin Press).

Bagordo, A. (2003) *Reminiszenzen früher Lyrik bei den attischen Tragikern: Beiträge zur Anspielungstechnik und poetischer Tradition* (Munich: Beck).

Barker, E. (2004) 'The Fall-out from Dissent: Hero and Audience in Sophocles' Ajax', *G&R* 51: 1–20.

Barlow, S. A. (1981) 'Sophocles' *Ajax* and Euripides' *Heracles*', *Ramus* 10: 112–28.

Barlow, S. A. (1989) 'Stereotype and reversal in Euripides' *Medea*', *G&R* 36: 158–71.

Barlow, S. A. (1996) *Euripides'* Heracles (Warminster: Aris and Phillips).

Barrett, J. (2002) *Staged Narrative: Poetics and the Messenger in Greek Tragedy* (Berkeley: University of California Press).

Belfiore, E. (2000) *Murder Among Friends: Violation of Philia in Greek Tragedy* (Oxford; New York: Oxford University Press).

Bergren, A. L. T. (1989) '"The Homeric Hymn to Aphrodite": Tradition and Rhetoric, Praise and Blame', *Cl. Ant.* 8: 1–41.

Billings, J. (2021) *The Philosophical Stage: Drama and Dialectic in Classical Athens* (Princeton: Princeton University Press).

Blondell, R. (1999) 'Introduction', in R. Blondell, M.-K. Gamel, N. S. Rabinowitz and B. Zweig (eds), *Women on the Edge: Four Plays by Euripides* (London: Routledge) 149–68.

Blondell, R. (2010) '"Bitch that I Am": Self-Blame and Self-Assertion in the Iliad', *TAPA* 140 (1): 1–32.

Blundell, M. W. (1989) *Helping Friends and Harming Enemies: A Study in Sophocles and Greek Ethics* (Cambridge: Cambridge University Press).

Boedeker, D. (1991) 'Euripides' Medea and the vanity of ΛΟΓΟΙ', *CPhil.* LXXXVI: 95–112.

Boedeker, D. (1997) 'Becoming Medea: Assimilation in Euripides', in J. J. Clauss (ed.), *Medea* (Princeton: Princeton University Press) 127–48.

Bond, G. W., ed. (1981) *Euripides Heracles* (London: Oxford University Press).

Bongie, E. B. (1977) 'Heroic elements in the *Medea* of Euripides', *TAPA* 107: 27–56.

Bowie, E. L. (2001) 'Ancestors of Historiography in Early Greek Elegiac and Iambic Poetry?', in N. Luraghi (ed.), *The Historian's Craft in the Age of Herodotus* (Oxford; New York: Oxford University Press) 45–66.

Bowman, L. M. (1999) 'Prophecy and Authority in the *Trachiniai*', *AJPhil.* 120: 335–50.

Bowra, C. M. (2001) *Greek Lyric Poetry from Alcman to Simonides* (Oxford: Clarendon Press).

Brown, C. G. (2006) 'Pindar on Archilochus and the Gluttony of Blame (Pyth. 2.52–6)*', *JHS* 126: 36–46.

Buccheri, A. (2016) 'Deiknūnai tēn phūsin: valider l'identité filiale dans le *Philoctète* de Sophocle', *Cahiers Mondes anciens: Histoire et anthropologie des mondes anciens.*

Buchan, M. (2008) '"Too difficult for a single man to understand": *Medea*'s out-jutting foot', *Helios* 35: 3–28.

Budelmann, F. (2000) *The Language of Sophocles: Communality, Communication, and Involvement* (Cambridge; New York: Cambridge University Press).

Bundy, E. L. (1962) *Studia Pindarica, I–II* (Berkeley: University of California Press).

Burian, P. (1985) 'Logos and Pathos: The Politics of the *Suppliant Women*', in P. Burian (ed.), *Directions in Euripidean criticism: A collection of essays* (Durham, NC: Duke University Press) 129–55.

Burian, P. (2013) 'Polyphonic Ajax', in K. Ormand (ed.), *A Companion to Sophocles* (Malden, MA; Oxford: Wiley-Blackwell) 69–83.

Burnett, A. P. (1971) *Catastrophe Survived: Euripides' Plays of Mixed Reversal* (Oxford: Clarendon Press).

Burnett, A. P. (1973) 'Medea and the tragedy of revenge', *CPhil.* 68: 1–24.

Burton, R. W. B. (1980) *The Chorus in Sophocles' Tragedies* (Oxford: Clarendon Press).

Cairns, D. L. (1993) *Aidōs: The Psychology and Ethics of Honour and Shame in Ancient Greek Literature* (Oxford: Clarendon Press).

Cairns, D. L. (2002) 'The Meaning of the Veil in Ancient Greek Culture', in L. Llewellyn-Jones (ed.), *Women's Dress in the Ancient Greek World* (Swansea: Classical Press of Wales) 73–93.

Cairns, D. L. (2006) 'Virtue and Vicissitude: the Paradoxes of Ajax', in D. Cairns and V. J. Liapis (eds), *Dionysalexandros: Essays on Aeschylus and His Fellow Tragedians in Honour of Alexander F. Garvie* (Swansea: Classical Press of Wales) 99–132.

Calame, C. (1990) *Thésée et l'imaginaire athénien: légende et culte en Grèce antique* (Lausanne: Payot).

Calame, C. (2001) *Choruses of Young Women in Ancient Greece: Their Morphology, Religious Role, and Social Functions* (Lanham, MD: Rowman & Littlefield).

Calame, C. (2005a) *Masks of Authority: Fiction and Pragmatics in Ancient Greek Poetics*, tr. P. M. Burk (Ithaca, NY: Cornell University Press).

Calame, C. (2005b) 'The Tragic Choral Group: Dramatic Roles and Social Functions', in R. Bushnell (ed.), *A Companion to Tragedy* (Oxford; Malden, MA: Blackwell) 215–33.

Calame, C. (2013a) 'Choral Polyphony and the Ritual Functions of Tragic Songs', in R. Gagné and M. Hopman (eds), *Choral Mediations in Greek Tragedy* (Cambridge; New York: Cambridge University Press) 35–57.

Calame, C. (2013b) *The Poetics of Eros in Ancient Greece*, tr. J. Lloyd (reprint edition) (Princeton: Princeton University Press).

Calder, W. M. (1971) 'Sophoclean Apologia: *Philoctetes*', *GRBS* 12: 153–74.

Campbell, D. (1993) *Greek Lyric, Volume V: The New School of Poetry and Anonymous Songs and Hymns* (Boston, MA: Harvard University Press).

Campbell, David A., ed. (1992) *Greek Lyric, Volume IV: Bacchylides, Corinna, and Others*, tr. D. A. Campbell (Boston, MA: Loeb Classical Library).

Carden, R. (1974) *The Papyrus Fragments of Sophocles, An Edition with Prolegomena and Commentary* (Berlin; Boston: De Gruyter).

Carey, C. (1991) 'The Victory Ode in Performance: The Case for the Chorus', *CPhil.* 86: 192–200.

Carey, C. (2009) 'Iambos', in F. Budelmann (ed.), *The Cambridge Companion to Greek Lyric* (Cambridge: Cambridge University Press) 149–67.

Carey, C. (2012) 'The Victory Ode in the Theatre', *BICS* 55: 17–36.

Carey, C. (2013) 'Comedy and the Civic Chorus', in E. Bakola, L. Prauscello and M. Telò (eds), *Greek Comedy and the Discourse of Genres* (Cambridge: Cambridge University Press) 155–74.

Carey, C. (2018) 'Narrative, Authority, and Blame', *Mouseion* 15: 7–27.

Carlevale, J. (2000) 'Education, "Phusis," and Freedom in Sophocles' *Philoctetes*', *Arion* 8: 26–60.

Carson, A. (1990) 'Putting Her in Her Place: Woman, Dirt, and Desire', in D. M. Halperin, F. Zeitlin and J. J. Winkler (eds), *Before Sexuality: The Construction of Erotic Experience in the Ancient Greek World* (Princeton: Princeton University Press) 135–69.

Carter, D. M., ed. (2011) *Why Athens? A Reappraisal of Tragic Politics* (Oxford; New York: Oxford University Press).

Carter, D. M. (2013) 'Finglass, P. J. 2011. Sophocles: Ajax. Cambridge, Cambridge University Press. x, 612 pp. Pr. £110.00 (hb). ISBN 9781107003071.', *Mnemosyne* 66: 139–41.

Chong-Gossard, J. H. K. O. (2008) *Gender and Communication in Euripides' Plays: Between Song and Silence* (Leiden: Brill).

Clear, R. (2013) 'Family, Duty and Expectation: A Case for the Joint Performance of Pindar's "Isthmian" 2 and "Pythian" 6', *Mnemosyne* 66: 31–53.

Collard, C. (1972) 'The Funeral Oration in Euripides' *Supplices*', *BICS* 19: 39–53.

Collard, C. (1975) *Supplices, I–II: Introduction and Text; Commentary* (Groningen: Bouma).

Collins, D. (2006) 'Corinna and Mythological Innovation', *CQ* 56: 19–32.

Conacher, D. J. (1956) 'Religious and Ethical Attitudes in Euripides' Suppliants', *TAPA* 87: 8–26.

Conacher, D. J. (1967) *Euripidean Drama: Myth, Theme and Structure* (Toronto: University of Toronto Press; London).

Cook, K. (2021) 'Memories of Glory: Poetry, Prose, and Commemoration in the Heraclidae', in K. Mawford and E. Ntanou (eds), *Ancient Memory: Remembrance and Commemoration in Graeco-Roman Literature* (Berlin, Boston: De Gruyter) 71–88.

Craik, E. M. (1980) 'Sophokles and the Sophists', *L'Antiquité Classique* 49: 247–54.

Crane, G. (1990) 'A Change of Fashion, and Euripides' "Medea" 190-203', *Mnemosyne* 43: 435–8.

Cropp, M. J. (1986) '*Heracles*, *Electra*, and the *Odyssey*', in M. J. Cropp, E. Fantham and S. E. Scully (eds), *Greek Tragedy and Its Legacy: Essays Presented to D. J. Conacher* (Calgary: University of Calgary Press) 187–200.

Csapo, E., and W. J. Slater (2009) *The Context of Ancient Drama* (Ann Arbor, MI: University of Michigan Press).

Davidson, J. (1995) 'Homer and Sophocles' *Philoctetes*', *BICS* 40: 25–35.

Davidson, J. (2001) 'Sophocles' *Philoctetes*: The Encounter of the Generations', *WJA* 25: 27–39.

Davie, J. N. (1982) 'Theseus the King in Fifth-Century Athens', *G&R* 29: 25–34.

Davies, M. (1991) *Sophocles, The Trachiniae* (Oxford: Clarendon Press).

Davies, M., and P. Finglass (2015) *Stesichorus: The Poems* (Cambridge; New York: Cambridge University Press).

Dee, N. M. (2015) 'The Athenian Reception of Evadne's Suicide in Euripides's *Suppliants*', *ICS* 40: 263–79.

Deicke, W. (1999) 'Zur Interpretation des sophokleischen *Philoktet*: Hartmut Erbse gewidmet', *Hermes* 127: 172–88.

Delgado, J. A. F. (2015) 'Mégara entre retórica y folclore (EUR. "HF" 451-496)', *Quaderni Urbinati di Cultura Classica* 111: 93–101.

Derderian, K. (2000) *Leaving Words to Remember: Greek Mourning and the Advent of Literacy* (Leiden: Brill).

Detienne, M. (1996) *The Masters of Truth in Archaic Greece*, tr. J. Lloyd (Cambridge (Mass.): MIT Press).

Dewald, C., and R. Kitzinger (2015) 'Speaking Silences in Herodotus and Sophocles', in C. A. Clark, E. Foster and J. P. Hallett (eds), *Kinesis: The Ancient Depiction of Gesture, Motion, and Emotion* (Ann Arbor, MI: University of Michigan Press) 86–102.

Dickson, K. M. (1993) 'Nestor Among the Sirens', *Oral Tradition* vol. 8, no. 1: 21–58.

Diggle, J. (1981) *Studies on the text of Euripides: Supplices, Electra, Heracles, Troades, Iphigenia in Tauris, Ion* (Oxford: Clarendon Press).

Diggle, J. (1984) *Euripidis: Fabulae, Vol. 1: Cyclops; Alcestis; Medea; Heraclidae; Hippolytus; Andromacha; Hecuba* (Oxford: Oxford University Press).

Dillon, M. (1991) 'Tragic Laughter', *CW* 84: 345–55.

Doherty, L. E. (1995) 'Sirens, Muses, and Female Narrators in the *Odyssey*', in B. Cohen (ed.), *The Distaff Side: Representing the Female in Homer's Odyssey* (Oxford; New York: Oxford University Press) 81–92.

Dué, C. (2006) *The Captive Woman's Lament in Greek Tragedy* (Austin, TX: University of Texas Press).

Dunn, F. M. (1997) 'Ends and Means in Euripides' *Heracles*', in F. M. Dunn, D. H. Roberts and D. P. Fowler (eds), *Classical Closure: Reading the End in Greek and Latin Literature* (Princeton: Princeton University Press) 83–111.

Easterling, P. E. (1977) 'The Infanticide in Euripides' *Medea*', *YClS* 25: 177–91.

Easterling, P. E. (1978) '*Philoctetes* and Modern Criticism', *ICS* 3: 27–39.

Easterling, P. E. (1982) *Sophocles Trachiniae* (Cambridge: Cambridge University Press).

Easterling, P. E. (1991) 'Men's κλέος and Women's γόος: Female Voices in the Iliad', *Journal of Modern Greek Studies* 9: 145–51.

Ebbott, M. (1999) 'The Wrath of Helen: Self-blame and Nemesis in the *Iliad*', in M. Carlisle and O. A. Levaniouk (eds), *Nine Essays on Homer* (Lanham, MD: Rowman and Littlefield) 3–20.

Euripides (1981) *Euripidis fabulae: Supplices, Electra, Hercules, Troades, Iphigenia in Tauris, Ion* (Oxford: E Typographeo Clarendoniano).

Färber, H. (1936) *Die Lyrik in Der Kunsttheorie Der Antike* (Munich: Neuer Filser-Verlag).

Farrell, J. (2003) 'Classical Genre in Theory and Practice', *New Literary History* 34: 383–408.

Fearn, D. (2007) *Bacchylides: Politics, Performance, Poetic Tradition* (Oxford; New York: Oxford University Press).

Finglass, P. J. (2006) 'The Hero's Quest in Sophocles' *Philoctetes*', *Prometheus: Rivista di studi classici* 32: 217–24.

Finglass, P. J. (2009) 'Two amputations in Sophocles', *Materiali e discussioni per l'analisi dei testi classici* 62: 223–30.

Finglass, P. J. (2011) *Sophocles' Ajax* (Cambridge; New York: Cambridge University Press).

Fitton, J. W. (1961) 'The *Suppliant Women* and the *Herakleidai* of Euripides', *Hermes* LXXXIX: 430–61.

Fletcher, J. (2013) 'Weapons of Friendship: Props in Sophocles' *Philoctetes* and *Ajax*', in G. W. M. Harrison and V. J. Liapis (eds), *Performance in Greek and Roman Theatre* (Leiden; Boston: Brill) 199–215.

Foley, H. (2003) 'Choral Identity in Greek Tragedy', *CPhil.* 98: 1–30.

Foley, H. P. (1981) 'The Concept of Women in Athenian Drama', in Foley, H. P. (ed.), *Reflections of Women in Antiquity* (Philadelphia: Gordon & Breach Science Publ.) 127–68.

Foley, H. P. (1985) *Ritual Irony: Poetry and Sacrifice in Euripides* (Ithaca, NY: Cornell University Press).

Foley, H. P. (1989) 'Medea's divided self', *Cl. Ant.* VIII: 61–85.

Foley, H. P. (2001) *Female Acts in Greek Tragedy* (Princeton: Princeton University Press).

Foster, M., L. Kurke, and N. Weiss (2019) 'Introduction', in *Genre in Archaic and Classical Greek Poetry: Theories and Models* (Leiden: Brill) 1–28.

Fowler, R. L. (1999) 'Three places of the *Trachiniae*', in J. Griffin (ed.), *Sophocles Revisited* (Oxford; New York: Oxford University Press) 161–75.

Fuqua, C. (1976) 'Studies in the use of myth in Sophocles' *Philoctetes* and the *Orestes* of Euripides', *Traditio* 32: 29–95.

Gagné, R., and M. G. Hopman (2013) *Choral Mediations in Greek Tragedy* (Cambridge; New York: Cambridge University Press).

Galinsky, G. K. (1972) *The Herakles Theme: The Adaptations of the Hero in Literature from Homer to the Twentieth Century* (Oxford; Malden, MA: Blackwell).

Gamble, R. B. (1970) 'Euripides' Suppliant Women: Decision and ambivalence', *Hermes* 98: 385–405.

Gardiner, C. P. (1987) *The Sophoclean Chorus: A Study of Character and Function* (Iowa City: University of Iowa Press).

Garland, R. (1992) *Introducing New Gods: The Politics of Athenian Religion* (Ithaca, NY: Cornell University Press).

Garrison, E. P. (1995) *Groaning Tears: Ethical and Dramatic Aspects of Suicide in Greek Tragedy* (Leiden: Brill).

Garvie, A. F. (1998) *Sophocles' Ajax* (Warminster: Aris and Phillips).

Gentili, B. (1988) *Poetry and Its Public in Ancient Greece: From Homer to the Fifth Century* (Baltimore: Johns Hopkins University Press).

Gibert, J. C. (1997) 'Euripides *Heracles* 1351 and the Hero's Encounter with Death', *CPhil.* 92: 247–58.

Goff, B. (1995) 'Aithra at Eleusis', *Helios* 22: 65–78.

Goff, B. (2004) *Citizen Bacchae: Women's Ritual Practice in Ancient Greece* (Berkeley: University of California Press).

Goff, B. (2010) 'Sons of the Shield: Paternal Arms in Epic and Tragedy', in P. Mitsis and C. C. Tsagalis (eds), *Allusion, Authority, and Truth: Critical Perspectives on Greek Poetic and Rhetorical Praxis* 7 (Berlin; New York: De Gruyter) 219–33.

Goldhill, S. (1986) *Reading Greek Tragedy* (Cambridge: Cambridge University Press).

Goldhill, S. (1991) *The Poet's Voice: Essays in Poetics and Greek Literature* (Cambridge: Cambridge University Press).

Goldhill, S. (1995) *Foucault's Virginity: Ancient Erotic Fiction and the History of Sexuality* (Cambridge; New York: Cambridge University Press).

Goldhill, S. (1996) 'Collectivity and Otherness: The Authority of the Tragic Chorus', in M. S. Silk (ed.), *Tragedy and the Tragic: Greek Theatre and Beyond* (Oxford: Oxford University Press) 244–56.

Goldhill, S. (2013) 'Choreography: The Lyric Voice of Sophoclean Tragedy', in R. Gagné and M. Hopman (eds), *Choral Mediations in Greek Tragedy* (Cambridge: Cambridge University Press) 100–29.

Gould, J. (1980) 'Law, Custom, and Myth. Aspects of the Social Position of Women in Classical Athens', *JHS* 100: 38–59.

Greengard, C. (1987) *Theatre in Crisis: Sophocles' Reconstruction of Genre and Politics in Philoctetes* (Amsterdam: Hakkert).

Gregory, J. (1991) *Euripides and the Instruction of the Athenians* (Ann Arbor, MI: University of Michigan Press).

Gregory, J. (2018a) 'Sophocles' Ajax and his Homeric Prototypes', in G. Xanthakē-Karamanou, A. Fountoulakis, A. Markantonatos and G. Vasilaros (eds), *Theatre World: Critical Perspectives on Greek Tragedy and Comedy: Studies in Honour of Georgia Xanthakis-Karamanos* (Berlin; Boston: De Gruyter) 137–56.

Gregory, J. (2018b) *Cheiron's Way: Youthful Education in Homer and Tragedy* (Oxford; New York: Oxford University Press).

Gregory, J. W. (1977) 'Euripides' Heracles', *YClS* 25: 259–75.

Grethlein, J. (2003) *Asyl und Athen: die Konstruktion kollektiver Identität in der griechischen Tragödie* (Stuttgart: Metzler).

Griffin, J. (1986) 'Homeric Words and Speakers', *JHS* 106: 36–57.

Griffith, M. (2001) 'Antigone and Her Sister(s): Embodying Women in Greek Tragedy', in A. Lardinois and L. McClure (eds), *Making Silence Speak* (Princeton: Princeton University Press) 117–36.

Griffith, M., and D. M. Carter (2011) 'Introduction', in D. M. Carter (ed.), *Why Athens?* (Oxford: Oxford University Press).

Griffiths, E. M. (2002) 'Euripides' *Herakles* and the Pursuit of Immortality', *Mnemosyne* 55: 641–56.

Griffiths, E. M. (2006) *Euripides'* Heracles (London: Duckworth).

Griffiths, E. M. (2020) *Children in Greek Tragedy: Pathos and Potential* (Oxford; New York: Oxford University Press).

Halleran, M. R. (1985) *Stagecraft in Euripides* (London: Croom Helm).

Hardwick, L. (1993) 'Philomel and Pericles: Silence in the Funeral Speech', *G&R* 40: 147–62.

Harvey, A. E. (1955) 'The Classification of Greek Lyric Poetry', *CQ* 5: 157–75.

Heath, M. (1999) 'Sophocles' *Philoctetes* a Problem Play?', in J. Griffin (ed.), *Sophocles Revisited: Essays Presented to Sir Hugh Lloyd-Jones* (Oxford; New York: Oxford University Press) 137–60.

Heath, M., and E. OKell (2007) 'Sophocles' *Ajax*: Expect the Unexpected', *CQ* 57: 363–80.

Heiden, B. (1989) *Tragic Rhetoric: An Interpretation of Sophocles' Trachiniae* (Bern; Frankfurt am Main: Lang).

Heiden, B. A. (1984) 'The Tragic Rhetoric of Sophocles' *Trachiniae*', PhD, Cornell University.

Henrichs, A. (1994) '"Why should I dance?": Choral Self-referentiality in Greek Tragedy', *Arion* 3: 56–111.

Henrichs, A. (1996) 'Dancing in Athens, Dancing on Delos: Some Patterns of Choral Projection in Euripides', *Philologus* 140: 48–62.

Herington, J. (1985) *Poetry into Drama: Early Tragedy and the Greek Poetic Tradition* (Berkeley: University of California Press).

Hesk, J. (2000) *Deception and Democracy in Classical Athens* (Cambridge: Cambridge University Press).

Hesk, J. (2003) *Sophocles:* Ajax (London: Duckworth).

Hesk, J. (2006) 'Homeric Flyting and How to Read It: Performance and Intratext in *Iliad* 20.83–109 and 20.178–258', *Ramus* 35: 4–28.

Hesk, J. (2011) 'Euripidean εὐβουλία and the Problem of "Tragic Politics"', in D. M. Carter (ed.), *Why Athens?* (Oxford; New York: Oxford University Press) 119–44.

Hesk, J. (2013) 'Leadership and Individuality in the Athenian Funeral Orations', *BICS* 56: 49–65.

Hirsch, E. (2014) *A Poet's Glossary* (Boston; New York: Houghton Mifflin Harcourt).

Holmes, B. (2008) 'Euripides' Heracles in the Flesh', *Cl. Ant.* 27: 231–81.

Holst-Warhaft, G. (2002) *Dangerous Voices: Women's Laments and Greek Literature* (London: Routledge).

Holt, P. (1981) 'The Debate-Scenes in the *Ajax*', *AJPhil.* 102: 275–88.

Hornblower, S. (2004) *Thucydides and Pindar: Historical Narrative and the World of Epinikian Poetry* (Oxford; New York: Oxford University Press).

Hose, M. (2009) 'Philoktet: Von der Schwierigkeit der Wiedereingliederung', *Philologus* 152: 27–39.

Hutchinson, G. O. (2012) 'Image and World in Epinician Poetry', in C. Carey, P. Agócs and R. Rawles (eds), *Reading the Victory Ode* (Cambridge: Cambridge University Press) 277–302.

Huxley, G. (1967) 'Thersites in Sophokles, Philoktetes 445', *GRBS* 8: 33–4.

Janka, M. (2004) *Dialog der Tragiker: Liebe, Wahn und Erkenntnis in Sophokles'* Trachiniai *und Euripides'* Hippolytos (Munich: Saur).

Jebb, S. R. C. (1908) *Sophocles:* The Trachiniae (Oxford: Oxford University Press).

Kamerbeek, J. C. (1980) *The Plays of Sophocles:* The Philoctetes (Leiden: E. J. Brill).

Kampakoglou, A. (2018) 'Epinician Discourse in Euripides' Tragedies: The Case of *Alexandros*', in R. Andújar, T. R. P. Coward and T. A. Hadjimichael (eds), *Paths of Song* (Berlin, Boston: De Gruyter) 187–218.

Katz, M. A. (1994) 'The Character of Tragedy: Women and the Greek Imagination', *Arethusa* 27: 81–103.

Kavoulaki, A. (2008) 'The Last Word: Ritual, Power, and Performance in Euripides' *Hiketides*', in M. Revermann and P. J. Wilson (eds), *Performance, Iconography, Reception: Studies in Honour of Oliver Taplin* (Oxford; New York: Oxford University Press) 291–317.

Kavoulaki, A. (2011) 'Choral Self-awareness: On the Introductory Anapaests of Aeschylus' *Supplices*', in L. Athanassaki and E. Bowie (eds), *Archaic and Classical Choral Song* (Berlin, Boston: De Gruyter) 365–90.

Kennedy, R. F. (2009) *Athena's Justice: Athena, Athens and the Concept of Justice in Greek Tragedy* (New York: Peter Lang).

Kirkwood, G. M. (1941) 'The Dramatic Unity of Sophocles' *Trachiniae*', *TAPA* 203–11.

Kirkwood, G. M. (1982) *Selections from Pindar: Edited with an Introduction and Commentary* (Chico, CA: Scholars Press).

Knox, B. M. W. (1961) 'The Ajax of Sophocles', *Harv. Stud.* 65: 1–37.

Knox, B. M. W. (1964) *The Heroic Temper: Studies in Sophoclean Tragedy* (Berkeley: University of California Press).

Knox, B. M. W. (1977) 'The Medea of Euripides', *YClS* XXV: 193–225.

Köhnken, A. (1971) *Die Funktion des Mythos bei Pindar: Interpretationen zu sechs Pindargedichten* (Berlin; New York: De Gruyter).

Kokkini, D. (2010) 'Admetos as Everyman in Euripides' *Alkestis*', in L. Langerwerf and C. Ryan (eds), *Zero to Hero, Hero to Zero: In Search of the Classical Hero* (Newcastle: Cambridge Scholars Publ.) 28–48.

Konstan, D. (2007) 'War and Reconciliation in Greek Literature', in K. A. Raaflaub (ed.), *War and Peace in the Ancient World* (Oxford; Malden: Blackwell) 191–205.

Konstantinou, A. (2012) 'The Lioness Imagery in Greek Tragedy', *Quaderni Urbinati di Cultura Classica* 101: 125–41.

Kornarou, E. (2008) 'The Display of the Dead on the Greek Tragic Stage: The Case of Euripides' *Supplices**', *BICS* 51: 29–38.

Kosak, J. C. (2006) 'The Male Interior: Strength, Illness, and Masculinity in Sophocles' *Philoctetes*', *Bulletin of the Institute of Classical Studies. Supplement* 49–64.

Kousoulini, V. (2019) 'Restraining her Song and Saving the Oikos? Nurses in Euripides' *Medea*, *Hippolytus*, and *Andromache*', *Skenè: Journal of Theatre and Drama Studies* 5: 19–42.

Kovacs, D. (1996) *Euripidea altera* (Leiden: Brill).

Kovacs, D. (1998) *Suppliant Women; Electra; Heracles* (Cambridge (Mass.): Harvard University Press).

Kovacs, D. (2001) *Euripides* Cyclops; Alcestis; Medea (Cambridge, MA; London: Harvard University Press).

Kowalzig, B. (2004) 'Changing Choral Worlds: Song-Dance and Society in Athens and Beyond', in P. Murray and P. Wilson (eds), *Music and the Muses* (Oxford: Oxford University Press) 39–66.

Kranz, W. (1933) *Stasimon* (Hildesheim: Georg Olms Verlag).

Kratzer, E. A. (2013) 'A Hero's Welcome: Homecoming and Transition in the *Trachniae*', *TAPA* 143: 23–63.

Kraus, C. S. (1991) '"Λόγος μεν ἔστ' ἀρχαῖος": Stories and Storytelling in Sophocles' *Trachiniae*', *TAPA* 121: 75–98.

Kraus, C. S. (1999) 'Dangerous Supplements: Etymology and Genealogy in Euripides' *Heracles*', *PCPhS* 44: 137–57.

Kurke, L. (1991) *The Traffic in Praise: Pindar and the Poetics of Social Economy* (Ithaca, NY: Cornell University Press).

Kyriakou, P. (2011) *The Past in Aeschylus and Sophocles* (Berlin; Boston: De Gruyter).

Lada-Richards, I. (1998) 'Staging the Ephebeia: Theatrical Role-Playing and Ritual Transition in Sophocles' *Philoctetes*', *Ramus* 27: 1–26.

Langerwerf, L., and C. Ryan, eds (2010) *Zero to Hero, Hero to Zero: In Search of the Classical Hero* (Newcastle: Cambridge Scholars Publishing).

Lardinois, A. (2011) 'The Parrhesia of Young Female Choruses in Ancient Greece', in L. Athanassaki and E. Bowie (eds), *Archaic and Classical Choral Song: Performance Politics and Dissemination* (Berlin; Boston: De Gruyter) 161–72.

Lardinois, A. P. M. H. (1995) 'Wisdom in Context: The Use of Gnomic Statements in Archaic Greek Poetry', PhD, Princeton University.

Larmour, D. H. (2005) 'Corinna's Poetic Metis and the Epinikian Tradition', in E. Greene (ed.), *Women Poets in Ancient Greece and Rome* (Norman, OK: University of Oklahoma Press) 25–58.

Lawrence, S. E. (1978) 'The Dramatic Epistemology of Sophocles' "Trachiniae"', *Phoenix* 32: 288–304.

Lee, K. H. (1982) 'The Iris–Lyssa scene in Euripides' *Heracles*', *Antichthon* 16: 44–53.

Lee, K. H. (1986) 'Helen's Famous Husband and Euripides' *Helen* 1399', *CPhil.* 81: 309–13.

Lee, M. M. (2015) *Body, Dress, and Identity in Ancient Greece* (New York: Cambridge University Press).

Levett, B. (2010) 'Verbal Autonomy and Verbal Self-restraint in Euripides' *Medea*', *CPhil.* 105: 54–68.

Llewellyn-Jones, L. (2003) *Aphrodite's Tortoise: The Veiled Woman of Ancient Greece* (Swansea: Classical Press of Wales).

Lloyd, M. (1992) *The Agon in Euripides* (Oxford: Clarendon Press).

Lloyd-Jones, S. H., and N. G. Wilson, eds (1990) *Sophocles Fabulae*, 2nd edn (Oxford: Oxford University Press).

Loraux, N. (1981) *L'invention d'Athènes: Histoire de l'oraison funèbre dans la cité classique* (École des Htes Ét. en sc. soc. Centre de rech. hist. Civilisations & Sociétés; LXV) (Paris: Mouton).

Loraux, N. (1986) *The Invention of Athens: The Funeral Oration in the Classical City* (Cambridge, MA: Harvard University Press).

Loraux, N. (1987) *Tragic Ways of Killing a Woman*, tr. A. Forster (Cambridge, MA: Harvard University Press).

Loraux, N. (1994) *The Children of Athena: Athenian Ideas about Citizenship and the Division Between the Sexes* (Princeton: Princeton University Press).

Loraux, N. (1998) *Mothers in Mourning: With the Essay, Of Amnesty and Its Opposite*, tr. C. Pache (Ithaca, NY: Cornell University Press).

Loraux, N. (2002) *The Mourning Voice: An Essay on Greek Tragedy*, tr. E. T. Rawlings (Ithaca; New York: Cornell University Press).

Loraux, N. (2006) *The Invention of Athens: The Funeral Oration in the Classical City* (New York: MIT Press).

Loraux, N. (2014) *The Experiences of Tiresias, The Feminine and the Greek Man* (Princeton: Princeton University Press).

Luschnig, C. E. (2007) *Granddaughter of the Sun: A Study of Euripides'* Medea (Leiden: Brill).

Machin, A. (1981) *Cohérence et continuité dans le théâtre de Sophocle* (Haute-Ville, Québec: Serge Fleury).

Machin, A. (1989) 'Prestation des serments et présentation des personnages dans le théâtre de Sophocle', in *Actualité de l'Antiquité: Actes du colloque organisé à l'Université de Toulouse-Le Mirail par la revue Pallas, décembre 1985* (Éd. du CNRS) 221–32.

Mackie, H. S. (1996) *Talking Trojan: Speech and Community in the* Iliad (Oxford: Rowman & Littlefield).

Maddalena, A. (1963) 'La Medea di Euripide', *RFIC* 41: 129–52.

Martin, R. P. (1989) *The Language of Heroes: Speech and Performance in the* Iliad (Ithaca: Cornell University Press).

Martin, R. P. (2003) 'Keens from the Absent Chorus: "Troy to Ulster"', *Western Folklore* 62: 119–42.

Maslov, B. (2015) *Pindar and the Emergence of Literature* (Cambridge: Cambridge University Press).

Mastronarde, D. J. (1979) *Contact and Discontinuity: Some Conventions of Speech and Action on the Greek Stage* (Berkeley: University of California Press).

Mastronarde, D. J. (1986) 'The Optimistic Rationalist in Euripides: Theseus, Jocasta, Teiresias', in M. J. Cropp, E. Fantham and S. E. Scully (eds), *Greek Tragedy and Its Legacy: Essays presented to D. J. Conacher* (Calgary: University of Calgary Press) 201–11.

Mastronarde, D. J. (1994) *Euripides* Phoenissae (29) (Cambridge; New York: Cambridge University Press).

Mastronarde, D. J. (2002) *Euripides* Medea (Cambridge; New York: Cambridge University Press).

Mastronarde, D. J. (2010) *The Art of Euripides: Dramatic Technique and Social Context* (Cambridge; New York: Cambridge University Press).

Mattison, K. (2015) 'Sophocles' *Trachiniae*: Lessons in Love', *G&R* 62: 12–24.

McCallum-Barry, C. (2014) 'Medea Before and (a little) After Euripides', in D. Stuttard (ed.), *Looking at* Medea*: Essays and a Translation of Euripides' Tragedy* (London; New York: Bloomsbury Academic) 23–34.

McClay, M. F. (2021) 'Becoming κλεινός in Crete and Magna Graecia: Dionysiac Mysteries and Maturation Rituals Revisited', *CQ* 71: 108–18.

McClure, L. (1999a) *Spoken Like a Woman: Speech and Gender in Athenian Drama* (Princeton, NJ: Princeton University Press).

McClure, L. (1999b) '"The Worst Husband": Discourses of Praise and Blame in Euripides' *Medea*', *CPhil.* 94: 373–94.

McDermott, E. A. (1991) 'Double Meaning and Mythic Novelty in Euripides' Plays', *TAPA* 121: 123–32.

McNeal, R. A. (1978) 'Structure and Metaphor in Pindar's Fourth "Isthmian"', *Quaderni Urbinati di Cultura Classica* 28: 135–56.

Meltzer, G. S. (1994) '"Where Is the Glory of Troy?" "Kleos" in Euripides' "Helen"', *Classical Antiquity* 13: 234–55.

Mendelsohn, D. A. (2002) *Gender and the City in Euripides' Political Plays* (Oxford: Oxford University Press).

Michelakis, P. (2002) *Achilles in Greek Tragedy* (Cambridge; New York: Cambridge University Press).

Michelini, A. (1991) 'The Maze of the Logos: Euripides, "Suppliants" 163/ 249', *Ramus* 20: 16.

Michelini, A. (1994) 'Political Themes in Euripides' *Suppliants*', *AJPhil.* 115: 219–52.

Mikalson, J. D. (1991) *Honor Thy Gods: Popular Religion in Greek Tragedy* (Chapel Hill, N. C.: University of North Carolina Press).

Mikellidou, K. (2015) 'Euripides' *Heracles*: The Katabasis-Motif Revisited', *GRBS* 55: 329–52.

Mills, S. (1997) *Theseus, Tragedy, and the Athenian Empire* (New York: Oxford University Press).

Mills, S. (2020) *Drama, Oratory and Thucydides in Fifth-century Athens: Teaching Imperial Lessons* (New York: Routledge).

Minadeo, R. W. (1993) 'Theme and Plot in the *Philoctetes*', *Studi Italiani di Filologia Classica* 11: 87–105.

Minchin, E. (2007) *Homeric Voices* (Oxford: Oxford University Press).

Montiglio, S. (2000) *Silence in the Land of Logos* (Princeton: Princeton University Press).

Moore, H. L. (1994) *A Passion for Difference: Essays in Anthropology and Gender* (Cambridge: Polity).

Morgan, K. (2013) 'Praise and Performance in Plato's Laws', in A. Peponi (ed.), *Mousike, Performance and Culture in Plato's Laws* (Cambridge: Cambridge University Press) 265–93.

Morrison, A. D. (2012) *The Narrator in Archaic Greek and Hellenistic Poetry* (Cambridge: Cambridge University Press).

Morwood, J. (2007) *Euripides'* Suppliant Women (Oxford: Oxbow Books).

Morwood, J. (2008) *The Tragedies of Sophocles* (Exeter, UK: Bristol Phoenix Press).

Morwood, J. (2012) 'Euripides' "Suppliant Women", Theseus and Athenocentrism', *Mnemosyne* 65: 552–64.

Mossman, J. (2001) 'Women's Speech in Greek Tragedy: The Case of Electra and Clytemnestra in Euripides' *Electra*', *CQ* 51: 374–84.

Mossman, J. (2011) *Euripides'* Medea (Oxford: Oxbow).

Mossman, J. (2012) 'Women's Voices in Sophocles', in A. Markantonatos (ed.), *Brill's Companion to Sophocles* (Leiden; Boston: Brill) 489–506.

Most, G. W. (1994) 'Simonides' Ode to Scopas in Contexts', in J. P. Sullivan and I. J. F. de Jong (eds), *Modern Critical Theory and Classical Literature* (Leiden: Brill) 127–52.

Mueller, M. (2015) *Objects As Actors: Props and the Poetics of Performance in Greek Tragedy* (Chicago: University of Chicago Press).

Murnaghan, S. (1989) 'Trials of the hero in Sophocles' *Ajax*', in M. M. Mackenzie and C. Roueché (eds), *Images of Authority: Papers Presented to Joyce Reynolds on the Occasion of her Seventieth Birthday* (Cambridge: Cambridge University Press) 171–93.

Murnaghan, S. (1999) 'The Poetics of Loss in Greek Epic', in M. Beissinger and J. Tylus (eds), *Epic Traditions in the Contemporary World: The Poetics of Community* (Berkeley: University of California Press) 203–20.

Murnaghan, S. (2009) 'Tragic Bystanders: Choruses and Other Survivors in the Plays of Sophocles', in J. R. C. Cousland and J. R. Hume (eds), *The Play of Texts and Fragments: Essays in Honour of Martin Cropp* (Leiden: Brill) 321–33.

Murnaghan, S. (2016) 'The Euripidean Chorus', in L. K. McClure (ed.), *A Companion to Euripides* (Oxford: John Wiley & Sons, Ltd) 412–27.

Nagy, G. (1979) *The Best of the Achaeans: Concepts of the Hero in Archaic Greek Poetry* (Baltimore; London: Johns Hopkins University Press).

Nagy, G. (1990) *Pindar's Homer: The Lyric Possession of an Epic Past* (Baltimore: The Johns Hopkins University Press).

Nagy, G. (1996) *Homeric Questions* (Austin, TX: University of Texas Press).

Nagy, G. (2011) 'A Second Look at the Poetics of Re-enactment in Ode 13 of Bacchylides', in L. Athanassaki and E. Bowie (eds), *Archaic and Classical Choral Song: Performance, Politics and Dissemination* (Berlin; Boston: De Gruyter) 173–206.

Nagy, G. (2013) 'The Delian Maidens and Their Relevance to Choral Mimesis in Classical Drama', in R. Gagné and M. G. Hopman (eds), *Choral Mediations in Greek Tragedy* (Cambridge: Cambridge University Press) 227–56.

Nagy, G. (2017) 'A Sampling of Comments on Pindar Nemean 7', *Classical Inquiries* [https://classical-inquiries.chs.harvard.edu/a-sampling-of-comments-on-pindar-nemean-7/] Accessed: 25/04/2023.

Nagy, G. (2020) 'On the Shaping of the Lyric Canon in Athens', in B. Currie and I. Rutherford (eds), *The Reception of Greek Lyric Poetry in the Ancient World: Transmission, Canonization and Paratext* (Leiden; Boston: Brill) 95–111.

Nagy, G. (2021) 'How Pindar's Homer Might Save from Harm the Heroic Glory of Ajax', *Classical Inquiries* [https://classical-inquiries.chs.harvard.edu/how-pindars-homer-might-save-from-harm-the-heroic-glory-of-ajax/] Accessed: 16/02/2023.

Niehaus, I. (2012) 'Gendered Endings: Narratives of Male and Female Suicides in the South African Lowveld', *Culture, Medicine, and Psychiatry* 36: 327–47.

Nooter, S. H. (2012a) *When Heroes Sing: Sophocles and the Shifting Soundscape of Tragedy* (Cambridge; New York: Cambridge University Press).

Nooter, S. H. (2012b) 'Poetic Speakers in Sophocles', in K. Ormand (ed.), *A Companion to Sophocles* 91 (Malden, MA; Oxford: Wiley-Blackwell) 204–19.

O'Higgins, D. (1989) 'The Second Best of the Achaeans', *Hermathena* 147: 43–56.

O'Higgins, D. (1991) 'Narrators and Narrative in the *Philoctetes* of Sophocles', *Ramus* XX: 37–52.

O'Higgins, L. (2003) *Women and Humor in Classical Greece* (Cambridge: Cambridge University Press).

Ormand, K. (1999) *Exchange and the Maiden: Marriage in Sophoclean Tragedy* (Austin, TX: University of Texas Press).

Padilla, M. W. (1994) 'Heroic Paternity in Euripides' *Heracles*', *Arethusa* 27: 279–302.

Page, D. L. (1938) *Euripides'* Medea (Oxford: Clarendon Press).

Pallantza, E. (2005) *Der Troische Krieg in der nachhomerischen Literatur bis zum 5. Jahrhundert v. Chr* (Stuttgart: Steiner).

Papadimitropoulos, L. (2007) 'Heracles as Tragic Hero', *CW* 101: 131–8.

Papadopoulou, T. (1999) 'Subjectivity and Community in Greek Tragedy: The Example of Euripides' Heracles", in S. Patsalidis and E. Sakellaridou (eds), *(Dis)placing Classical Greek Theatre* (Thessaloniki) 297–307.

Papadopoulou, T. (2001) 'Revenge in Euripides' *Heracles*', in F. Budelmann and P. Michelakis (eds), *Homer, Tragedy and Beyond: Essays in Honour of P. E. Easterling* (London: Society for the Promotion of Hellenic Studies) 113–28.

Parks, W. (2014) *Verbal Dueling in Heroic Narrative: The Homeric and Old English Traditions* (Princeton: Princeton University Press).

Parry, H. (1965) 'The Second Stasimon of Euripides' *Heracles* (637–700)', *AJPhil.* 86: 363–74.

Pavlou, M. (2012) 'Pindar and the Reconstruction of the Past', in J. Marincola, L. Llewellyn-Jones and C. A. Maciver (eds), *Greek Notions of the Past in the Archaic and Classical Eras* (Edinburgh: Edinburgh University Press) 95–112.

Pearson, A. C. (1924) *Sophoclis Fabulae* (Oxford: Clarendon).

Perkell, C. (2008) 'Reading the laments of *Iliad* 24', in A. Suter (ed.), *Lament: Studies in the Ancient Mediterranean and Beyond* (Oxford; New York: Oxford University Press) 93–117.

Perysinakis, I. (1994) 'Sophocles' Philoctetes and the Homeric epics [An anthropological approach]', *Mètis: Anthropologie des mondes grecs anciens* 9: 377–89.

Perysinakis, I. N. (1992) 'Sophocles: *Philoctetes* and the Homeric Epics', *Δωδώνη* XII:.

Phillippo, S. (1995) 'Family Ties: Significant Patronymics in Euripides' *Andromache*', *CQ* 45: 355–71.

Pickard-Cambridge, A. W., J. Gould, and D. M. Lewis (1968) *The Dramatic Festivals of Athens* (London: Oxford University Press).

Podlecki, A. J. (1966) 'The Power of the Word in Sophocles' *Philoctetes*', *GRBS* 7: 233–50.

Pomeroy, S. B. (1975) *Goddesses, Whores, Wives and Slaves: Women in Classical Antiquity* (New York: Schocken).

Poster, C. (2006) 'The Task of the Bow: Heraclitus' Rhetorical Critique of Epic Language', *Philosophy & Rhetoric* 39: 1–21.

Pozzi, D. C. (1994) 'Deianeira's Robe: Diction in Sophocles' *Trachiniae*', *Mnemosyne* 47: 577–85.

Pucci, P. (1980) *The Violence of Pity in Euripides'* Medea (Ithaca, NY: Cornell University Press).

Pucci, P. (1994) 'Gods' Intervention and Epiphany in Sophocles', *AJPhil.* 115: 15–46.

Pucci, P. (2003) *Filottete: Testo greco a fronte* (Rome: Mondadori).

Rabinowitz, N. S. (1993) *Anxiety Veiled: Euripides and the Traffic in Women* (Ithaca; London: Cornell University Press).

Rabinowitz, N. S. (2004) 'Politics of Inclusion/Exclusion in Attic Tragedy', in F. McHardie and E. Marshall (eds), *Women's Influence on Culture in Antiquity* (New York: Routledge) 40–55.

Rabinowitz, N. S. (2014) 'Women and War in Tragedy', in P. Meineck and D. Konstan (eds), *Combat Trauma and the Ancient Greeks* (New York: Palgrave Macmillan).

Race, W. H. (1983) 'Negative Expressions and Pindaric ΠΟΙΚΙΛΙΑ', *TAPA* 113: 95–122.

Rawles, R. (2011) 'Eros and Praise in Early Greek Lyric', in L. Athanassaki and E. Bowie (eds), *Archaic and Classical Choral Song: Performance, Politics and Dissemination* (Berlin; Boston: De Gruyter) 139–60.

Rawles, R. (2013) 'Aristophanes' Simonides: Lyric Models for Praise and Blame', in E. Bakola, L. Prauscello and M. Telò (eds), *Greek Comedy and the Discourse of Genres*, 1st edn (Cambridge: Cambridge University Press) 175–202.

Rehm, R. (1988) 'The Staging of Suppliant Plays', *GRBS* 29: 263–307.

Rehm, R. (1989) 'Medea and the λόγος of the heroic', *Eranos* 87: 97–115.

Rehm, R. (1994) *Marriage to Death: The Conflation of Wedding and Funeral Rituals in Greek Tragedy* (Princeton: Princeton University Press).

Rehm, R. (1996) 'Performing the Chorus: Choral Action, Interaction, and Absence in Euripides', *Arion* 4: 45–60.

Rehm, R. (2002) *The Play of Space: Spatial Transformation in Greek Tragedy* (Princeton: Princeton University Press).

Rehm, R. (2006) 'Sophocles on Fire: To Pur in *Philoctetes*', in I. J. F. De Jong and A. Rijksbaron (eds), *Sophocles and the Greek Language: Aspects of Diction, Syntax and Pragmatics* (Leiden: Brill) 95–107.

Roberts, D. H. (1989) 'Different Stories: Sophoclean Narrative(s) in the *Philoctetes*', *TAPA* 119: 161–76.

Rodighiero, A. (2012) *Generi lirico-corali nella produzione drammatica di Sofocle* (Tübingen: Narr Dr. Gunter).

Roisman, H. (2005) *Sophocles:* Philoctetes (London: Duckworth).

Roisman, H. M. (1997) 'The Appropriation of a Son: Sophocles' *Philoctetes*', *GRBS* 38: 127–71.

Roisman, H. M. (2001) 'The Ever-Present Odysseus: Eavesdropping and Disguise in Sophocles' *Philoctetes*', *Eranos* 99: 38–53.

Roisman, H. M. (2004) 'Women's Free Speech in Greek Tragedy', in I. Sluiter and R. Rosen (eds), *Free Speech in Classical Antiquity* (Leiden: Brill) 91–114.

Romilly, J. de (1961) *L'évolution du pathétique d'Eschyle à Euripide* (Paris: Presses Universitaires de France).

Rose, P. W. (1976) 'Sophocles' Philoctetes and the Teachings of the Sophists', *Harv. Stud.* 80: 49–105.

Rose, P. W. (1992) *Sons of the Gods, Children of Earth: Ideology and Literary Form in Ancient Greece* (Ithaca; London: Cornell University Press).

Rose, P. W. (1995) 'Historicizing Sophocles' Ajax', in B. Goff (ed.), *History, Tragedy, Theory: Dialogues on Athenian Drama* (Austin, TX: University of Texas Press) 59–90.

Rosenbloom, D. S. (2001) '"Ajax is μέγας:" Is That All We Can Say?: review article', *Prudentia* 33: 109–29.

Rosivach, V. J. (1976) 'Sophocles' *Ajax*', *The Classical Journal* 72: 47–61.

Rusten, J. S. (1989) *The Peloponnesian War, Book II* (Cambridge: Cambridge University Press).

Rutherford, I. (1994) 'Apollo in Ivy: The Tragic Paean', *Arion* 3: 112–35.

Rutherford, I. (2011) 'Singing Myth: Pindar', in K. Dowden and N. Livingstone (eds), *A Companion to Greek Mythology* (Chicester: Blackwells) 109–23.

Rutherford, I. C. (2001) *Pindar's Paeans: A Reading of the Fragments with a Survey of the Genre* (Oxford; New York: Oxford University Press).

Rutherford, R. B. (2012) *Greek Tragic Style: Form, Language, and Interpretation* (Cambridge; New York: Cambridge University Press).

Ryzman, M. (1991) 'Neoptolemus' Psychological Crisis and the Development of Physis in Sophocles' *Philoctetes*', *Eranos* LXXXIX: 35–41.

Sammons, B. (2021) 'Five Times Seven: Cataloguing the Seven against Thebes in Four Greek Tragedies', in R. Laemmle, C. Scheidegger Laemmle and K. Wesselmann (eds), *Lists and Catalogues in Ancient Literature and Beyond* (Berlin; Boston: De Gruyter) 305–26.

Sanders, E. (2013) 'Sexual Jealousy and *Eros* in Euripides' *Medea*', in E. Sanders, C. Thumiger, C. Carey and N. Lowe (eds), *Erôs in Ancient Greece* (Oxford: Oxford University Press) 41–58.

Schein, S. L. (1982) '*Electra*: A Sophoclean Problem Play', *Antike und Abendland* 28: 69–80.

Schein, S. L. (1984) *The Mortal Hero: An introduction to Homer's* Iliad (Berkeley: University of California Press).

Schein, S. L. (2006) 'The *Iliad* and *Odyssey* in Sophocles' *Philoctetes*: Generic Complexity and Ethical Ambiguity', *Bulletin of the Institute of Classical Studies* 49: 129–40.

Schein, S. L. (2013) *Sophocles'* Philoctetes (Cambridge; New York: Cambridge University Press).

Schmitt, R. (1967) *Dichtung und Dichtersprache in indogermanischer Zeit* (Wiesbaden: Harrassowitz).

Scodel, R. (1999) 'Verbal performance and Euripidean rhetoric', *ICS* 24: 129–44.

Scodel, R. (2009) 'The Persuasions of Philoctetes', in J. R. C. Cousland and J. R. Hume (eds), *The Play of Texts and Fragments* (Leiden: Brill) 49–61.

Scully, S. (1996) 'Orchestra and Stage and Euripides' "Suppliant Women"', *Arion: A Journal of Humanities and the Classics* 4: 61–84.

Seaford, R. (1986) 'Wedding Ritual and Textual Criticism in Sophocles' *Women of Trachis*', *Hermes* 114: 50–9.

Seaford, R. (1987) 'The Tragic Wedding', *JHS* 107: 106–30.

Seaford, R. (1994) *Reciprocity and Ritual: Homer and Tragedy in the Developing City-state* (Oxford; New York: Oxford University Press).

Seaford, R. (2019) 'Looking at the Isolation of Ajax', in D. Stuttard (ed.), *Looking at* Ajax (London: Bloomsbury Academic) 83–9.

Segal, C. (1977) 'Sophocles' *Trachiniae*: Myth, Poetry, and Heroic Values', *YClS* 25: 99–158.

Segal, C. (1981) *Tragedy and Civilization: An Interpretation of Sophocles* (Norman, OK: University of Oklahoma Press).

Segal, C. (1986) *Interpreting Greek Tragedy: Myth, Poetry, Text* (Ithaca, NY: Cornell University Press).

Segal, C. (1989) 'Song, Ritual, and Commemoration in Early Greek Poetry and Tragedy', *Oral Tradition* vol. 4, no. 3: 330–59.

Segal, C. (1992) 'Tragic Beginnings: Narration, Voice, and Authority in the Prologues of Greek Drama', *YCS* 29: 85–112.

Segal, C. (1993) *Euripides and the Poetics of Sorrow: Art, Gender, and Commemoration in* Alcestis, Hippolytus, *and* Hecuba (Durham, NC: Duke University Press).

Segal, C. (1994) *Singers, Heroes, and Gods in the 'Odyssey'* (Ithaca; London: Cornell University Press).

Segal, C. (1995) *Sophocles' Tragic World: Divinity, Nature, Society* (Cambridge, MA: Harvard University Press).

Segal, C. (1996) 'Euripides' *Medea*: Vengeance, Reversal and Closure', *Pallas* 45: 15–44.

Segal, C. (1998) *Aglaia* (Lanham, MD: Rowman & Littlefield).

Segal, C. (2000) 'The Oracles of Sophocles' *Trachiniae*: Convergence or Confusion?', *Harv. Stud.* 100: 151–71.

Seidensticker, B. (1990) 'Euripides, *Medea* 1056-80, An Interpolation', in M. Griffith and D. J. Mastronarde (eds), *Cabinet of the Muses: Essays on Classical and Comparative Literature in Honor of Thomas G. Rosenmeyer* (Atlanta: Scholars Press) 89–102.

Silk, M. S. (1985) 'Heracles and Greek Tragedy', *G&R* 32: 1–22.

Sissa, G. (2020) 'Mighty Mothers: Female Political Theorists in Euripides' *Suppliant Women* and *Phoenician Women*', in A. Sharrock and A. Keith (eds), *Maternal Conceptions in Classical Literature and Philosophy* (University of Toronto Press) 193–223.

Skinner, M. B. (1983) 'Corinna of Tanagra and Her Audience', *Tulsa Studies in Women's Literature* 2: 9–20.

Smith, W. D. (1966) 'Expressive Form in Euripides' *Suppliants*', *Harv. Stud.* 71: 151–70.

Snell, B., and H. Mähler (1987) *Pindari Carmina cum fragmentis* (Leipzig: Teubner)

Sorum, C. E. (1986) 'Sophocles' *Ajax* in Context', *CW* 79: 361–77.

Sourvinou-Inwood, C. (2003) *Tragedy and Athenian Religion* (Lanham, MD: Lexington Books).

Spelman, H. (2018) *Pindar and the Poetics of Permanence* (Oxford, New York: Oxford University Press).

Stafford, E. J. (2012) *Herakles* (London: Routledge).

Stallbaum, G., and M. Davarius, eds (1960) *Eustathii Commentarii ad Homeri Iliadem et Odysseam.* (4 v.) (Hildesheim: G. Olms).

Starobinski, J. (1974) *Trois fureurs* (Paris: Gallimard).

Steiner, D. (1986) *The Crown of Song: Metaphor in Pindar* (Oxford: Oxford University Press).

Steiner, D. (1994) *The Tyrant's Writ: Myths and Images of Writing in Ancient Greece* (Princeton: Princeton University Press).

Steiner, D. (1999) 'To Praise, Not to Bury: Simonides fr. 531P', *The Classical Quarterly* 49: 383–95.

Steiner, D. (2005) 'Nautical Matters: Hesiod's Nautilia and Ibycus fragment 282 PMG', *CPhil.* 100: 347–55.

Steiner, D. T. (2010) 'The Immeasures of Praise: The Epinician Celebration of Agamemnon's Return', *Hermes* 138: 22–37.

Stelow, A. R. (2020) *Menelaus in the Archaic Period: Not Quite the Best of the Achaeans* (Oxford: Oxford University Press).

Stinton, T. C. W. (1986) 'Sophocles, *Trachiniae* 94–102', *CQ* 36: 337–42.

Storey, I. C. (2008) *Euripides:* Suppliant Women (London; New York: Bloomsbury Academic).

Storey, I. C. (2016) '*Andromache*', in L. McClure (ed.), *A Companion to Euripides* (Oxford: John Wiley & Sons, Ltd) 122–35.

Swift, L. (2010) *The Hidden Chorus: Echoes of Genre in Tragic Lyric* (Oxford: Oxford University Press).

Swift, L. (2011) 'Epinician and Tragic Worlds: The Case of Sophocles' *Trachiniae*', in E. Bowie and L. Athanasakē (eds), *Archaic and Classical Choral Song: Performance, Politics and Dissemination* (Berlin: De Gruyter) 391–414.

Swift, L. (2013) 'Conflicting Identities in the Euripidean Chorus', in R. Gagné and M. Hopman (eds), *Choral Mediations in Greek Tragedy* (Cambridge: Cambridge University Press) 130–54.

Swift, L. (2020) '*Phoenician Women*', in A. Markantonatos (ed.), *Brill's Companion to Euripides* (Leiden: Brill) 343–59.

Taplin, O. (1978) *Greek Tragedy in Action* (London: Methuen).

Thomas, O. (2018) 'Music in Euripides' *Medea*', in T. Phillips and A. D'Angour (eds), *Music, Text, and Culture in Ancient Greece* (Oxford: Oxford University Press) 99–120.

Thury, E. M. (1988) 'A Study of Words Relating to Youth and Old Age in the Plays of Euripides and Its Special Implications for Euripides' *Suppliant Women*', *Computers and the Humanities* 22: 293–306.

Toher, M. (2001) 'Euripides' "Supplices" and the Social Function of Funeral Ritual', *Hermes* 129: 332–43.

Torrance, I. (2013) *Metapoetry in Euripides* (Oxford; New York: Oxford University Press).

Torres-Guerra, J. B. (2015) '*Thebaid*', in C. Tsagalis and M. Fantuzzi (eds), *The Greek Epic Cycle and its Ancient Reception: A Companion* (Cambridge: Cambridge University Press) 226–43.

Tyrrell, W. B., and L. J. Bennett (1999) 'Pericles' muting of women's voices in Thuc. 2.45.2', *CJ* 95: 37–51.

Vernant, J.-P. (1979) 'Πanta Kaλa D'homere a Simonide', *Annali della Scuola Normale Superiore di Pisa: Classe di Lettere e Filosofia* 9: 1365–74.

Vernant, J. P., and Vidal-Naquet, P. (1988) *Myth and Tragedy in Ancient Greece* (New York; Cambridge, Mass: Zone Books; Distributed by MIT Press).

Vidal-Naquet, P. (1988) 'Sophocles' *Philoctetes* and the Ephebeia', in P. Vidal-Naquet and J. P. Vernant (eds), *Myth and Tragedy in Ancient Greece* (New York; Cambridge, Mass: Zone Books; Distributed by MIT Press) 161–79.

Visvardi, E. (2015) *Emotion in Action: Thucydides and the Tragic Chorus* (Leiden; Boston: Brill).

Wade, P. (1994) 'Man the Hunter: Gender and Violence in Music and Drinking Contexts in Colombia', in P. Gow and P. Harvey (eds), *Sex and Violence: Issues in Representation and Experience* (London: Routledge) 115–37.

Wakefield, G. (1794) *Tragoediarum delectus: Hercules Furens, Alcestis, Euripideae: et Trachiniae, Sophoclea. (Ion, Euripidea, Philoctetes, Sophoclea; et Eumenides, Aeschylea.) In scholarum usum edidit et illustravit G.W. Gr., Lat. F.P.* (2 tom. Londini).

Walker, H. J. (1995) *Theseus and Athens* (Oxford; New York: Oxford University Press).

Walsh, G. B. (1979) 'Public and Private in Three Plays of Euripides', *CPhil.* 74: 294–309.

Weiberg, E. L. (2018) 'The Writing on the Mind: Deianeira's Trauma in Sophocles' *Trachiniae*', *Phoenix* 72: 19–42.

Weiberg, E. L. (2019) 'Learning to Bear Witness: Tragic Bystanders in Sophocles' *Trachiniae*', in A. Karanika and V. Panoussi (eds), *Emotional Trauma in Greece and Rome* (London: Routledge) 177–91.

Weiss, N. (2020) 'Generic Hybridity in Athenian Tragedy', in M. Foster, L. Kurke and N. Weiss (eds), *Genre in Archaic and Classical Greek Poetry: Theories and Models* (Leiden; Boston: Brill) 167–90.

Wells, J. B. (2009) *Pindar's Verbal Art: An Ethnographic Study of Epinician Style* (Cambridge, MA: Harvard University Press).

Wender, D. (1974) 'The Will of the Beast: Sexual Imagery in the *Trachiniae*', *Ramus* 3: 1–17.

West, M. L., ed. (1989) *Iambi et elegi Graeci ante Alexandrum cantati* (2nd edn, aucta atque emendata) (Oxford; New York: Oxford University Press).

West, M. L., ed. (2003) *Greek Epic Fragments from the Seventh to the Fifth Centuries BC* (Cambridge, Mass: Harvard University Press).

Whitby, M. (1996) 'Telemachus Transformed? The Origins of Neoptolemus in Sophocles' "Philoctetes"', *G&R* 43: 31–42.

Whitman, C. H. (1958) *Homer and the Heroic Tradition* (Cambridge: Harvard University Press).

Whitman, C. H. (1974) *Euripides and the Full Circle of Myth* (Cambridge, MA: Harvard University Press).

Willcock, M. M. (1995) *Pindar: Victory Odes: Olympians 2, 7, 11; Nemean 4; Isthmians 3, 4, 7* (Cambridge; New York: Cambridge University Press).

Williams, B. (1993) *Shame and Necessity* (Berkeley, CA: University of California Press).

Williamson, M. (1990) 'A Woman's place in Euripides' *Medea*', in A. Powell (ed.), *Euripides, Women and Sexuality* (London: Routledge) 16–31.

Winnington-Ingram, R. P. (1960) *Euripide: sept exposés et discussions* 6 A. Rivier, J. C. Kamerbeek, H. Diller, A. Lesky, R. P. Winnington-Ingram, G. Zuntz, and V. Martin (eds) (Entretiens sur L'antiquité Classique) (Vandoeuvres-Genéve: Fondation Hardt pour l'étude de l'antiquité classique).

Winnington-Ingram, R. P. (1980) *Sophocles: An Interpretation* (Cambridge: Cambridge University Press).

Wohl, V. (1998) *Intimate Commerce: Exchange, Gender, and Subjectivity in Greek Tragedy* (Austin, TX: University of Texas Press).

Wolff, C. (1979) 'A Note on Lions and Sophocles, Philoctetes 1436', in G. W. Bowersock, W. Burkert and M. Putnam (eds), *Arktouros: Hellenic Studies presented to Bernard MW Knox on the Occasion of his 65th Birthday* (Berlin: De Gruyter) 144–50.

Worman, N. B. (2000) 'Infection in the sentence: the discourse of disease in Sophocles' *Philoctetes*', *Arethusa* 33: 1–36.

Wright, M. (2018) *The Lost Plays of Greek Tragedy (Volume 2): Aeschylus, Sophocles and Euripides* (London; New York: Bloomsbury Academic).

Wróblewski, W. (1972) 'Die Begriffe ἀρετή und ἄριστος in den Epen Homers', *Eos: Commentarii Societatis Philologae Polonorum* LX: 21–39.

Yoshitake, S. (1994) 'Disgrace, Grief and Other Ills: Herakles' Rejection of Suicide', *JHS* 114: 135–53.

Young, D. C. (1971) *Pindar Isthmian 7: Myth and Exempla* (Leiden: Brill).

Zeitlin, F. I. (1990) 'Thebes: Theater of Self and Society in Athenian Drama', in J. J. Winkler and Froma I. Zeitlin (eds), *Nothing to Do with Dionysos?: Athenian Drama in Its Social Context* (Princeton, NJ: Princeton University Press) 130–67.

Zeitlin, F. I. (1996) *Playing the Other: Gender and Society in Classical Greek Literature* (Chicago, IL: University of Chicago Press).

Zuntz, G. (1955) *The Political Plays of Euripides* (Manchester: Manchester University Press).

Index

Page numbers followed by 'n' refer to notes.